About the Author

Susan Knight has been living in Ireland since 1977. She has published two novels, *The Invisible Woman* (1993) and *Grimaldi's Garden* (1995). She is also the author of several radio plays, including the P.J. O'Connor prize-winner, *Mr Moonlight* (1986). Her one-act stage play, *Amazon*, was performed at the Andrews Lane Theatre as part of a festival of women's writing. Another play, *Don't Drink the Milk*, won the O.Z. Whitehead award. She has written comedy scripts for stage and television, including for *Nighthawks*, *The Basement* and *The Late Late Show*. As a freelance journalist, she has written extensively for several papers, including, most recently, *The Sunday Tribune*. With a PhD in Russian literature, she now teaches adult classes in creative writing at the People's College, Dublin, and University College Dublin. She lives in Dublin with her husband and three children.

Where the Grass is Greener

Voices of Immigrant Women in Ireland

Edited by
Susan Knight

Oak Tree Press
Dublin

Oak Tree Press
Merrion Building
Lower Merrion Street
Dublin 2, Ireland
http://www.oaktreepress.com

A catalogue record of this book is
available from the British Library.

ISBN 1 86076 213 1

Cover painting: Detail from *Once Upon a Time*, © Catherine Kollefrath
O'Leanacháin. Reproduced here with kind permission of the artist.

Printed in the Republic of Ireland by Colour Books Ltd.

Contents

Contents

Acknowledgements

I would first like to thank my agent, Jonathan Williams, for his persistence, advice and support during the writing of this book; David Givens, Brian Langan, Maureen McDermott and Leonie Lawler of Oak Tree Press for their enthusiasm, efficiency and good humour; my family, Des, Karl, Jenny and Leo, for putting up with my frequent absences and for bringing me down to earth when necessary. I am most grateful to Catherine O'Leanacháin for permission to use one of her paintings on the front cover. I should also like to thank everyone around the country who helped me contact and track down my interviewees; without them, there would be no book. And above all, I want to thank the wonderful women themselves — all sixty-one of them — who constantly amazed me with their willingness to take someone who was a total stranger into their homes and hearts.

To all the women interviewed here, with profound thanks

Introduction

Ireland, an island off an island, has up until very recently stayed remote
from change. When I came to live here in 1977, I thought I had stepped
back in time in so many ways. Later I found it could be charming, but at
first I was appalled. There was something monolithic about the place:
from the all-pervasive influence of the Catholic church — infusing not
only the spiritual life of the people but the education and political sys-
tems as well — to the faces in the street, all the one colour, the one
look, the one voice. I'm exaggerating, of course, but not much. Despite
the fact that I myself could pass through the crowd unnoticed, I felt like
an alien, something I had never experienced in other places, where difference was embraced. In Ireland, the strong feeling I got was that if you
weren't part of it, forget it. One morning, a short while after I arrived, I
met an Englishwoman at a bus stop, who had been here for many years.
"They never accept you," she said to me.

I myself am of mixed English and Danish parentage and came over
with my Irish partner — who up to then had been working in London —
and our eleven-month-old baby. Like some of the women interviewed,
my experiences, especially in the early years, didn't tally with expectations. The preconceived image of the friendly, easy-going Irish con-
trasted sharply with neighbours who squinted through their net curtains
and called the guards the first night we arrived because the removal van
stayed parked in our driveway.

Over the years, things improved, mainly because of my own deter-
mination to make a life here. Eventually, we moved to a house on an
estate where most of the families had young children. But I still remember the dreadful loneliness of the first two years, when my second baby

died a cot death and I had no close friend to turn to. And that's a refrain constantly echoed in these interviews: you can't get close to the Irish; you think you've made a friend, but the next day you're ignored. Not that after 24 years I find it still the case, but as a foreigner, you have to learn to make adjustments. It takes time. It takes getting used to.

This collection of interviews with foreign women living in Ireland has a double agenda. On the one hand, to uncover a mosaic of stories, less ordinary and extraordinary, but never ordinary; to glimpse into the lives of some of the exotic people who are becoming more and more visible on the streets of our cities, towns and villages. On the other, to see Ireland at this transitional moment in its history through other eyes. I have chosen to interview only women because they are traditionally the more passive members of society and therefore have a particular angle of vision. Many have come not of their own choice but accompanying partners, husbands and boyfriends, both Irish and non-Irish, who are here to work or find an alternative lifestyle. And if they haven't come because of that, the perception is still, in this not totally liberated society, that they must have.

It should be emphasised that many — the majority even — are delighted to be in Ireland and have no regrets. Others have been disappointed, their expectations not fulfilled. Like a series of snapshots, Ireland is captured through their eyes in some attractive, some flattering, some uncomfortable, even ugly poses. Alongside Ireland of the Welcomes is the Ireland that punches a pregnant refugee woman to the ground. Alongside the magic, the spirituality is the culture of cute hoorism and of religious bigotry. Alongside the easy-going, laid-back quality of life, is the Ireland where no one, particularly tradesmen, keeps an appointment, where people prefer to lie than tell the truth in case they hurt your feelings.

I have endeavoured to provide a spread of nationalities, but inevitably there will be gaps — in such an eclectic collection as this, it would be impossible to be comprehensive. Nevertheless, thirty-one nationalities are represented. Also, I deliberately aimed for a random choice of subjects: people I happened on, friends and acquaintances of friends and acquaintances, a network of tenuous connections spreading across the country. Some of the women interviewed have been in Ireland for decades and have seen enormous changes. Some are newly arrived, part of the wave of workers and refugees who hope that a new richer Ireland will extend a helping hand. Certain individuals tell terrifying or very personal tales, and for that reason some have chosen to maintain anonymity. This was a courtesy offered to ensure that the women would talk frankly. Nonetheless, in interviewing refugees in particular, I was very aware that they probably wouldn't be prepared to tell the full story, even under a false name.

I have also tried to achieve a broad geographic spread, although it wouldn't be practical to aim to cover every corner of the country. Inevitably, the majority of interviews are from the Dublin area, where most people live, as well as the urban centres of Cork, Galway and Limerick. Such rural areas as Donegal, Mayo, Cork, Limerick, Kilkenny, Tipperary, Roscommon and Wicklow are also represented. I took a difficult decision to exclude the North, because, after all, interviewees are responding to the experience of living in the Republic, with its jurisdiction, its religion, its social policies. To have some token women from the North would seem to me a distortion of the complex experience of living there.

The interviews took place over a period of two years, although more than half of them are much more recent. The procedure I adopted was a taped conversation, each woman responding to a set of basic questions — where she is from; what brought her to Ireland; what her expectations were; whether these have been fulfilled or whether anything surprised her; what she likes; what she dislikes, and so on. Frequently, the conversation would open out into a wider discussion, which I would run with. I then transcribed and edited the interviews into readable monologues because, after all, the way people speak is generally full of digressions, non-sequiturs and repetition, not to mention, in the case of people whose first language isn't English, mistakes of grammar and vocabulary. However, I also endeavoured to maintain the individual voice of each of the women and showed the final version to each interviewee for approval.

For the purposes of convenience, the book is subtitled "Voices of Immigrant Women in Ireland". However, it should be pointed out that this is somewhat misleading. Not all the women are in Ireland to stay:

some are students and some have come for work experience, intending to go home or move on. On the other hand, some arrived intending to stay only for a brief while and many years later find themselves still here. Indeed, I myself would fall into that category. (I didn't even bother to put my son's name down for national school in 1977, because I didn't think we would be here long enough for him to avail of it. Now he has a son of his own.)

Regarding the position of women, Ireland today is undoubtedly a more accommodating place than it ever was before. If you doubt that, read Irene F. But as so many of these interviewees indicate, you still have to get out there and do the work yourself. That so many are managing to raise themselves up is a tribute to a place where, as I heard over and over, anything is possible. And yet this little book can only reflect the state of affairs at a moment in time that is already passing. Even as I write, the tiger that has drawn so many people here is padding the country carrying disease on its paws, and may not be burning quite so bright as it once did. For some, that will be a relief. As Marie Campion says, "I can't wait until the bubble bursts and we again have the time to sit down with a cup of tea."

It was commented to me how the Irish abroad always hanker to return — they sing their songs and weep into their inferior foreign Guinness. Perhaps it reflects on the ultimately engaging quality of the country how few of the interviewees want to go back where they came from. Beautiful, exasperating Ireland. It gets under your skin.

Susan Knight
Dublin
May 2001

Engracia Alteza
Filipino

Engracia is a small, compact person who looks incredibly youthful for someone in her mid-fifties, with seven grandchildren. She has short dark hair and a serious face that frequently breaks into a wide smile. She sits in an armchair in the foyer of Jurys Hotel, Ballsbridge, Dublin, and casts an approving eye around. Her English is accurate but heavily accented. She is quiet, perhaps deceptively so, for she has recently set up her own business, an employment agency for Asian workers.

My name is Engracia Alteza, Siony for short. I am from Luzon in the Philippines, quite near to Manila. I've been in Ireland for fourteen years now, mostly as housekeeper to one Irish family. Last year I left to set up my own agency, which was quite painful for all of us, as I had become part of the family. When I first came here, I didn't know anything about Ireland. It was my employer's wife who taught me everything. She also helped me with my English. In my country there are many different languages, so English is used as the second language. We are forced to speak it all the time in school but at home we speak Tagalog.

It was never my plan to come here to Ireland. I was working in an agency in the Philippines and there was this Arab family who wanted to employ a Filipino who could speak English. As a joke I said, 'How about me?' I was interviewed and passed the test. I was nearly forty, with four children, and I had to leave them behind. It was heartbreaking. But that's how it is in my country. It's very poor and we have to go abroad to earn enough money for the family. I was to spend three months in Bahrain to get to know the children of my employers and help them to learn English. The parents would then come to fetch us back to Ireland. They were both doctors, working in Dublin.

Ireland was a big change after the Middle East. The cold here used to be a big problem for me. I didn't want to get out of bed. I wanted to go around all the time with my duvet over my shoulders. But I'm used to it now. And in the Middle East I had to wear clothes that covered me completely. Even jeans weren't allowed — they weren't considered modest enough. When I came here, it was the opposite. The women expose everything.

I only stayed with the Arab family for a few months. They used to lock me in the house when they went out, saying that Dublin was too dangerous to be wandering around in. What they did was illegal of course but, you see, I had no rights at all. They had taken away my passport. I had no idea they were like that: in the Philippines they seemed very nice, very liberal. Suddenly when we were here, they changed. The only times I was allowed out was with the family. It was very lonely for me. I knew no one here. At that time, there were only about two or three other Filipinos in the whole country.

The first chance I got to go out on my own was on my birthday. This is how it happened. One day I was in Herbert Park, sitting on a bench while the children played on the grass. My mind was far, far away. Some people sitting next to me asked if I was OK. I told them I was but they didn't believe me. They asked me if I knew anyone in the country and when I said 'No', they gave me the number of a Columban priest who had worked in the Philippines for eight years. A week passed before I had the chance to ring this person. When eventually I did, I begged him to help me get out of the situation I was in and started to cry. At first he thought I was messing. But I kept ringing him and eventually he asked me to meet him. I told him it was impossible but he said, 'Find a way.' My birthday was coming up, so I asked the family if I could go out by myself to church. They said I could, but for one hour only. However, instead of going to church, I met this priest. I burst into tears again as I explained everything to him and he said, 'Please don't cry.'

I went back to the family for the sake of the children, but all the time I was planning how to leave. It took me two more months to arrange it.

After I had gone, the family reported me to the police as missing. The police asked them how old I was and when they heard that I was in my forties, they just said that I had probably run off with a boyfriend [*she laughs*]. At first the priest took me in as a housekeeper and gave me money to buy clothes. I didn't have any money because I had never been paid. That was another thing. In the Philippines I had been told I would be earning 250 dollars a month. When I got to Bahrain this couple wanted me to sign a document all in Arabic and I refused, not knowing what it might be. They said if I didn't I would be put in prison. What could I do? I signed it. Apparently, it was a new contract in which I agreed to be paid 40 dollars a month. But I didn't even get that, not a penny.

After a while, this priest helped me to find another position with a family. Unfortunately, they moved to England and I couldn't go with them without my passport. Finally, I found the family with whom I was to spend the next fourteen years and they helped me to get my passport back. They simply phoned the Arab doctor and asked if he knew me and if he had my passport. When he said 'Yes', they said, 'Don't you know you are breaking the law, holding on to someone else's passport?' Then they drove me to the hospital where he was working and we picked up the passport, with no more problems.

My experience isn't unique. Many Filipino women have similar problems with Arab employers. I know of one woman here who, like me, ran away. But she had to go back. They got word to her that her sister, who was in the Middle East, would suffer if she didn't return. Then they took her back to the Middle East as well. I don't know what happened to her. I haven't heard. Maybe . . . [*She draws a finger across her throat significantly*] It has happened. I know it has. I had a lucky escape.

In the end, the hard time I experienced turned out to be fruitful. It brought me to Dublin, where I am now very happy. All the Irish people I have met have been nice to me. They have helped and supported me. Now my children have finished their education and have grown up, my eldest son and my youngest son have come to work here, too. My daughter came over for a while but couldn't find work in her profession as a civil engineer, so she went back. Sadly, my husband died last year, on St Valentine's Day, of a heart attack. I used to go home once a year to see him. Now I am going back for the anniversary of his death.

I decided to set up the agency partly because of my son. He is qualified in computer science but couldn't get work in that area and had to settle for a job as a waiter. It was suggested to me that there was an opening for someone to try to get placements here for qualified people from non-EU countries. I thought to myself, 'That's a good idea', so I set up my agency which deals mainly with Filipinos. Originally, I had an Irish partner because I wasn't allowed to set up business myself. She died of cancer last year and I had to try to find some way to keep going. Again I approached my Columban priest and he helped me find a new partner. This man is only part-time, however, with his own business, so effectively I do most of the work with the help of my son. It was difficult at first to try and convince companies to employ Asians but it is getting easier. And we are learning as we go along. It took us three months to process the papers of the first group, who came here to work in a hotel in Bray. Now we know better what to do and the business is building up, mainly through word-of-mouth. We started with housekeepers, chambermaids, hotel workers and now we are branching out. We have recently placed some civil engineers with a big company here and now we are trying to get the attention of IBM.

At present my office is in my one-room apartment. The bed is on one side, the computer, photocopier and so on are on the other side. I shall have to find office space soon because it's too small. It's particularly inconvenient if I have an early morning appointment. I have to get up and make the place perfect, so as to create a good impression.

We look after the welfare of our workers, particularly when they first arrive. We meet them from the airport and find accommodation for them. That can be very expensive, especially if we have to buy duvets and sheets and towels for all of them. I prefer it if the accommodation is provided by the employer. Then the new arrivals sometimes have a little difficulty adjusting — for instance, to the food. In the Philippines, the staple diet is rice: rice for breakfast, rice for lunch, rice for supper. One of my people got very excited the other day when he saw something new on his plate: not roast potatoes, not baked potatoes, not chips. He started eating it. 'Siony,' he said to me, 'it was mashed potatoes!'

There's a big Filipino community here now. We've formed a group to organise activities. There's going to be a Mr and Miss Valentine's Dance soon. Because quite a few of our people are gay, I suggested Miss Gay Valentine, but it didn't catch on. Next year we are hoping to have a float for St Patrick's Day, with people wearing traditional costumes from different parts of the country, maybe playing some of our music. It would be really nice.

You can be a housekeeper all your life if you want, but I decided to try and improve myself so I started to learn about computers. I went to a place near St Stephen's Green and explained that I was a total beginner. Sometimes I felt bad because everyone else could do so much more than I could. But I got there in the end. Sometimes I am surprised when I think about myself: from a housekeeper to someone who is learning something new every day. It's great.

Elizabeth B *

Ivory Coast

Elizabeth is in her early thirties, with a beaming smile. Her hair is short. She has an open and pleasant manner and seems very intelligent, answering questions in a considered way. She sits in the Parents' Room of her children's school in central Dublin, when she has been making buns with some of the other mothers. Her English is excellent.

I'm from Abidjan, the capital of the Ivory Coast in West Africa, next to Liberia and Guinea. Towards the north, we are bordered by Burkina Faso; to the east is Ghana. The Ivory Coast is quite big, about the same size and shape as France, and in fact it used to be a French colony. Because my mother is from the English-speaking part of Cameroon, I grew up speaking both languages, English and French.

I came to Ireland because of the political problems we had back home. That was the push that led me to look for somewhere safer to live. My immediate family is my two kids, myself and my husband, although he isn't here at present; he's in France. Back home he was in politics, although he was also a businessman. And he's studied computer science. As for me, I used to be a secretary but here I'm a homemaker. If I'm given permission to work, I'd prefer to do that. Sitting down doing nothing is quite boring for somebody who has been used to working. It's a big change for us and was difficult at first but now we're settling down OK.

I've been here for almost a year and hope by next month to have a more positive view of what will happen. Either we'll join my husband in France or he'll come here. At the moment, everything is upside down. We're here as refugees and so far nothing has been done. Any reply would be better than just hanging about waiting.

At first I found the people quite distant, but once you get to know them better, that changes. Our own culture is different. We are brought up to be open. And we are used to the extended family. Here when you say 'family', people think of the immediate family, the nuclear family. But for us it's a big thing. If I'm walking on the street with my cousin and I meet someone, I say, 'Meet my sister' or 'Meet my brother'. I wouldn't even use the word 'cousin'. Everybody is brother and sister.

In September, this anti-racism organisation started running a pro-gramme for refugees to have lunch with Irish families. It was great for us. We were placed with very nice people who still call round to visit, to see how we're getting on. I live in the city centre but this lady lives out in Goatstown, towards the mountains. She has invited us over a couple of times since the original meeting. At Hallowe'en, she wanted my kids to go and spend the night so that they could go out with the other children and play and have fun. This was new for them. Back home, we don't celebrate Hallowe'en. For us the important date is 1 November, All Saints' Day. We remember our dead and visit their graves, clean them and put fresh flowers there. We go to church and then have a big meal. Just to commemorate our dead.

I was brought up as a Catholic but now I'm a born-again Christian. Here I attend a Pentecostal church on Westland Row. They are very friendly there. From time to time we've come across racial abuse in Ire-land. I don't think society will ever be rid of that, no matter what the government tries to do. Nevertheless, I don't worry too much about it because I'm a positive person.

The children have no problems at all in this school. There are so many different cultures, different nationalities mixing together here. It's really very good. And the parents can meet here, too. My daughter is nearly nine and my son is four-and-a-half. Back home they went to an international school, where you have a lot of expatriate children together. My daughter left the Ivory Coast three years ago, which is when the problems started there. I had to send her to my sister in England. When I came here, I fetched her too. At first, as with anyone, she was homesick for England but now she has settled down and made lots of new friends.

I used to visit my sister on holidays fairly regularly. In fact I've been to several European countries, even to America. So before I came here, although I hadn't really stayed in any European country for more than a month, I knew more or less what to expect. Of course, I was only ever here during the summer, so I'd never experienced the snow we had recently, for example.

Of course, I keep in touch with my family back home. It was difficult for a time but now there's a period of calm. The problems are still there but my family has moved on to Ghana so it's easier to get in contact with them.

Renu C *

Indian

Renu is twenty-five, with sleek black hair, tied back. She is wearing jeans and a sweater but says that she often wears a sari, particularly when going out. She is radiantly happy, expecting her first baby in two weeks' time. Her mother-in-law, with whom Renu evidently has an excellent relationship, shares in the conversation. She and her husband are over from Tanzania for the birth and to help out after the baby is born. The red-brick bungalow, where Renu lives, is set in rolling countryside a few miles from Limerick city. Homemade Bombay mix and Indian sweetmeats are served with tea for the guest. Renu speaks very good English, with a slight Limerick intonation.

My husband has been in Limerick for eighteen years — he studied here as a student at the University and now teaches. Several years ago he asked his parents to choose him an Indian wife. We are Sikhs — not very religious, but we observe the tradition of arranged marriages. My husband even asked for the approval of his grandfather. It's a matter of respect.

I come from a new town called Chandigarh, three hundred kilometres from Delhi, which in India is quite near. When I came here, I spoke no English. In my country, people can often read and write the language but can't speak it fluently, although that's changing now. The last time I went to India to visit my family it seemed to me that speaking English was becoming more common, even among people in shops and restaurants. For myself, I worked hard to pick it up. I've been here four years now, four years and two days. We used to live in Henry Street, in the centre of Limerick, and we moved to this house last year. I'd never been to Ireland before. Actually, before I went to Tanzania, I'd never been out of my country. My first impression was of the friendliness here. People have been very kind and helpful and there is nothing that I dislike, except that I miss my family.

I'm going to have the baby in Limerick hospital. The staff there are very good, very helpful. I've been going to antenatal classes and you can ask anything you want and they'll explain it to you.

I joined the International Women's Club after I had been here one year. I had been going to a college in town to improve my English and the club was great for getting to know people and to give me conversation practice.

My husband has an Irish passport now and earlier in the year I got a job as a sales assistant in a petrol station. I worked there for about seven months. It was good for me because I found it very quiet here and wanted to go out. At work I met the same people every day and that helped my English. At first I couldn't understand the accent but everyone was very patient. And because I didn't smoke, I had no experience of the names of cigarettes but gradually I learned all about them. Because I would wear a badge with my name on it, people would ask how to pronounce it, whether it meant anything.

There seems to be a good attitude to India here. Some know more about it than others but people are always saying how much they would like to go there.

We have loads of Irish friends because my husband has been here so long. The wives of his friends took care of me when I first arrived and showed me around and explained the customs. In India, we don't celebrate Christmas, so I had never seen a Christmas tree before. Now I even put decorations up. We also celebrate our New Year, which occurs around October. It's called Diwali.

The members of the International Women's Club take it in turns to prepare national dishes, and show the others how to do it, so that we get to make and taste each other's food: English, Italian, Indian, French. It's very hard to be a vegetarian when you are in a foreign country, so we aren't strict about it, although my father- and mother-in-law keep to the diet. I still don't like ham, but I will eat most things. In general it's difficult to keep up our religion but we have a shrine in the home and practise our devotions every morning.

I had a baby shower recently. I didn't know what it is and was told that it's the custom in America with a first baby. My friends prepared it secretly. I was working but was off on Friday and they said, 'There's a class on Friday. Would you like to come?' So I said I would. When I arrived, they produced all these presents for me. It was a lovely surprise. I couldn't stop myself crying.

I don't wear a sari much here because it's too windy. But when I go out somewhere special, I'll dress up in one. [*Renu shows an album of wedding photographs, with herself beautifully dressed in traditional clothes.*] My hands had a henna design painted on them for the wedding ceremony. They say in India: when the henna comes out dark, you'll get on with your mother-in-law. [*She and her mother-in-law laugh affectionately with each other.*]

One thing in India, we know we have to respect our parents and abide by their wishes with regard to arranged marriages. Sometimes these break up but the parents will always try and get the couple to stay together. Here there doesn't seem to be the same respect. And then my husband was very helpful to me, to get me to adjust to this new life. Some Indian husbands don't allow their wives to go out and make friends. But my husband encouraged me, even though sometimes I wouldn't be back in time to make his lunch. I would leave something for him, of course. Of course, he has lived here so long that he is not like the usual Indian man.

Marie Campion
Czech

Marie is a small, energetic woman in her forties. She has dark hair, parted in the middle and wears rimless glasses, which give her a very Middle-European appearance. She speaks excellent English very fast, her Czech accent overlaid with Irish intonation. Her manner is warm and friendly, and she has definite views on a range of subjects. She is personally acquainted with the owner of the café in the north Dublin suburb where she sits drinking strong coffee and he comes over to say hello. As she says, she likes to be part of the life of the local community and does her shopping in the small neighbourhood shops rather than in supermarkets, which she hates. All these cosy circumstances are in sharp contrast to the story she has to tell. She runs a clinic for Eating Distress, lectures widely and has written a book on the subject.

I'm originally from Czechoslovakia, the Czech Republic as it is now. I still use the old name because I'm very conservative about it. I'm actually from a place two miles from the border and studied in Slovakia. I loved it there. The present division is artificial and Slovakia has suffered because of it.

Because I was always very religious, I wanted to study medicine so that I could work in the missions but I was told I could only go to Charles University in Prague if I gave up my religion. They gave me twenty-four hours to decide and I refused. I ended up studying economics, tourism and hotel management, which was permitted to me. Me and thirty-five communists. They chucked me out after four years anyway. It's a long story.

When I think of what we endured for our religion in Czechoslovakia. I had to pass the school on my way to church and the next day would be called up before the headmaster. We had get up at dawn to go to 5 a.m. mass because that was the only one at which they didn't have spies.

In the mid-seventies I left my country illegally on a forged passport and was living in Germany. I remember my mother phoning me one Christmas to say that I was the only one in my class not yet married and was there any chance of me getting a man. At the time I was twenty-four. So along came this handsome Irish man, tall with beautiful blue eyes, and asked me out. I wanted to leave Germany so he invited me to Ireland. But because I'd been granted asylum in Germany, the only way to stay here was to get married. I didn't think twice about it. When I look back now, I don't think I was quite sane at that period. My marriage effectively lasted one day, the wedding day. Although I didn't know it, my husband needed me too — he was gay at a time when it was illegal in Ireland.

I hated it here at first. I couldn't speak English but I had a ten-year prison sentence on my back for the way I left my country and couldn't return. My father came over for my wedding and loved it here. When he went for walks around Kerry, where we were living, people would smile and ask, 'How are you?' He thought that was wonderful. In Czechoslovakia you were afraid even to say hello, in case there was some hidden motive behind it. Anyway, my father told me, 'You know, Marie, if you want to live in this country, you have to become like the Irish. You seem to expect the Irish to become like the Czechs.' It took me a long time to discover that he was right.

In the meantime, my husband and I emigrated to Australia, where we set up a restaurant, which did well financially. But it was too far mentally for me: I'm European through and through. Anyway, it was in Australia that I finally realised how much I love Ireland and the people I knew here. It was there, too, I learnt the real reason why the marriage wasn't working. My husband admitted his problems to me, including his homosexuality, his alcoholism, his schizophrenia. At the same time, he was very violent. It's easy to say, you should do this and that, you should leave, but when you're inside the situation, you see things differently. I only came to my senses on the night I was pushed back over the edge of the balcony with a knife at my throat. After that, I returned to Ireland on my own. My baby daughter had been left here with my in-laws. That was the biggest mistake I ever made in my life. I felt so guilty. But my husband had told me I wouldn't be a good mother and I believed him because I was very vulnerable. I had even attempted suicide a few times, and I said to myself, *My God, I can't even die properly.*

Because of my religion, I had been prepared to continue living with my husband. The knife at my throat forced me to think of my daughter. Because she is Irish, I decided to stay in this country. I found a furnished flat in Dublin. I had nothing, not even a change of clothes, because one day when he was in one of his states my husband had torn everything up. We'd had a joint account but when I came to collect my share of the money, I discovered it was all gone. You can see how mental I was in those days: I'd trusted him. All I had was the clothes I was wearing, one baby and £250. I got no support from anyone. His mother wouldn't accept the truth about her son, especially as I was four years older than him and a foreigner. It had to be my fault. So one day the two of us, mother and child, went to church. I love empty churches and particularly in Ireland where I hear from the altar such different things from Czechoslovakia that it is hard for me to believe it's the same religion. Anyway, that was when I got this idea to open a restaurant. But I had to start from nothing. I bought a bike. I started to bake home-made bread and made sandwiches which I took round offices to sell. I was like one of these refugees, bringing my baby with me and leaving her at reception if I couldn't get a neighbour to mind her. It was humiliating, but I didn't see that I had any other choice. Gradually things turned around and after two years I was able to open a coffee shop in Harcourt Street. Then I got another one, and a house in Clontarf and was employing twelve people, so it was going well.

I had to get loans for the restaurants. The bank manager was a very good customer of mine, who believed in me. But the last one nearly ruined me because it turned out there was a problem with the lease. I owed about £210,000 and had to remortgage the house. We were closed for a long time and I lost the clientele, lost the house, lost everything. I was desperate but Gerry said, 'Haven't you still got your head?' I'd met Gerry, who was to be my second husband, when he was working across the road from the restaurant. For many years we were just friends.

I thought about what he said and my first preference to study medicine. At the time I was recovered from an eating disorder which I'd had since childhood: anorexia, bulimia, you name it, I'd had it. They give it different labels but it was all the same, all in the mind. At the age of eleven I'd been hospitalised. The so-called best experts told me I would never be cured. Then one day in the middle of a binge, I read an article in a magazine about a woman who had overcome a problem like mine. It gave me such hope. I started getting myself together through self-help. So then my dream was to set up a clinic to help others. After the restaurant business went bankrupt, I started doing courses in counselling, massage, nutrition, anatomy, aromatherapy.

Finally I leased a premises and waited for people to come in. It took a while to build up but after three years I was so busy that I couldn't take on any more clients. In 1999, we got over 5,000 phone calls. Then I started to write a book. This was another dream of mine. I was working all day and writing at night and running home in the middle of the day to cook dinner for Gerry's father, who was living with us, and who insisted on meals on the table at a certain time. It was crazy. So I decided more people needed to be able to do the work I was doing, and I shifted to training. Now in that little office there are twelve of us, including myself and Gerry. It just proves that anything can be done.

I've an office at home now and I've started another book. I prepare material for various organisations. I deal mostly with children now: my youngest patient was just three years old. These are usually very super-sensitive children, full of anxiety, negativity, self-destructive thoughts. There's never just one reason.

I love nearly everything here, even the weather, I'm embarrassed to say. In Czechoslovakia it's either too hot or too cold. Here for the first ten years I didn't even have an overcoat. I'm very aware, nevertheless, that Ireland is becoming more materialistic. I've been ten years in counselling now and I see the changes. This rich time results in depression, emptiness and psychological problems of all sorts. The problem in the past was that there were no jobs. Now the problem is that people don't even have the time to say hello. I can't wait until the bubble bursts and we again have the time to sit down with a cup of tea.

Something I can't understand here: people don't vote and then they give out about the government. In Czechoslovakia we had to vote, but they told us who to vote for. I feel very strongly about this. Either you don't give out or you try to do something about it. I always talk to the canvassers at the door and ask what they are going to do, for example, about mental illness. I check it out before the elections. Then I am so proud to vote. We make a day out of it and go for a drink afterwards.

I tried to get an annulment for three years but it was difficult because I had no witnesses, except my husband's mother and she refused to give evidence. It was humiliating for me. Every time I left the archbishop's palace, I felt like Mary Magdalene. Eventually I got divorced through the Dominican Republic and remarried in the United States. But even just a year and a half ago, in confession, I was told I should leave Gerry because I was living in sin — even when I told them I have two children! That's why I don't have a high opinion of the Catholic Church here, to the extent of putting my children in the Protestant school. There are a lot of good Catholics here and I like the fact that what happened in the past is now coming out. But I don't go to the local church. I don't like the way they are always asking for money. However, I would never give up my faith and have been attending Clarendon Street church every Sunday for ten years.

At the same time, it's changing but not yet enough. When I was in Kerry I was organising dinners between Protestants and Catholics; I felt very passionate about it and I asked the priest to announce it from the pulpit. He was astonished that I should even consider such a thing and refused. At the same time, he was announcing GAA parades and children's swimming, yet he wouldn't do this. Another time, I wanted to do something nice for the priest and I made him a lovely Christmas cake, even though at the time I didn't have any money. He took one look and said 'God, we have so much. You eat it.' It confused me so much. And then to see them driving around in their big cars . . .

Despite that, I love this country so much now. You know the question: *Where is home?* I never missed Czechoslovakia the way I missed Ireland when I was in Australia. Then my life for so long was so hectic that I never had time to think about it. When I started on my recovery, I found myself asking questions: *Who am I? Where do I belong?* Even now, I get goose-pimples flying back from abroad and seeing Howth from the plane, the mountains round Dublin.

And my two dreams have come true: to set up the clinic and publish a book. In it some of my patients tell the stories of their recoveries. It's entitled *Hope.* So now I'll have to find some new dreams.

Natalie Capitaine

French

Natalie is a tall woman in her early thirties. She has wavy red-blonde hair and a pale complexion. She apologises for her poor English — she is attending a Basic English course at the People's College in Parnell Square in Dublin — but in fact, despite a pronounced French accent, it is competent enough. She is thoughtful about her responses to questions and has an air of quiet self-possession.

I'm from near Paris and have been in Ireland for about eight months now. Previously I came over to study as a student and found Dublin very interesting, such a small town in comparison with Paris. Last year, I was a little bit fed up with France and wanted a change, so I decided to try and find a job here. Just now I'm working for Xerox, in the finance section, and for the moment it's OK. In France I was an estate agent and before that a personnel assistant. I like to have direct relations with clients but here I'm on the telephone all the time. At the moment my English isn't fluent enough, so I'm working in the French department. As a result my English unfortunately isn't improving as fast as I would like because I just don't have much opportunity to use it. I speak English with my flatmates but they are foreigners, too, Spanish and Italian. It's not easy to talk with Irish people in pubs because they are always in groups and it can be very noisy. Sometimes it's OK. When I introduce myself and they hear my accent, they want to know where I'm from. In general, people are friendlier than in France.

The atmosphere was different when I came as a student, more exciting. I suppose working here, I'm finding it a little disappointing. I don't have time to study or go out much during the week, I'm too tired. And the cost of living is very high. I found it difficult to rent a suitable apartment. If you want your own place, you either have to be very far from the centre or to pay a lot of money. One big advantage, however, is that the flats are furnished. In France they would be empty.

In the first three months I was here I moved three times. At first I was in Dunboyne, which is very far out. Then I was sharing with five other people in a house in Castleknock. It was convenient for work but such a boring place, with nothing to do. So then I found a place in the city centre. I share with three others, which suits me because I don't like to live alone. On the other hand, at the moment they are three men, which is a problem because they don't clean up after themselves. Sometimes I feel like a mother, telling them what to do and tidying up. One is moving out soon and I hope the next flatmate will be a girl.

Another thing that struck me: in France we aren't used to drinking all the time, just a little wine with dinner. It's amazing to see the amount people here drink. I enjoyed it at first, going out to the pub all the time but I don't want to end up an alcoholic. In France I'd meet friends round a table for a meal where you can have a good conversation; it's not too noisy. But it's not like that here. The Irish prefer to go to a pub and you have to accept that's the way it is. You can't change the culture. As for boyfriends, I've been out with some Irish men but again they just want to drink. It would be nice to go out somewhere else sometimes, maybe to a restaurant.

In France I had lots of interests. Here, well, it's better than a year ago. I can go to the cinema, the libraries, museums, travel round Ireland. All the same, the very fact that Dublin's such a small town means that after a while it gets a bit boring. I don't think I'll stay here for the rest of my life. There are more opportunities for me in France.

I find girls different here. Their clothes are very attractive, even flashy. I would feel very conspicuous wearing such clothes myself. As well as the fact that it's so cold and yet they wear so little. French people all find it amazing. In our country only girls who aren't respectable dress in such a way.

Transport is difficult. I work in Blanchardstown, far from the centre, and the bus service is poor. In France there'd be a bus every ten minutes. And then we have the metro. I have to get up early in the morning, at 6 a.m., to make sure of a bus that will get me to work on time.

People here have definitely got less friendly, even since last year, since so many foreigners started coming in. They aren't used to it. You notice it in shops, where the assistants don't have any patience with you any more. In five or ten years, it will be just like Paris. Still, for the moment I'm happy enough. I'll stay for the time being. Eventually I'd like to go to another country, to see what it's like there, maybe to Barcelona, somewhere the sun shines. None of my family has ever lived abroad before. At first they thought it was a little bit dangerous but soon got used to it. They are proud of me. In their eyes, I'm a pioneer.

Glenda Cimino

American

Glenda lives in an amazing old cottage, dating from 1811, in Donny-brook, south Dublin. It incorporates the shell of a church, which Glenda thinks is even older. Piled high with clutter — books and papers, parts of old set designs, paintings and posters — the place is like an Aladdin's cave. Glenda is a small, dark, plumpish woman with a Mediterranean look that comes straight from her Sicilian ancestors. She speaks quickly and is highly articulate.

I was born in Atlanta, Georgia, part of the post-war baby boom. My father was Italian-American and my mother Scots-Irish. When I was seventeen, I left home for good and went away to college in Florida. I got to spend time in South America as part of the programme there. When I got my degree, I went off to do a postgrad degree in Sociology at Columbia University and spent a few months in Chile.

It was at the time when I was trying to write up my PhD and was teaching my first course — in urban sociology at Queen's College — that I was caught up in a lot of political unrest because of the Vietnam war. I was also doing a karate class in preparation for the revolution! All the people I'd started that with dropped out except me. In the class there was this Irish-American guy called Jack, and one time I accidentally punched him on the nose, something you're not supposed to do under any circumstances. When I checked to see if he was all right, I discovered he had these beautiful blue eyes.

We got to know each other and pretty soon Jack moved in with me. We were thinking of going to Mexico but meantime he showed me these letters he'd received from a man living in Wicklow, with an address at Tinahely or Shillelagh or something. A very beautiful and poetic address. This was a man of about sixty called Max, whom Jack had met one night on a rooftop in Morocco. They'd exchanged addresses and corresponded for two years. Max was a yoga expert with a herb garden, who was teaching himself Arabic by listening to his short-wave radio. He invited us to come over and visit him for as long as we liked. So, two months after we met, Jack and I decided to take off for Ireland. And that's why, when people ask me what brought me here, I say it was because of the chance meeting between two people I didn't know in a country I've never been to.

I had vague ideas I might work here. My flat was in a good area of New York, near Columbia University, and very cheap. But strangely enough, I gave it up. In those days it was difficult to find such a place and you'd never give it up if you were planning to return. And yet I can't remember ever making a conscious decision. I just sold all my things and never looked back, except that I had dreams for fifteen years that I still owed rent.

Max met us in Wicklow and took us to a one-roomed pub. I thought Wicklow was the most quaint and wonderful place I'd ever seen; and yet at the same time amazingly civilised. We decided to buy a house, with Max's help, and lived there for a couple of years. When Jack went back to America, I stayed on. Max had become like a father figure to me — my mother had left my own father when I was two and I was never close to my stepfather. But then Max was killed in a terrible road accident and I decided to leave Ireland, because the circle that had gathered around him scattered like the beads of a broken necklace.

I felt really bereaved by Max's death and was all set to take up a teaching job in upstate New York. But I made the mistake of first going to Listowel Writers' Week, to Brendan Kennelly's poetry workshop, where I met a young poet and we started a relationship. At the same time I was offered a job in Dublin that I hadn't applied for. It suddenly seemed that the weight of the scales was very much in favour of staying in Ireland.

I worked for five years with the Combat Poverty Agency as senior re-search officer, which was challenging because I really didn't feel I knew enough about Ireland. I actually ended up doing research for ten years, initially with the Language Attitude Survey, then with Combat Poverty and finally with the European Community. The Language Attitude Survey was an extensive study of people's attitudes to and usage of the Irish language. I had been hired because I was neutral, with no axe to grind. But eventually I got very disillusioned with that research because the results were not believed. We'd indicate that the survey proved such-and-such and then these politicians would come along and claim something different, whatever suited them. They'd also disregard our recommendations and come up with their own. I think I walked myself into a corner taking on evaluation research, because after all no one really wants to be evaluated.

So then in the early eighties my boyfriend and I got together with a group of people and set up Beaver Row Press. It was a co-operative publishing house devoted to bringing out the work of new poets. We were very idealistic and made the decision not to put our own writing out first, which in retrospect was a mistake. I think the Arts Council would have looked much more kindly on us if we had been publishing our own work. As it was, we got very little grant aid from them. And while I loved the work, my own writing suffered. The press was never profitable and no one made a living out of it, so gradually the group fell apart. I kept going but stopped publishing in 1991 because it was too burden-some on my own. I now see how much easier it would have been if desktop publishing had been available at that time.

Nevertheless, it was a very interesting experiment. In all, we brought out the work of about twenty-seven poets, many of whom had never been published before, but who later became well-known, such as Paula Meehan, Anne Hartigan and Tony Curtis. Brendan Kennelly gave us a couple of his books to publish. I never regretted that period of my life, although there have been moments when I would have appreciated the comfort and security of an academic career. A lot of the people I taught in the States went on to get their theses and are now in very good posi-tions, unlike me. I'm still living on the edge. Then again, I used to have a neighbour who'd come to me and say, 'You know, Glenda, the rich, they don't be happy.'

I wanted my daughter, who was nine and who had been born in Ireland, to have some experience of living in the States and in 1991 I had the opportunity to take up a research job in Florida, writing up the history of my old college. It didn't turn out quite as I expected but it was certainly a learning experience. I was eventually replaced, and after that found a job as copy editor for a very right-wing newspaper in Florida. I got fired from that when I went on a trip to Cuba. I'd had this idea that one of the reasons I'd been mouldering in Ireland was because I wasn't a native. What I now discovered was that nepotism exists everywhere. Even though I was from America, I wasn't from Florida, I wasn't from that particular community, and had nobody backing me, relatives or people in power. But I cut my losses and did a series of secretarial jobs. Then I got a regular column with a by-line in a local arts magazine, and started publishing cartoons in an environmental paper so it looked like things were opening up for me, that I had a little niche. The group I mixed with then I'd call psychological exiles. They were living in America but were alienated from a lot of what was going on. I'm still in touch with several of them.

Then I was in a car crash. It's easy to see how quickly a life can go downhill. I had to have two operations. I had to give up my job and go on social welfare. The driver who hit us hadn't been properly insured and I was cheated by my attorney. I'd been waiting for things to get better but decided I should try to get back to Ireland fast before things got worse.

People here had kept in contact for the four years we were away. They said, 'Everything's different now', and kind of hinted that I might be better off staying where I was — while in the States, I was getting the opposite message. I suppose it's true: the grass is always greener . . . but then it literally is in Ireland, isn't it? So I came back in 1995, only to be told in the social welfare office that I couldn't sign on; that I had no right to be here. I showed them my open visa and my permit and the social welfare card I'd had from before, giving me permission to work. The woman employee said, 'You shouldn't have that' — and tore it up in front of me! It seemed that Ireland had tightened up its rules in the years

I'd been away. Anyway, after a lot of agony and running around, I found that because my daughter was an Irish citizen, I automatically had the right to work here, but not before I'd been publicly humiliated. I was shocked by the experience.

I did secretarial temping then all over Dublin for a while. There aren't many city streets that I don't know. And for the last year I've been a student of multimedia. I mix with a lot of teenagers now, at college and because my daughter is sixteen and brings her friends home. I can see there's discrimination against youth here. For example, before I went back to the States, I'd done a project with kids in St Teresa's Gardens, in the inner city. These were all school drop-outs. They'd tell me things about going to town and being stopped by the guards, who'd say to them, 'You're off your turf.' This ghettoisation thing is still around.

But I love living in Ireland. It's changed me for the better. Many things that happened to me over the years in America were traumatic and almost no one there helped me with it. It was only when I got to Ireland that I began to work on myself: examine what had made me what I was, and what I loved about who I was. All the same, for a long time I thought that if I went back to New York, I'd immediately become neurotic again. That the difference was not in me but in my context.

My aspirations now are to finish some of my projects. I'm a member of so many groups. Artists' Anonymous, for one. It's based on Alcoholics Anonymous; we meet once a month to give each other support and talk through the problems we're having with our writing. It can help you move on. Personally, I find it very difficult to finish anything and now I can see how my early experiences have contributed to this.

You can look back on your life and see the opportunities you threw away. You can also look at what happened to you and see why it is. I think it's important not to have regrets. People have asked me if I'm bitter about the losses I've had in my life, but after all, very few people have everything their way. Most are from dysfunctional backgrounds in one way or another, so I don't think it's acceptable to use that as an excuse for anything. We should perhaps love more and judge less. I feel very creative now: what little things I've finished have tended to get published. One thing that made me proud: I was included in the *Salmon Anthology of Twentieth-Century Irish Women Poets*.

I think I've always been a bit of an outsider, everywhere I've lived. So being an outsider here was a feeling I was perfectly at home with. I've never been in a place where I've felt one hundred per cent part of the community and in fact I've often wondered if it's ever really possible. Still, my first Irish boyfriend was from a family of about ten kids and I thought that was perfect. They used to have these parties where they'd dance and sing together, and I loved being a part of that. I've missed them all as much or more than I've missed him.

Ana Cosma *

Romanian

Ana is aged thirty-four, pretty with long dark curly hair and a golden complexion. She is dressed all in black and receives me in the spotless kitchen of her home in suburban west Dublin where she lives with her husband and two children. She apologises in advance for smoking so much and throughout the interview is evidently restraining herself from lighting up constantly. She is very nervous at first, as well as being quite intense, but gradually begins to relax. She speaks in a soft, slow voice, accurately but with a pronounced Romanian accent. Outside the afternoon heavens open in a massive downpour.

I come from Constanza, which is a beautiful place on the Black Sea. We left Romania ten years ago and we've been in Ireland for four years. What can I say: it is an honour and I am forever grateful to have been given the chance to live and work here. Nowhere has felt more like home than Dublin.

As a Romanian woman living in Ireland, I have been thinking a lot recently about the relative positions of women in our two countries. As nations we're not very different culturally but as family units there's a great deal of difference. Even under the communists there were many families, mine included, resembling those of the Ireland of thirty or forty years ago, based on high moral principles and religion. The mother would be expected to stay at home and rear the children. There were other lifestyles, of course, but I can't speak for them. I was very strictly brought up. So I came here as a housewife, obedient and orderly, with dreams of course, but I put them to one side. Then I started looking around at the way Irish women live today, at the typical Irish wife and mother. It was nice to see them knowing what they want, making time for themselves independent of their duties to their husbands and families. But I never thought about changing my own life until one night a year ago, at New Year, when my husband made a toast, thanking God for giving him the chance to fulfil all his dreams. Suddenly I realised that I was no part of any of his dreams. It was very painful to learn that for thirteen years I had barely existed for him. So then I started to ask myself this question, 'What is my place, as a woman? Where do I stand? What do I represent?' It's a big question with no answer. Do you think your book will be able to answer this question?

I was very young when we got married; I was eighteen, a child myself. In those days in my country, it was difficult for a girl to get to know boys. There was no way you could go out with them to a restaurant or a party. You had to keep your dignity if you wanted one day to be a respected wife. So he was my first and last boyfriend. We married and started building a life together. We were very much on our own because both our families were against the marriage. Neither of us had anything and whenever we earned a little money, we would buy something for our flat. First a bed, then two forks and two knives and so on. Probably he wouldn't have made it so well on his own.

Being at home all the time is new for me: most of my life I have worked very hard outside the home. I used to go to work, study at the same time, and be a mother and a wife. Nobody ever helped me in the house or stayed with my children when they were sick. I brought my share of money into the family but had no control over it. For example, I never had the freedom to pick out the dresses I truly liked. My husband would come with me to buy clothes: he'd never like the things I liked, and so, because he was paying, I would have to accept his choice. I never went into a pub until last year in Ireland. He never took me out. Never. Any party or celebration would take place at home.

He has Irish men friends and goes out with them. The funny thing is that, until this year, he was considered by them the happiest man on earth, with a little wife who did what she was told. I had no identity of my own. Now I just can't understand why a man wouldn't treat a woman as his equal. We've faced many hard things over the years and it has always been me who has had to take responsibility for the big decisions. Even though I've also been the woman who cleaned, cooked three times a day and ironed everything, including socks.

My husband kept telling me my place was at home with the children. 'As long as I give you money,' he said, 'you don't need anything else.' That was the real moment at which I started to question my life, the fact that every single morning I would wake up thinking of the needs of the family and by the end of the day be too tired to think of myself. If I had never come to Ireland, I would have continued to live in misery. But now I have changed. Now I wake up every morning and after I've washed my face, I think of myself. As a Catholic I wouldn't consider leaving my husband under any circumstances. In any case, he is a good father and would make great sacrifices for the children. But he has his own life, which doesn't include me. I don't know why — lack of love, perhaps.

He was very tough until the day we had a big row and I threw all his clothes out of the window. He spent the night sleeping in the car. He never took me seriously until then, even though I am a bit ashamed about having done it.

Do I have friends here? When we first came here, we wanted to rent a flat and the landlord showed us something we didn't like, so we asked him if he had anything bigger. He said he did and I was preparing to write down the address when he said, 'Jump in the car, I'll take you there.' It was such a nice gesture. We have been friends ever since. For a long time, his wife was the only Irish woman I knew. It's only in the last year that I have tried to get in touch with other Irish women, even just other mothers on the estate, or in the shops. Now I have started to go out with my women friends. Another thing I have done over the past year is to take driving lessons. This is something that he never allowed me to do before. I am at last becoming self-sufficient.

I've always liked reading and writing. One day my husband found
something which I called my first novel. I had been writing now and
again the best things that came into my mind. And I was putting it together into something very nice. He read some of it and then destroyed
it. 'Why are you doing this?' he said. 'You don't need this sort of thing.'
Then a few months ago we had a barbecue and he told a neighbour who
works in publishing that I am a good writer. So now I keep thinking that
I should get back into it. It's hard in English but I don't want to write in
Romanian. Who would be interested? You say 'Russia' and people think
of Tolstoy, Dostoevsky, all these big names. You say 'France' and they
think of Victor Hugo, Alexandre Dumas. . . . You say 'Romania' and
people think of one word: 'gypsy'.

It's said that the Irish are racist. I don't believe that. I believe
that they are scared. In a very short time, from being a country where
very few foreigners lived, Ireland has become multicultural, a place
full of foreigners, refugees. Unless Irish people are in constant contact with these people, they are uncertain about what to say, what to
do. It's just a case of not knowing. Personally I have never seen hate
or prejudice in anyone's eyes. And the other side of it is that we foreigners must give Ireland our best. As long as you behave decently,
I don't think you should fear that the Irish will behave in a racist
manner.

That said, it's very difficult for Romanians to study here at college.
The authorities are afraid they will come here and then claim political
asylum. But it's wrong to treat everyone the same. We are very much
individuals. Many of the Romanians who are here at the moment are
the more unfortunate members of society, people who have nothing
back home. Their reasons to be here are mostly economic. Not many of
them are planning to stay. I like to keep away from these questions myself. There are occasions when I hear about things that certain Romanians have done that make me feel embarrassed. But of course there are
Irish people who do bad things, too. Every nation has its good and bad
people.

I don't want to go back to live in Romania. Don't get me wrong, I love my country and am a good Romanian. But I see my life here for many more years.

Ineke Durville

Dutch

Ineke is tall and slim with smooth light brown hair. Her hands, when she answers the door, are covered in soil because she has been gardening. The kitchen where she sits is airy and full of plants, with a big window overlooking the back garden of her north Dublin house. She has a serious manner and soft voice, offset occasionally by a sudden yelp of laughter. Her Dutch accent is almost imperceptible. The conversation is constantly interrupted by an attention-seeking large white and black cat.

In the seventies I was in college in The Hague studying social work, but I wasn't keen on the opportunities available there. So when in my second year at college I had to do a placement for a month, I thought of coming over to Ireland, which I'd visited a few times previously. At that time, agencies here were only just starting to employ social workers and this seemed to offer interesting scope for involvement in the development of new services, so I asked if I could do a longer placement in my third year. I came back then for six more months.

It was a breath of fresh air. There was excitement at all the possibilities. And there was none of the heavy politicisation we had in Holland. The students at my college there were mostly Maoist in outlook — you weren't allowed think in any other way — and this influenced the way the college operated. For example, I remember at the end of my first year we wanted to celebrate the anniversary of the founding of the college, but that was considered totally bourgeois. You couldn't have a party unless it was for something really worthwhile. So we got around it by holding a fundraiser for Tanzania. We actually raised 4,000 guilders, which was a lot at the time.

Days, weeks, used to be spent discussing the philosophy from which the service would be delivered. This was also the case with the agencies. There seemed to be no thought to involve the service users, to consider their needs and wishes. It wasn't like that here. It was much more practical. So at the end of my four years at college, I decided to come over to Ireland for good.

At first I worked in a café called Murph's, cleaning tables. If an inspector came to find out who was working there, we illegal aliens (as I was then, Ireland not having fully joined the EEC) had to pretend to be customers, get a coffee and sit down at a table. But very soon I got a job as a psychiatric social worker in a local health centre in Ballymun. At that time, the whole development was bringing the service down to a local level, involving people in the improvement of their own communities instead of coming in as an outside agency to tell them what they needed. Initially, all we had in Ballymun was a clinic, but as time went on, we got more activities for patients, and they'd see it as a place for linking in.

Life for me is very different here in Ireland. For example, in Holland most families are small, the family network loose, so my support group would be my friends. You never realise how important that is until you're gone from it. Here, it's the other way round: my colleagues would go home to their families for the weekends, but I wouldn't have that fallback. I can't say I felt lonely, but it was strange. After a few years, that feeling went, especially after I built up a good network of friends here too and met Rody, my husband.

I remember when I'd been here a few months, a friend came over from Holland. You know how, when you're walking down Grafton Street, you meet everyone you know. Loads of people were saying 'Hi, Ineke! How are you!' My friend was totally amazed. We had both lived in The Hague, which is a smallish place: 600,000 people. Even then I would rarely bump into someone I knew. People here are very friendly and easy and you link in quickly. I really like that and I would now find it hard to be back in Holland.

It was only when I got married and had children that it hit me how Catholic the country is. No one we knew was going to mass, but, when it came to it, few would actually stick to their guns and say, 'No, we're not going to get married in church.' Traditions are still strong here. We went to Holland and had a civil marriage ceremony in the town hall the day the Pope came to Ireland, so we missed all the fun — wasn't that terrible!

A friend of mine had her children baptised — that was the one concession she made — but then never did any more. She said it was nearly worse because her family then had this expectation that she would send them to communion and confirmation. Before you have a child, you don't think about these things too much but then this little baby arrives and you say, 'Am I going to have to bring her up as a Catholic or do I fit her into this Protestant school?' What are the options? It really puts it on the line, because it's fine for me to be different but it's difficult for children. A colleague at work told me about the Dalkey School Project[*] and I went down to see them. They were very welcoming. Then I called the first meeting in our house to set up a similar school on the northside of the city. All these people whom I had never seen before suddenly arrived, squashed into our little house. It was really exciting, great fun. A lot of them are still my friends. And through the school, the children learned to deal with being different, the big thing being the tolerance of difference.

I was just thinking whether or not Ireland has changed over the years. Certainly on the surface it seems to have changed a lot. But when I said to a friend recently that work has got much more difficult, she replied that it was always difficult. What's different is that before it was a different generation from mine enforcing all those rigid rules. I always felt that people from my own generation would be more open to new ways of looking at things. For instance, in the

---

[*] The first multi-denominational national school project to be recognised by the government. The school, run by a committee of parents and others who did not want sectarian schooling for their children, opened in 1978.

health field the original idea was of starting from the ground up, supporting communities to help themselves. I have been working in some very deprived communities and if you see how people have got themselves together through hard work and education, there is great movement on that level. But then there's a big gap. At the top — and now it's my generation at the top — they are still carrying on as if that's not happening, still not involving and listening to people on the ground. All that has changed is that they have learned management language — about targets and inputs and outputs — which doesn't take account of people at all.

Being brought up in Holland, where there's mixed schooling in primary, mixed schooling in secondary, I never had the assumption that there were things I as a woman couldn't do. But I also think that you get to an age where you become philosophical about life; you realise that there are certain things you can't change that fast. Of course, a lot has been achieved when I think of the differences with my mother's generation. There's no question now about women working or studying, and if you look at local communities, it's the women who have got up, who are going to courses, who are moving miles ahead. The men are left behind, stuck in a time warp. They still think they can run things by laying down the law. It's hard to reach them. Their function isn't there any more — the heavy jobs, dock work for instance, are gone — and it's sad to see how they have such difficulty adjusting to those changes.

The marriage bar hasn't been gone that long, since 1972, is it? Before that, if a woman civil servant got married, she had to give up her job. Of course, it's understandable that men have been reluctant to give up their privileges. I mean, I'd love a housewife, wouldn't you? Someone to cook a nice dinner and say, 'Sit down and have a drink.' Why would I give that up if I had it?

About going back, I think you outgrow your own culture. There's a lot of freedom and ease in Ireland. In Holland, there is on the one hand this tolerance of difference and on the other the expectation that you will obey the rules. If the traffic light is red, you don't cross the road. Dutch children are in bed by seven o'clock. My brother's colleague, a doctor, took his child out of school to go on a winter sports' holiday, the only time he could get off work. He had to go to court over it. And I said to myself, 'God, aren't I glad to live in Ireland! Isn't Ireland lovely!'

Isabel E *

Russian

Isabel is an extremely pretty, dark-haired woman in her twenties. She and her family are seeking residence permits in Ireland and in the meantime are staying in a converted hotel in West Cork. The hotel is warm but run-down and the nearby village has plenty of scenery but few shops and no regular public transport system. The family — Isabel, her husband and their two children — live in two rooms but are hoping to move soon to a more spacious apartment in a nearby town. During the interview, she holds baby Alan in her arms while her daughter and niece — who is here with her father — sit beaming beside her. There are many interruptions because we are in the dining room of the hotel. Isabel is trying to coax the children to eat their dinner. Her English is halting with a soft Russian blur to it, but she has a reasonable command of vocabulary and grammar and she smiles and laughs a lot, to make up for the gaps.

We left our country because we had been having troubles there and have been in Ireland seven or eight months now. We are from North Ossetia. It's in the Caucasus in the south of Russia, neighbouring the republic of Chechnya, where there is a big war. Before coming here we were in Belgium for some time. It was difficult for me there because I don't speak any French.

When we first came to Ireland we stayed in Cork but the authorities advised us to come here. Now we are hoping for a residence permit and

I think we will get it because of our baby. He was born in Ireland and so we are entitled to apply for it. We called him Alan because we wanted to find a name for him which would be suitable both here and in our country. In our republic, Alan is the most popular boy's name. The province we come from is called Alaniya, you see, after our ancestors who lived there.

Alan was born in Cork city. They were good to me in the hospital but I was surprised that the equipment was not much better than you would find in Russia. Cork is the second city, isn't it? I thought it would be more modern.

I like Ireland, much more than Belgium. I have heard that some Irish people don't want refugees to come to the country but personally I haven't experienced any problems. Our manager here helps us with everything; he is very good. And the kitchen staff, who are Irish, are friendly. This is a little village where everyone knows everyone, so they are aware when new people arrive. They smile and say hello to us in the street. Some of them are very kind. For example, my daughter is studying in the national school, which is quite far away, maybe twenty or thirty minutes' walking distance. Some parents from the village help us by picking up the children every morning and giving them a lift there and back again. My daughter likes the school and has many friends.

We eat here in the canteen because, even though we have a little kitchen in the apartment, we can't afford to buy food from the shops. I hope it will be different in town, where there is more selection. As for going to the local pubs, how could we afford it on £15 per week?

I am grateful to the Irish government but don't think they are doing enough for us. To leave us staying in a hotel for months on end is not good. It's very isolated here. Very beautiful, of course. In summer we were walking every day but now in winter it rains so much, we have to stay in. For me it isn't so bad because I have the children to look after, but for some of the others, all they can do is just sit waiting for their cases to be reviewed. There are about thirty people living here at the moment. We would prefer to be in Dublin or Cork but had no choice. The month we spent in Cork city, we received no money, no assistance, and when the woman from Social Welfare heard that we were staying with our friends — Russians we had met in Cork, also refugees — she said that it was not allowed. Our friends would be fined or something if we stayed on. That's why we came here.

We aren't allowed to work yet, but I hope that will change after we get our residence permits. First, we'd like to do some language courses to improve our English. Someone comes here once a week to give a class but it isn't enough. I am a dentist by training and that's why to get work I need to have better English.

The procedure is very slow. After so many months we don't even know when our interview will be. We just sit and wait. Some people here have already had their interviews but now they have to await the decision.

I miss Russia of course. My parents are there, my sisters and their families, many friends. I'd like to go back to visit after things have been settled here. We phone home every week. It was actually not so hard for me there economically. I had a good job, enough money. But for most people, life is very difficult, both politically and economically. My husband was trained as a geologist but had to work in the factory as a lathe operator.

Suzanne Eckhardt

German

Suzanne is small, in her late thirties. She has short, fair, curly hair and a slightly harassed expression, perhaps because the kitchen in which she sits in a small house in an estate on the outskirts of Limerick city is regularly crossed by a succession of chatty small boys. Two of them, with white blonde hair, are her own; the rest their friends. She speaks rapidly and fluently and has a warm and friendly manner.

I came over here originally in 1980, from a place just north of Frankfurt. My intention was to stay for one year and learn English. The connection was rather interesting. I'm a watchmaker by trade — it's in the family. We have a shop at home. About thirty years previously, my grandfather had employed someone who had emigrated to Ireland, and he still had the address. So he wrote and asked if this man could arrange a job for me, because it's not something that you can get very easily. He not only got me a job but also a flat, which at the time was also quite difficult to obtain. That man was Fritz Eckhardt, Wilfred's — my husband-to-be's — father.

I had flown over at short notice with only a small bag and had no radio or TV or anything like that in the flat, so Fritz told me to come over any time I liked for company in the evenings. As well as Wilfred, there was a daughter the same age as me, both of them born in Ireland.

Wilfred and I had started going out together very soon after I first came over and I stayed on in fact for two years. I hadn't said to my parents that I was involved with a guy here and basically I decided that anyway the most sensible thing would be to finish off my training and do my Master's. My employment prospects would then be much better. Also, Wilfred and I would be able to see more clearly how we felt about each other.

After a year, I came back to the same place where I had been working before and even to the same flat. It really worked out extremely well. Wilfred and I got married in 1986. I stayed in the same job for many years and then last year moved to a new place where I continue to work part-time, four half-days and one full day a week. I've worked like that since Hans, my eldest son, was one.

I still remember the first day I arrived in Ireland. Aer Lingus was on strike, so I couldn't fly to Shannon and had to take a train from Dublin to Limerick. I had little English at the time and was sitting on the train next to a man who was doing his best to have a conversation with me. When we got to Limerick he said, 'One thing you've got to experience is a pint of Guinness.' He took me for a pint in the Railway Hotel. At that time, I thought it was horrible. But times have changed. It's something you have to get used to. Anyway, then Fritz picked me up and drove me through Limerick. I still remember it was raining that night and my first impression was how filthy it all was.

After a few days I felt much better about everything. I was working with three women who were absolute dotes. One of those ladies unfortunately died recently: she was elderly even when I started working there. My first boss, who's now retired, was also great to work for, very kind, with a real personal touch.

Now I'm repairing clocks and watches. That whole thing has changed so much, since the advent of quartz watches. There aren't as many mechanical watches as before, and less care goes into the manufacture of them, so it can get frustrating.

Unfortunately, in general, life here has got a lot faster. One little thing can illustrate this: shortly after I first came over there was a murder here. It wasn't just a one-day wonder. People talked about it for ages because it was so unusual. Now, of course, the whole society has got a lot more violent. There doesn't seem to be the same morality. Everyone's giving out about the church now, but I feel that the world was a better place when people went along with its teaching. I myself attend the Church of Ireland and am a member of the choir. Through that I got to know a lot of people as well, so many really good people. I also have great neighbours.

There are a lot of positive changes, of course: people are better off. Limerick city itself has improved immensely. It's never looked as good before as it does now. The whole place has been cleaned up.

One thing that really saddens me is the North. I've travelled up there a few times and can't understand how people can hate each other so much. Hopefully now things there will get better.

I don't miss Germany too much, but I am a very family person and it was difficult for me, particularly when Hans and Stefan were born. I felt it was such a pity that my family wasn't around, because it was such a joyful time. And then there's a problem if something major happens, like when my grandfather, whom I loved very much, was dying. I was supposed to go over in the middle of May and on the first of April my dad rang and said that if I wanted to see my grandfather alive, I should go at once. So I did and he was still able to recognise me. He died a few days after I went back and I wasn't able to return for the funeral. I felt so lonely and even after many years, I still don't feel that I have buried him. In fact, last year my uncle and brother died within a few days of each other. My brother was only forty, with three children. It was very sad. But at least on this occasion I made sure I was able to go over for the funerals. There's something about a family being together on such an occasion to share the grief and take part together in the rituals that somehow makes it all more bearable. People recall the good times, the funny stories which otherwise might stay forgotten. That's what I missed when my grandfather died.

It's a strange thing but it seems to me that the longing to go home increases over the years. I was talking about this to another German woman who has been living here since the war. Just recently her last friend back home died. She was filled with this longing for what we call *heimat*. I don't think there's an adequate translation for this word. My own mother is Austrian and I know she feels the same. The trouble is that even when you go back, you find that you've lost something, the sense of belonging to one place. I've been thinking about all this recently, even though I have a good life and a good job here and am in general very happy.

It was strange how I found my new job. I was visiting a German friend who lives in Omagh and told her that I was thinking of giving up watchmaking. She was very insistent that I shouldn't, since it's such a rare skill these days. So anyway she mentioned me to a friend of hers who then just happened to meet a man he knew, a jeweller from Limerick, and asked him to keep me in mind if he ever had any work for me. This was a family business, a father and son who were both watchmakers, which is why I hadn't bothered approaching them for work. It turned out, however, that the father was thinking of going into semi-retirement, if only he could find someone to replace him. It all fitted together so well. I absolutely love working for them. They were very kind to me when my brother died and even phoned me in Germany to see if I was all right. That sort of caring means a lot.

Irene F *

American

Irene is in her mid-thirties, pale with brown hair. She sits in the Irish Film Centre café in Dublin and dispassionately tells the horror story of her early life. She has a clear voice and talks rapidly, smoking throughout the interview.

I was born in the States, in Chicago. My parents are Irish and they returned here in 1972. I stayed here until 1980 and then went back to the States. I finally moved back in 2000. Now that it's changed so much, I think I can live here at last.

A lot happened to me when I was a teenager, which had to do with society in Ireland at that time. The summarised version is that I got pregnant and was put in one of those convents down the country; the baby was taken off me for adoption and I became a drug addict. I went back to the States at the age of seventeen and stayed an addict for many years. Now, as an adult, I'm in recovery and in a role reversal; I'm a social worker, working with young drug addicts on the streets. So I'm seeing it all from a very different angle.

Both my parents came from a poor farming background. They emigrated to the States in the fifties and my dad did quite well. He came back here during the boom of the seventies but then lost everything in the eighties. Still, while I was growing up they were able to send me to a private school. My mother was a very strict Catholic and my dad enjoyed a drink: a typical Irish household, full of whiskey bottles and rosary beads. Sex wasn't discussed and I was extremely innocent. I remember being told by the nuns not to sit on a boy's lap on the way to a football match because you could get pregnant that way. I couldn't figure it out. In fact, I didn't think you could get pregnant unless you were married. That's how limited my education was.

When I was about fifteen I started hanging around with a crowd of kids who dressed in cool clothes and smoked hash. They call it peer pressure but for me it was somewhere I felt at home. My mother didn't allow me to mix with them, so I had to wait until everyone was asleep and then sneak out the window, across a roof and over the walls to the park where my friends were playing loud punk rock music, smoking joints and drinking cider. And then I'd go to convent school the next morning.

I fell in love with this guy when I was sixteen. He was beautiful and wild and dangerous. He fell madly in love with me too and we had this passionate affair. My mother got wind of it and forbade me from seeing him. Of course I didn't listen. One of the other people in the group told me maybe I should get birth control and I asked what for? We thought we knew everything but we were babies really. She came with me down to this place in Harcourt Street but they wanted my name, address and home number and, because I was under eighteen, they wanted to contact my mother for permission. I hightailed it out of there. The next thing I knew, I found myself pregnant. I remember praying to the Virgin Mary to make my period come. I said, 'You were a single mother. You know what this was like. Please make it go away.'

My boyfriend thought it was great. We'd go and live in this squat in town and sell beads on Grafton Street and live happily ever after. I was good in school and had been put a year ahead, so I was already doing my Leaving Cert. When I think of the torment I was going through at that time! Eventually one morning I burst into tears and told my mother. She was very calm and cool and told me to stay in bed until my father came home. I had to lay in bed for eight hours waiting to hear my father's boots on the concrete in the backyard.

He said to me 'I hear you're in trouble. What are you going to do?'
And suddenly all these ideas I'd had about living in a squat seemed
ridiculous. I was taken to the convent down the country and wasn't to
tell anyone. The story was that I would be away on a secretarial
course.

We weren't given any birthing classes. We weren't told what
would happen during the birth or afterwards. There was no social
worker, only mass in the morning and the rosary several times a
day, and chores to do. I still can't stand the smell of boiled cab-
bage. One of the other women there was insane and didn't know
how she'd got pregnant. She would say, 'A spirit visited me.' In
retrospect, I think she was a victim of incest. She used to play the
piano but only knew one song, *Feelings*, which she'd play over and
over. One time she tried to jump out of a window and the next day
was taken away. I never saw her again. My parents visited every
Sunday and brought me a porter cake. But we never talked about
the situation. To this day we haven't talked about it.

It was while I was in the convent that all those hippies in the park,
including my boyfriend, got into heroin. I'd run away several times
and kept hoping my boyfriend would come and get me, but when I
saw what was happening to him, it dashed my hopes. I gave birth by
myself in Holles Street. It was very lonely. At that time they kept you
in hospital for five days and I got really attached to the baby. When
my mother came to fetch me, she had to get the nurses to pull me off
him. At home, my father poured me a shot of whiskey and said, 'I'd
say you need a drink.' That was all he ever said to me on the subject.

I was still determined at this stage to keep the baby. I had six
weeks to make up my mind and in the meantime he was placed in a
halfway house. I was allowed visit him every day. During those six
weeks, I could see the way things were going with my friends. The
whole situation had deteriorated: heroin was their daily life. One of
my friends died on his eighteenth birthday. The first time he used
heroin, he died. I wanted money in order to keep the baby, so these older
junkies talked me into going into chemists and stealing prescriptions,
which they'd then pay me for. I got arrested, of course. My parents

had to come and get me out of the police station. At that point, I didn't care. I thought there was nothing else they could do to me. A girlfriend of mine had stolen someone's chequebook, so I used it to go around town and buy things for the baby. I filled this squat my boyfriend was staying in with baby gear. The next day the six weeks were up. But when I went down to the squat, everything was gone. He'd sold everything I'd got for the baby for heroin. That was an awakening for me: I saw I couldn't bring my baby to this. I went down and signed the papers for a full adoption, so that he'd go to a good family, which in retrospect was the best thing to do, because I wasn't capable of looking after him on my own. And after I'd signed the papers, I asked my boyfriend to give me some heroin. Because I'd seen that whatever it was they were taking gave them oblivion and they didn't care about anything any more. I stayed a heroin addict for thirteen years after that.

The next thing, my parents sent me off to the States with 50 dollars, to start a new life. When the plane took off from Dublin that day, I thought of Ireland as a hateful place and swore I'd never come back.

I had a few jobs over the years but basically got deeper and deeper into my addiction. I was still grieving terribly for my baby. In 1992, I came back to Ireland for nine months but I didn't like it and went to Paris. I loved the lifestyle there. It was there I got into recovery and started dealing with my grief. I began building up a relationship again with my parents and got interested in counselling and psychotherapy. Then I went back to school in France and trained to be an addictions counsellor and started working. Incidentally, my boyfriend stayed a drug addict all those years and in 1992 he was arrested, and hanged himself in a cell in Mountjoy. He'd been one of thirteen children in a two-bedroomed house, the father an alcoholic, and, as I subsequently discovered from talking to his little brother, they'd all been terribly sexually abused by an older brother. A typical pattern for an addict, as I know now.

In 1995 I went back to the adoption agency. The same nun was there. She told me to leave a letter on file in case my son ever came looking for me. In 1997, I contacted the agency again and this time all

the nuns were gone. The Social Services had taken over and all those
homes in the country had been shut down. Suddenly it was OK to be a
single mother. People were talking about divorce and abortion and
birth control. To me, Ireland seemed at last to have moved into the
twentieth century.

The woman in the agency was very helpful and in fact contacted
the adoptive family. They were thrilled to hear from me and sent me
an album of photographs. They told me through the agency that my
son was doing well and planning to go to university. For me, that
seemed enough, to know that he was healthy and happy. Last year, I
got a letter from him and, though we haven't met, I think we will this
year. I haven't told my parents and won't. My mother hasn't mentioned the subject in twenty years and is now nearly seventy. And
while Ireland has changed, she hasn't. I'm one hundred per cent sure
that to this day she still thinks she did the right thing. And in her own
way, she did.

I began to see that there were lots of interesting things happening here in my field. I think the fact that my boyfriend had died in
prison in Mountjoy had made me always want to come back and
work with drug addicts in Dublin and so, when I saw an ad offering
work in addiction counselling for six months, I applied and got the
job. At the same time, I did a birth mothers' course at Barnardo's,
basically a course to teach us about our rights, what the law is, and
the process towards reunion with our children. It was so interesting
for me because never in my life before had I met another woman
who'd given up her baby for adoption. And it was another sign that
Ireland was progressing. Suddenly it was no longer that dark, grim,
don't-tell-secrets-in-case-the-neighbours-find-out kind of society.

I'm working now in an education programme for addicts, trying
to get across to them that a better life is possible. The stuff I see on a
daily basis is horrendous. I deal with groups of ten at a time and always at least one member of the group has been sexually abused. I
work a lot with young homeless kids. There's nowhere for people
like that to go, nowhere for victims of incest. Despite the boom,
there's something massively lacking in Irish society now. There's

still a dark underside that the government is trying to ignore. The solution is seen as the methadone programme. It puts a big band-aid on the problem. They say you're on maintenance, you're stable. What that means is that instead of the kids taking drugs on the street, they take them in a clinic. The thinking is there's less risk of them spreading AIDS to the general population and less likelihood of them committing crimes. Which isn't true. I was on methadone myself. The clinic is a meeting place. You'd go to there in the morning so you wouldn't be sick any more. And you'd meet these people who'd tell you where to go off and get money to do heroin later anyway. Visit any methadone clinic any morning of the week and see two or three hundred people waiting with their little kids, filthy and mal-nourished. This is the high point of their day; this is as good as it gets.

Methadone is OK as a detox, just for a short time, but they keep you on it here for seven or eight years. It's terribly addictive. It rots your teeth, it rots your bones. It takes away your motivation. France is as bad in that they also think methadone is a wonder drug. But the dif-ference there is that the social system is fabulous. There's no such thing as 'homeless'. You're provided with an apartment immediately. Here we're trying to get these people off drugs, but every night they're going back to some flophouse where all these other people are using drugs. And there's no place else for them to go. You hear all the time about the great Dublin nightlife. But I don't see that. I see hundreds of people huddled up on the bridges or in doorways or on the steps of the Custom House.

So, instead of dealing with the problem properly, the govern-ment is saying: 'Here's a lifetime's supply of free opiates.' They're not saying it's possible to have a life where you can have dreams, travel, be creative. The best they can offer is that you're stable. I have people come to me all the time who want to get off metha-done, but their doctors won't let them. They tell them they're not ready. It makes me very angry.

The actual physical withdrawal from methadone is far more pain-ful than from heroin itself. How I finally got off drugs, I went cold turkey. I was sick for three or four days and then it was over. I was free. But they make you believe that you can't do this. That you're dependent. If I hadn't got into recovery I think I'd be dead by now. As it is, I have a rich full life. All the same, I think things here will change. We have success stories and there's a lot of hope. I'm starting with a new group tomorrow and that's always very exciting — to see how many make it.

Eiman Fadul

Sudan

Eiman is in her twenties and, unlike the other Muslim women present, has her head uncovered, revealing fashionably crimped hair. She is an MSc student of Engineering Hydrology at the National University of Ireland, Galway, and sits in the recreation room of a large prefab, where she also has some of her lectures. She speaks heavily accented English, but has a good command of the language. The foreign male students circle round, smiling in confusion: they cannot work out why they are not being interviewed too.

This is my first time to come to a European country. What struck me was that everywhere you have to hurry, everything is on time and you have to rush not to miss your train or bus, for example.

At the beginning I found it difficult to meet many Irish people, which was a pity because I wanted to improve my English. In our flat we were all from the same culture, speaking Arabic; we went to school every day and mixed with the same people. There was one reception party but again it was all the same people.

Then I had the chance to share a flat with four Irish girls and, to be frank, they are all so friendly. The only problem is that they have different Irish accents and it took time for me to manage to understand them. In general, it's difficult to understand what people say, but they are good about repeating themselves if you ask them. It's a new experience for my flatmates to meet someone from Sudan and we've had valuable discussions about tradition, habits and religion in Sudan and in Ireland. Most Irish people I meet know very little about my country and I had the chance to tell them about it. In Sudan, although it is considered a poor country, people know plenty about other countries, but this is not so common here in Ireland

In Islam, women are supposed to cover their hair and bodies. Some do that in an over-exaggerated way and some are not so strict about it. As you know, in any religion, not all the people follow all the rules to the letter. My country is not as strictly Muslim as some others and, like many other women in my country, I choose fashionable dresses which can do the job. In any case, I think that people's outward appearance is not a sign of their religion or how good or bad are they: what they believe inside their hearts is the most important. I don't break any other rules.

In fact, I've had some difficulties in practising Islamic duties, such as praying five times a day on time, since I am out most of the day at school. As well as that, we have to fast one month per year for many hours a day (from sunrise till sunset) and because this was during our exams, we had to fast even more hours than necessary, which affected our concentration.

Not drinking is a problem, because if you want to meet people here, that's what they do: they go to pubs, to nightclubs, which we are not used to. At first it got a bit boring for me. The course is very intensive but you can't work all the time. I thought it was impossible to have a nice time outside the class, except sometimes going to the cinema. Then people told me that I can go to pubs with my friends without having to drink alcohol; I can simply have Coke or water, so that's that what I do and now have the opportunity to meet more people.

However, frankly I've had some difficulties. There have been occasions when I felt embarrassed. For example, on one occasion I was having some snacks with Sudanese friends in McDonald's and, as usual, people there with their kids were giving us strange looks. This time a drunken man came in from outside and moved towards us, insulting us and shouting at us to get out of the country, until some of the staff managed to get rid of him. I felt so upset and unwelcome; nobody apologised to us and we just left.

Another thing I notice is that when I go shopping, some of the security guards in the shops look at me suspiciously and follow me until I leave. Maybe they do that because they believe that African people are starving in their countries and may behave in uncivilised way.

But to be honest, the best friend I've ever had in my life is an Irish girl and after I've gone back home, we plan to meet up in Cairo.

Helen G *

Australian

Helen, a tallish woman in her mid-fifties, lives in an old house on an acre of land in County Roscommon. She has short brown hair, a round, friendly face and serious manner. Her soft voice has a recognisable but not broad Australian accent. Her husband died twelve years ago and she has had to rear three children by herself.

I'm from Adelaide in South Australia and have been here for over twenty years. I was working in London and came over first to visit friends who'd left to live in Ireland. I just adored it. There was something about the quality of the sky and the shape of the hills that reminded me of Australia. In the English countryside all the roads are bendy, with houses and villages round every corner. The ability to travel for any distance without all that had been lost to me, but when I came here I found empty roads that just go straight to the horizon. OK, here the horizon might not be very far away, but still. . . . I even rediscovered the night sky, although the stars are different. There's also a lot of Irish in the Australian psyche and if I was thinking about where I felt most at home, it would certainly be in Ireland. All the time I've been here I've never been patronised, which, as a 'colonial', I constantly was in England.

After that first trip, I used to come regularly for holidays to stay with my friends. One time they had another visitor over from England: we fell in love and decided to come here and live.

At that time in the early seventies, there was nobody going up our road except a man with a donkey and cart. It would have been maybe forty years behind England then but it's catching up quickly. I think there are huge opportunities in Ireland to learn from Europe's mistakes. For example, there are a lot of complaints about foreign nationals coming in, buying up large old houses on lakeshore fronts and then preventing local people's access to the lake where their forefathers have fished for maybe hundreds of years. Legislation has been passed in one of the Scandinavian countries — Denmark, I think — to stop that happening. Everyone here is rushing on with the Celtic Tiger and not looking at the implications.

There have also been lots of positive changes: for instance, all the festivals that are happening in just about every little town. Culture is no longer something that happens only in Dublin or Galway. However, I don't think Ireland is becoming a more pluralist society. It seems like it on the surface but not when push comes to shove. One of the things that really struck me when I first came to Ireland was someone asking me if I was a Protestant. It wasn't a word that meant anything to me and made me very uncomfortable. I grew up in a society where there were Methodists and Baptists and members of the Church of Christ and Presbyterians and Roman Catholics and no one paid any attention to what you were. I've got used to it here but still don't like it. I think it's easier for me being a non-Catholic in Ireland because I'm a foreigner.

On the other hand, not going to mass in a small country area brings about exclusion. That's the place where announcements are made about the doctor being on holiday or the schools closing — lots of general events.

I'm a Buddhist. My practice is part of my daily life. Most of those in the same school of Buddhism as me live in Dublin but there are six of us who meet twice a month to practice together, to study writings. If people round here knew about it, I'd probably be classed as a pagan, but it's not something that would come up in casual conversation. The locals make assumptions because they know I'm not a Catholic and don't go to the local Church of Ireland, so probably think I'm a pagan anyway. The people I work with, who know I'm a

Buddhist, don't have a problem with it. Again, I think that being an Australian makes it easier. Actually, Irish people take it for granted because I don't have a German accent that I'm English. There's a kind of lightening in their attitude when they find I'm not. Well, we're only forty miles from the border here.

One time a local man said that it was great seeing foreigners refurbishing ruined houses that were empty and lonesome, and raising families in them. But he added that it will be crunch time when the boys grow up and want to marry local Catholic girls. That stuck in my mind: we will never be part of the community completely. I've heard about somebody from Leitrim being referred to as a blow-in — having come a few miles down the road. So what hope is there for us!

All the same, I don't feel the 'them' and 'us' thing all the time. I feel very much a part of Ireland. I have the right to vote in national and local elections, and always use my vote, looking at the candidates in terms of what they'd be likely to do for women and for the environment.

Since my husband died, I've been working with women's groups and run some training courses. Irish women are changing dramatically. When I started, it would have been exclusively middle-aged women doing personal development or stress management or assertiveness training. Now I'm running courses in places like Longford attended by women from council estates. Their status — is that the word? — is different. More women are seeing that there is a life beyond the family and a lot of them are struggling to find out what that is. The thing that impresses me is the huge bond that they form among themselves. All the things that come out — cases where there is drunkenness in the home, the isolation that they have gone through for years and years — they at last find a way to work through. They start to look at their own needs. And you see it even in the way that at first the class has to finish by 12.30 p.m. so that they can get back and have the dinner on the table. As the course develops, they might say, 'We'll leave him some sandwiches.' Then finally, 'He can make his own sandwiches.'

I don't think Irish men are changing so much. They tend to see personal development as a women's thing and for some men, living isolated lives in rural Ireland, life can be very difficult. The suicide rate among males in the West is alarmingly high.

There are still certain attitudes about what women should or shouldn't be doing and there are problems for a woman raising a family alone. My husband died when our youngest was four. If I went into a pub on my own in Dublin, it would be OK. Here too, if I was with another woman. If I'd had a really hard day and wanted to call into the local on the way home and have a gin and tonic or a pint of beer by myself, I could do it because I know the publican and his wife, but there would be people who'd be speculating, 'Has she turned to the bottle? Is she easy game?'

I find the Irish very nosy and perhaps Australians are a bit naive. People used to ask me questions and I would gladly tell them all the details of my life. Now I've learnt to answer a question with another question, the way the Irish do themselves. Another thing: someone said to me, if you're seen to be doing well here then you're showing off; if you're not seen to be doing well, then you're mean. Whichever way, it seems you can't win. But that said, I wouldn't live anywhere else.

H *

Malaysian

H is tall and slim with glossy black hair. She is in her early thirties. A solicitor, she has an assured and pleasant manner and comes across as open and intelligent. The amiable drunk at the next table in the pub where we are eating lunch plagues her with questions — where is she from, and so on — which she answers with exquisite politeness. H works in central Dublin and lives with her architect husband and their young daughter in a small village outside the city.

I'm from Malaysia, not too far from Kuala Lumpur, but before coming to Ireland I lived in Singapore for eleven years. I did my A-levels there and stayed on. The short version of how I came to Ireland is that I married an Irishman. The longer version is that it took us several years to decide on the move. I met my husband at university in Singapore and we lived there after graduating. We were very happy. Things were comfortable and we had a nice flat. But after three or four years we started to ask ourselves whether we really wanted to spend the rest of our lives there and we decided we didn't. I suppose it all has to do with what you think about Singapore. If you were trying to create a little Utopia, you wouldn't be far from it there, but just because of that, life can be rather sterile. I suppose we sat down and thought OK, if we stay, this is what it's going to be like: the flat in the condominium, the Filipino maid, everything very predictable. We took into account all the factors. On the financial side, it didn't make sense to move: in Singapore you would pay less than a month's wages in a full year in taxes. But we had to balance that against quality of life. For example, it didn't seem to me the right place to raise a child. Many of my friends' children grew up speaking English with Filipino accents because they were always with the maid. Here my neighbour looks after my daughter when I am at work and that's great because I can see that they are genuinely attached to each other. Ireland is a good place to raise children; it's so family-oriented.

I suppose because I wasn't actually from Singapore, I could take a step back and look at the place objectively. Malaysia is like Ireland in that respect — less structured, more surprising. So we had to decide where else we wanted to live and for a long time Vancouver looked very interesting — we even went over there to check it out. The main problem was that the Canadian economy was weak. When we came over to Ireland in September 1996, we got a completely different impression. For example, we had sent faxes to various firms in Canada and Ireland asking if we could drop in for a chat with them during our visit. Whereas the response in Vancouver was muted, in Ireland people were enthusiastic and welcoming. It made it all much easier when we finally decided to move here.

I had of course been to Ireland before — in fact, we got married here — and it would have been my third or fourth time in the country, so I knew what I was letting myself in for. The greyness, the clouds pressing down on me. When we first arrived, four years ago, Ireland was very different from what it is today, less vibrant. The economy was already doing well but not like now. It's much more cosmopolitan. When I walk down the street I see a good mix of people, whereas then I was very much a minority. Of course, I still am. That's what I like about going to London. From the moment you get off the plane, there's a great sense of anonymity which I never get here. When I walk into a shop in Grafton Street, I'm made to feel how different I am. Of course, where I work and live, I am cocooned from what I hear is going on. Personally I've never experienced aggression or hostility.

It's hard to generalise but there's a cultural difference that's difficult to overcome. They say the Irish are warm and welcoming and it's true. But there's still a big difference between Irish people and foreigners. There's a perceived warmth which can be misleading: you can have a long conversation with someone and presume that you've made a friend but for the Irish person it doesn't necessarily mean anything, and this can be quite hurtful. Where I come from, once you have had that sort of interaction with a person, you know where you stand from then on. In this country, conversation rarely gets beyond a certain level. I suppose that's what life is like here and it's not right to be judgmental. It's just something I wasn't prepared for. In the office, the foreigners or people who have lived abroad seem to have a special connection. It's not a conscious thing but we seem to have more in common. Perhaps, after all, the same applies to Irish people: my mother-in-law is from Wexford but now lives in the North and after thirty years she half-jokes that she is still a blow-in.

That said, I have absolutely no regrets about moving here. I'm working as a solicitor and the switchover was easy for me, since law in both Singapore and Ireland is based on the UK system, taking into account local law and case law. But getting recognition was initially a bit of a bumpy ride. The system here is quite insular. I am admitted in England because special recognition is given there to solicitors from Hong Kong and Singapore. You're not required to sit any transfer tests as long as you have the relevant number of years' experience. Here in Ireland, on the other hand, you have to retake the tests altogether, which means in effect a degree course. I was exempted from that because I had been admitted in England, but it took a lot of persuasion to get them to let me take that route. It's more difficult now. I think they insist that you actually practice in England first.

In Singapore I was also writing scripts for television. That of course stopped when we moved here and in fact for the first couple of years I hardly wrote anything, because it takes time to get used to the way people speak. I'm just starting up now again. I recently finished a short film script and to my great delight placed it with a well-established production company. The person I first showed it to liked it at once. It's about two little boys in Donegal and what happens when a Nigerian man comes to lodge in their house. Although I never intended it to deal with issues of race, that's how it turned out. The two boys think the man is a space vampire and want to kill him, but by the end of the film they realise that he is human too, with a little son of his own in Nigeria. There are two versions: the longer, which is about twenty-five minutes, and the shorter, which is about twelve or fourteen minutes. We have submitted it for a couple of awards, 'Oscailte' and 'Short Cuts', and if we are successful, it will eventually be shown on TG4 or RTE. We've been shortlisted for the 'Oscailte' and we're hopeful.

My husband is from Fermanagh and, before we arrived, we considered living there, but the practicalities ruled it out. And then we thought of basing ourselves between Enniskillen and Dublin and commuting: he north and I south. We actually drew a straight line on the map and found Virginia, County Cavan, was exactly half-way between the two places. Coming from Singapore, I don't think we were fully aware of the geography involved! Where we're living now is a small place in the country, very quaint with a village green. We moved out of the city because otherwise it would have been no different from Singapore. Even in Vancouver we couldn't have bought a piece of land and built a house on it as we did here, because there were so many planning restrictions. We were lucky. This must be one of the few places in the world where that sort of thing is still possible.

I don't drink and I think in Ireland that's social suicide. At first, before my daughter was born, I used to go with friends to the pub, but after a few rounds of Guinness for them and Coke for me, I always got the feeling that the conversation had moved to a different level. I felt completely out of place. Pubs are so much a part of life here — and I'm going to sound like a killjoy here — it seems to me that Ireland has a drink problem and just doesn't recognise it. On the other hand, people here might go out for a drink at night and still turn up for work next day. However bad you feel there's no question of not turning up — you just go and have a bacon sandwich in the middle of the morning. That certainly wouldn't happen in Singapore.

Another thing that strikes me is that so many people are driving around on provisional licences. There was even an amnesty in the late seventies because the waiting list for tests was so long. That's scary. But now I'm becoming like an Irish driver myself — when I see a yellow light I find myself thinking the Irish way: *Go faster!* And if ever I do that and then look in my mirror, I find two more cars have gone through behind me! It's amazing.

I hanker for my own food. There is only one good Chinese restaurant in Dublin that I have found. As for Malaysian food, I cook it myself. At least most of the ingredients are now available through the Asia Market. I just wish the weather would perk up.

Selma Harrington

Bosnian

Selma, who looks to be in her thirties, is tall with short blonde curly hair. An architect by profession, she dresses very stylishly and wears eye-catching earrings with cats' faces on them. Her English is excellent with barely a trace of an accent. Her manner is warm and friendly and she laughs a lot. At the same time, she considers her answers thoughtfully and is clearly both intelligent and cultured. We meet a few days before Christmas, in a café in Ranelagh, a suburb of Dublin, where they serve the good strong espresso that Selma likes to drink. Loud Christmas music cuts across the conversation.

I'm originally from Sarajevo and have lived in Dublin effectively for about three years. But I visited here several times before that, first in 1991. My husband is Irish. We met in Zimbabwe where we were both working. Before that I hardly knew anything about Ireland, except for the Troubles. I had read Brendan Behan in school: *The Borstal Boy*. James Joyce was also compulsory school literature: *A Portrait of the Artist as a Young Man* and a bit of *Ulysses*; that was the extent of my acquaintance with Dublin. I suppose that's one aspect in which the West is deprived: there's little awareness of, for example, Slavic literature, Polish, Czech. Being smaller nations, perhaps we had that advantage, that we were striving to know more about the rest of the world. That said, the Irish people I met abroad were open-minded, cosmopolitan. Living here, I am finding other sides to the mentality.

I can't say that Ireland was a cultural shock, but speaking as an architect I suppose what struck me immediately was how the cities were largely untouched by the Second World War. Another difference is that in central European cities you see people out and about in the areas where they live, in the suburbs. My parents, visiting me in Clonskeagh after seven or eight years in the prison that was Sarajevo, asked, 'But where are all the people?' Day or night you hardly see anyone out on the streets. And that's typical of any residential area in Dublin. It's to do with planning, I suppose. Here all the people converge on the centre. Even the transport system operates that way.

In Yugoslavia, my work as an architect and in related areas such as furniture design meant that I was travelling a lot abroad to trade fairs. In the late 1980s, Zimbabwe was hosting a conference of non-aligned nations and, as a result, a group of Yugoslav professionals was invited to go there to work. Programmes on television showed us how beautiful Harare was. The proposition was also attractive financially, so I inquired about job opportunities and was offered some interesting work. This was at a time when the recession was starting to hit Yugoslavia, with resulting political problems and some signs of the future conflict. As it turned out, I left Sarajevo six months before the war broke out — fate, I suppose. I literally arrived with two suitcases and met my future husband within two weeks of my arrival.

That was when I started visiting Ireland, during our six-year stay in Zimbabwe. The first time I arrived on a Yugoslav passport with no visa requirements but then the war broke out in April and everything changed.

What happened in Yugoslavia is particularly sad because it functioned relatively well as a federation. We had a lot of pride in our country, a great sense of freedom and achievement. There were problems of course but we had our own industry, even our national car. There were no great divisions in society and in fact one of the differences that strikes me here, in this booming economy, are the numbers of people sleeping rough, which tells me that the community has disintegrated in some way.

You were asking about culture shock. One thing is the attitude I often encounter when people here find out I am from Eastern Europe. It seems that the changes that have occurred have swept away any perception of the positive aspects of the countries. For example, although it's accurate to say that I am a Bosnian Muslim, I find it quite offensive to be labelled in this way. Our society was in any case secular, accommodating people from a multitude of religious backgrounds: for example, Jewish settlers from the sixteenth century, expelled by the Spanish Inquisition, were given shelter in the then Turkish Empire. An architect friend of mine of that background was discussing with me the topic of how we are perceived abroad, and said, 'Selma, I assume you socialised in Sarajevo with people and not with Muslims or Croats or whatever.' He is an atheist but finds himself defined by his Jewishness. It's quite insulting in a way.

My first visit to Ireland was at Christmas and I was struck by the warm atmosphere. Because my country was socialist, our festival officially centred more on New Year. People ask how we celebrated Christmas in Bosnia. We used to go and visit my school friend's grandmother, who was of Czech origin, and who baked wonderful Christmas cookies. At that time, we weren't bothered about putting labels on anyone. My own grandmother, who was Muslim, would get gifts from the neighbours and send them baklava cake in return, to celebrate the end of Ramadan, since these two holidays can occur within a few days of each other. Now I find that my friends from before are still my friends, whatever their background. But I know that is not the case everywhere.

My parents stayed in Sarajevo throughout the war and luckily weren't directly affected. But my young cousin, the mother of two lovely girls, was walking along the street and a piece of mortar hit her in the back. She's paralysed now. Another cousin, who was a real golden boy, volunteered to defend the city. He'd go up into the mountains to try and break the siege and, after one action in June 1995 when they were coming back into the city, he was hit by a sniper and killed. What was tragic was that his father was trying to get him out — he even applied to me for help. But my cousin said to his father, 'No I don't want to leave.

Someone has to fight. Do you want to sit on your couch and wait until
they come to your door?'

It was unbelievable how culturally active people were in Bosnia
during the war. My mother saved the clippings to send me because she
knew I would be interested. On one occasion a 'Bosnian haiku' verse
was doing the rounds, which typified what life was like in Sarajevo,
with no running water, no electricity, having to burn furniture and old
shoes for heating. I translated it for a talk I gave in Zimbabwe. As far as
I remember, it went as follows: 'Spare the underwear/Humbly eat,
thinly shit/Wash your bottom parts a bit.' That was life during the siege,
in a nutshell.

During the war it was difficult to communicate with my family.
A letter could take six months to get through. Telephones were cut
off in July 1992. Sometimes satellite phones were working if you
were in Europe. But from Zimbabwe it was impossible. I was worried sick. So eventually I treated it as a sort of project, setting up a
network of communication through a chain of people I'd never met.
Our little parcels would circle the world to get into Bosnia. It was
quite an enterprise to decide what to put in a parcel that would be
small enough for people to agree to take. I ended up sending vita-
mins, pressed herbs, tea, coffee, things like that. Once I got some
liquid glycerine from a health shop, thinking it would be great for
use as a hand cream or something. It was taken out of the parcel because glycerine, as I realised later, could be used to make explosives!
I'd like to write about it all sometime, the parallel life I was leading
in a beautiful country, lovely weather, with a fantastic Irish guy: I
felt guilt all the time. Then my parents wrote to tell me that at least
with me away, they had one less worry.

There is a great sense of disappointment now. Even after the Day-
ton peace accord, tens of thousands of young people were leaving the
country. And there was no need for any of it. Under a different leader-
ship, Yugoslavia could have continued to function and might even
eventually have joined the EU — if there is any advantage in living in
the EU with its polluted environment and its poisoned meat. That's
one thing I find highly ironic: that you live in this supposedly

developed world and you can't trust your basics; it's disgraceful to have e-coli in your water or salmonella in your food. I have to say, I have strong reservations about the EU bureaucracy. The Irish enthusiastically adopted the benefits without addressing the downside. Maybe now it's time to slow down. What would be wrong with that? I worry about the country being so dependent on multinationals. Maybe that's a residue of my thinking from the old socialist Yugoslavia where we were striving to have control over our own destiny, for better or for worse.

Nevertheless, in general I like living here. Particularly now you can get good coffee, which has only been in the last few years! Dublin is like Sarajevo, still a nice manageable size. And I feel I can relate to Irishness. When you scrape a little at the superficial elements of it, it's not so different. Of course I miss my friends but when you have chosen the nomadic life, that's what you have to put up with. Anyone coming from countries where there was a stronger sense of community will be struck by its absence here, the obsession with privacy, at least in the big city like Dublin.

It's not easy to come close to people. Perhaps, even though Irish people might not like to hear this, it's a kind of relic of Anglo mentality — to keep yourself to yourself. One can be socialising for years with people, even visiting them in their homes but still wouldn't call them friends. Although that's another thing, in my language 'friend' is a big word. It's used here broadly, where *we* might use the word 'acquaintance'. Language is funny that way: I was talking to an Irish woman about something and she asked me, 'Are you happy about that?' And after considering for a while, I replied, 'Well, I'm not ecstatic.' So then she got worried. But it was just a question of translation. For me, 'happy' is another big word. I can be content, pleased, glad, satisfied, but 'happy' describes a rare moment.

Allowing for the fact that as a non-native speaker I am not in a position to judge the possibilities that language offers, I feel a little bit deprived sometimes. Adopting a different language as the means of communication, all that pool of expression is different, and maybe this affects interpersonal relationships as well. That said, where I work there are about thirty or so people and while I couldn't say I have friends among them in my sense of the word, yet they take the initiative to invite me to their homes, which is nice — something to build on.

I have found religion here more old-fashioned and rigid than anywhere else I have been, including Italy. But perhaps that's related to Irish history where religion had to play a role in maintaining identity. On the other hand, my husband's parents were fantastic from the start. At first they didn't know much about my background. Then they started hearing about the conflict on television. They had never seen a Muslim in their lives before they saw me. So then they asked my husband if I was going to convert. 'Why should she?' he asked and they fully accepted that. Denis's father died when we were still in Zimbabwe but he made a phone call, which was significant only later, in which he told Denis to make sure to tell me that I am the nicest girl he ever met. They never raised the subject of religion with me and for my part I accepted that different members of the family are religious to different degrees, to the extent of my attending ceremonies with them in church. I don't practice my religion much but still consider myself Muslim. For me the Islamic culture represents tolerance: that's what I got from my family. In any case I think that while different religions have different rituals, at heart they are the same. Sometimes I'm a bit fed up when I meet somebody new who has these fixed ideas about Muslims, so I tell them that I left my veil in the wardrobe.

I can't keep explaining to people how in the past in Bosnia we were so used to living with one another that we would take part in each other's celebrations. I suppose that's what every religion is preaching at the end of the day: respect for one's neighbour. That's the theory; the practice is often different.

When I first came to Ireland it was the time of *Riverdance*, that time when Ireland kept winning the Eurovision song contest. I even bumped into a Bosnian group one day in Dunnes Stores. That phenomenon in music and arts, the upsurge in applied arts, reminded me a lot of what we had in Sarajevo before the war: film directors like Kusturica, original rock groups, a period when we were asserting our identity, after so many years of servility. I got the same feeling of confidence when I came to Ireland. I'm not aware of it so much now. Now it's almost all about selling the image rather than substance, and that I don't particularly like.

I look at the architecture too. We've always admired Finland and Scandinavia. But here there's a sameness and blandness and no one seems to think there's anything wrong with that. Before I started in my present place of work, I took a day trip with a colleague, driving around County Kildare to look at the developments there. I was shocked. It seemed to me that the landscape was wounded. But there are lots of positive things too, and ways to complain, which is great. It'll be interesting to see what the future holds.

Sabena I *

Pakistani

Sabena sits in the living room of her large house in a fashionable area of south Dublin. A television with a giant screen is switched off during the interview but still dominates the room. Twenty-five-year old Sabena — the mother of three delightful and inquisitive children, aged seven, six and two — is very pretty, with long dark hair, tied back. She wears cream jeans and a black top, which look slightly out of place alongside the massive suite of upholstered furniture, the draped windows and chandelier. She seemed more at ease earlier in her kitchen, making the children's dinner, but gains confidence as she speaks. Her English is excellent, with a slight Dublin accent and turn of phrase, and she comes over as articulate and intelligent. A Muslim, she explains how because two female members of her husband's family already share her own original first name, she was given another on her marriage, to distinguish her from them.

I've been here eight years. My husband is a lot older than me, and has lived here for twenty-five years. Now he has Irish citizenship and so have I — for the last year.

It was an arranged marriage. I had never travelled outside my country before my husband came to fetch me. In fact, I had never even been to the nearest big city. I lived in the countryside, so you could call me a farmer's daughter. Definitely it was a big change coming to Ireland but it was OK because I was only seventeen. What I didn't take to was the culture here: the way people keep distant from their own families. Even when my children were born, there was nobody with me. My husband's family gave me no support. Where I was brought up, families stick together.

I got pregnant quickly, two months after my marriage. I didn't have a clue about it and it was tough. I've always loved babies: I'm the eldest among all my cousins and used to look after the smaller ones. But it's different when you have your own, full-time. And I was a very young mother. I had no problems with the hospital. The nurses, the doctors, the service, everything was fabulous, but after four days I had to come home and that's it, you have to start working. Back home, you'd relax for a couple of weeks after having a baby. The family would be there to look after everything.

When my first daughter was born, my mother-in-law was here. While I'm not saying it was no help at all, I still had to do everything for the baby myself. When she was two days old, she got so dirty I couldn't cope and started to cry and that was the only time my mother-in-law cleaned her. Just the once. My mother-in-law is extremely traditional; everything has to be done a certain way.

All my family, my grandparents, my uncles and aunts, live beside each other — you don't even feel they are in separate houses — so it was a huge shock coming here where, when parents get older, they go into nursing homes. That's very sad. I love old people, though perhaps I shouldn't say much because I don't love my mother-in-law. We didn't get on at all and she moved out. Actually, when I came to Ireland I had a dream. I was so happy and excited to find out that, because my husband is the oldest in the family, his mother would be living with us. I had always been close to my granny and I thought that if I was going to lose her, I would at least have someone here to take her place. It was OK for a couple of months and at first I confided in my mother-in-law. Then it all changed: she turned the family against me and told them I was lazy and didn't want to cook for them when I was sick during my pregnancy. She always tried to put me down. Everything I did was wrong. As for my sisters-in-law, because the brothers don't get on at the moment, their wives aren't supposed to talk to each other. So my dream never came true.

My husband loves his mother. Even today, he will say, 'My mother is my number one, not you.' It used to hurt me but when you hear the same thing over and over, you start ignoring it. I am glad he loves his mother and hope it will always be so. I tried to get on with her but it's very difficult when people don't like you. Even if they never say thank you, at least they don't have to criticise and blame you all the time. I would say that for any woman, it's better if you know the family you're coming to, know everything about them. There are many women of all cultures who are afraid to say what they are going through. For example, if what I am saying now appears in a book and is read by members of my family, I might think, 'Oh, my God! What will happen to me?' But I have to talk, to get it out of my system.

You learn the hard way: the bad experiences have made me stronger. And for the last two or three years it has been easier for me because I've got a few friends I can trust. If I'm in trouble, they're there for me. These are Irish, Asian, a good few people. If you are eager to find friends, it's no problem here.

I am not a strictly religious person and go to the mosque only occasionally. I consider that your religion is what you are, your personality, and I respect everyone's religion. I haven't had problems with Roman Catholicism, though in Ireland people generally don't know much about other cultures. When I went to my kids' school, they asked me what religion I was, out of curiosity. They wanted to know why, if you are Muslim, you want to send your children to a Catholic school. The only bad experience I had was that I put my daughter's name down for a certain school two years in advance and the week before she was supposed to start, they rang me and told me they couldn't take her because the school wasn't in my parish. They knew I was a foreigner and wouldn't understand about parishes and that. I asked them to help me but they said it wasn't up to them. They behaved in a very ignorant way towards me. Actually, it's funny because in our parish there's no school, so what were we to do? Thank God another, better, school took her at the last minute and there have been no problems since. But I got so much trouble from my husband over that. It even affected our marriage. I understand him, however. In our country, education isn't great, so he didn't want his child to lose even one day's schooling here. That's why he gave out to me so much.

When I came to Ireland, I couldn't speak one word of English; it's only in cities that people need English, not where I was living in a village. I remember after a few weeks here there was something wrong with the plumbing and I asked my husband to get a plumber for me. He refused — at that time we didn't have a telephone in the house — and gave me twenty pence in my hand and told me to phone the man myself. At the time I felt bad but now I realise it was good for me. I'd be well able to run a business now. I have never had a job here — I'm just a housewife. But there's a family business, a boutique, and sometimes I help with messages for my husband. I've just been to London for the day on his behalf. I love to do it — it keeps me busy.

Now people here are complaining about refugees coming in. I don't blame them, but they should realise that not all the foreigners are out begging on the street. You can get bad experiences from taxi drivers, saying that everyone should stay in their own country. I don't agree with that. They shouldn't forget there was a famine here once and the Irish went all over the world. We aren't going to abuse the country we come to, but at the same time we expect some respect and welcome. Over the last few years, the attitude has definitely changed for the worse and things people say and do can be hurtful.

I was so young when I came that sometimes when I think that I am from Pakistan, I wonder 'Am I really?' I feel like I've been brought up here.

Some of my neighbours are OK. They come and look at you and your house and if they think you are on their level, they are friendly with you. If not, they ignore you. Maybe it's everywhere but I've only experienced it here: the Irish don't regard people as people; they only respect money, background. That's definitely the case in the area where I live. They are more educated, with good jobs, and should know better, so it's even more terrible when they treat people like that.

For my kids, this attitude presents a big problem. Maybe I will go back home in the future. But it wouldn't be fair to do that to my kids. Their whole life is here, their experience. Imagine taking an Irish person, putting him in Pakistan and saying, 'Right, now live there.' How would he be able to cope?

An arranged marriage is normal for my culture and thank God for me it has worked out OK. But I wouldn't put my daughter through that. It will be her choice. My husband has more traditional views but I'll hope to change him.

I prefer the position of women here. At least women have rights. When I go out, I'm not allowed to visit the pub without my husband. Men have responsibilities for providing for the family, but I think women have an even greater responsibility — giving birth, raising the children. It's very important that they should have rights.

I'd love to do something for people here, to show them about other cultures. For example, there are many in the countryside here who have never tasted curry. Can you imagine that! For me, it's so funny.

Carol James

English

A small, slight woman in her fifties, Carol has a firm voice with a standard English middle-class accent. Although she talks quite freely, she is a private person and there are evidently aspects of her life which she doesn't wish to touch on. She loves to be outdoors on a fine evening and sits on the bank of the Lee, upstream from Cork city, amid woodland walks and sweeping trees, gazing at the flowing water.

I'm originally from a very small village in Oxfordshire: Steeple Aston. The first time I came to Ireland was for the Cork Film Festival in 1961. I was sixteen and just about to go to the London School of Film Technique. I came over with my first boyfriend and had a marvellous week. People went out of their way to be kind to us. We returned every year for about five years for the festival and then decided we wanted to see a bit more of the country, so we took a horse-drawn caravan tour from Cork all the way to Killarney and back: a two-week holiday and we walked all the way. It was organised like a sort of wagon-train: a couple of lads came with a chuck wagon to do the cooking, and we were just left to ramble. It was wonderful. You couldn't do it now with all the traffic on the roads.

It was a combination of events that brought me to live here. I had been working in the film industry for about fifteen years and was still making documentaries — on health and safety in coal mines, that sort of thing. I wanted to make features, but knew I never would. I didn't have whatever it was it took. So I was beginning to wonder what else I should do with my life. I still loved the countryside, even though I was living in London, but didn't want to go back to Oxfordshire. I'm not very good at going back to places. I thought of Ireland, how there's something magical about it, and decided to try it for three years and see what happened. I was living on a houseboat at the time, which I sold, and came over looking for a house to buy. The one I found was just outside Tralee, on the way down to Dingle, with a couple of acres. I had no idea what I was going to live on. There was only my mother and myself, no other relatives, and I was wondering how she would take my sudden disappearance, so I showed her some photographs of the place. She was amazed at how beautiful it was, with a view up to the mountains, sixteen miles of golden beaches, and asked if she could come as well. It had never even occurred to me that she'd want to.

We were mostly self-sufficient. I had ducks and goats. My mother was a great gardener: she'd work in the garden for about eight hours a day until she was seventy-five. We ended up supplying half the neighbourhood with fruit and vegetables. At that time, and probably still today, there was a whole collection of people doing exactly the same thing. I was only there two days when I was introduced to everybody else — Americans, Germans, French, anybody. We'd all go to the bog and dig together, working a sort of barter system. You know: 'You've got hens' eggs this week and we've got goats' cheese, so we'll swap.' It was idyllic but very hard work. After a while, too, there wasn't enough for my mind to be working on. Eventually I got involved in amateur drama. It was great fun. Then I started a theatre group in Tralee and the enthusiasm for that became my next 'thing'. I tend to go into new projects in sudden dives.

After my mother died, I didn't want to stay on in the place in Kerry. I did a video production course in Tralee but didn't take to video. One of the lads on the course was from Cork city and he told me I'd love it there. I remembered it from before, so I went down for a weekend and visited the Cork Arts Theatre. I hadn't been there ten minutes when someone came up to me and asked me if I'd be interested in working for a local theatre company. It was only a FÁS scheme but there was a house going with it. So I said yes. Such things are meant to be, I'm convinced of it, particularly when you take wrong turnings and say to yourself: *My God, what am I doing here?* Suddenly you realise that if you hadn't been there, you wouldn't have turned the next corner to end up in the place where you were supposed to be. I've been here eight years. And I'm now doing Fine Arts in Crawford College, just as a result of seeing a notice in the library.

I don't necessarily see myself staying in Ireland. I love it but at the same time if something else came up, I could move on at a whim. Even today, the weather earlier on was so bad, I was saying to myself, 'This bloody country! I've got to go somewhere where it's sunny.' We'll see. I don't live in the past and I don't think too much about the future. I'm very much for now and pitch everything into what I'm doing at a given moment.

When I first came here, Ireland was about twenty years behind everywhere else but we've kind of leapt those years without any intermediary period to get used to things. Floods of EU money, everyone suddenly eating pasta, that sort of thing. You think, my God, what happened? Now we're all just part of a vast global mob. For me, coming here in the seventies was like going back to my childhood, to the rural community life, even though as a foreigner you'd never be fully accepted here. Still, at least people were welcoming. There was terrific innocence, loyalty and trust. That has gone now. We've just come of age, I suppose.

There was some slightly anti-British feeling in Kerry, all right; certain places I knew not to visit, not with my accent. And there was some resentment about outsiders coming in and taking over, which we tend to do, bossing people about, reorganising them. It seems to be something they like at first, the fact that you have ideas and can get things going. At the same time, you'd come home and wonder if you'd overdone it. With the Irish there's a wonderful tendency to sit around and have endless discussions. Nothing gets done but they talk themselves into believing they've achieved something. That can be very frustrating. On the other hand, there's an advantage in things being small. Everyone knows everyone and if you want to start something up, you can make it happen.

I still like it. If I didn't, I wouldn't be here. There's a quality about the people you don't find elsewhere. The story I frequently tell is that, when we first came to the film festival, there was a club where the ordinary punter could go and meet the stars and the directors. For students like us, it was marvellous. But when my boyfriend and I came down on the first day to collect our tickets for the club, there was this seventeen- or eighteen-year-old boy behind the counter. 'You do know it's strictly evening dress?' he asked. We were horrified. The idea of coming from London with a back pack carrying a formal suit! Actually, I was all right: I had a dress with me. But my friend had nothing suitable. So anyway the boy told us to come back later that night to the desk and to ask for him. He then went home to Cobh and borrowed a suit off an older brother who sang in a male voice choir. Then he brought the suit back to Cork and handed it over to my boyfriend for the week. There was no question of cleaning it after or anything like that. We were two people out of the blue and he did this for us for no other reason except to be helpful. That's the way it was here.

Francine K *

Dutch

Francine is tall and blonde with smudgy black mascara and pale blue nails. She is in her early twenties. She makes strong Dutch coffee in the small apartment in the centre of Limerick city, which she shares with her Irish boyfriend. She speaks rapidly in a soft voice with very little Dutch and a great deal of Limerick in her accent. Her manner is friendly, unaffected and interested.

I'm from the north of Holland, a town called Groningen, near the German border. At the moment I'm working in a call centre in Shannon but I hope to study in Cork. I want to do the last year of my psychology degree at University College Cork.

I first came here two years ago but went back to Holland for six months. Now I think I'm going to stay. I was home again recently for ten days and didn't like it at all, even though I'd saved for ages and was really looking forward to it. It's bad because you always like to have a home base and now I don't feel I have it any more.

Limerick's great. Perhaps if I'd gone somewhere else first I would have had a different feeling about it because everyone who's not from Limerick is supposed to hate it, but I think it's a lovely little city.

I met my boyfriend in Israel. He had been working there for five years and was dying to come home, so I said I'd return with him. I actually didn't like it here at first. It was very difficult. My boyfriend had forgotten his English — he had better Hebrew. We had to start from the bottom and were living in a tiny little bed-sit. I was working in packaging: standing up all day and fitting polystyrene shapes round TVs, that sort of thing. I was there three months and nearly went mad. I hated Limerick, I hated everything. At that time, it was very difficult to get a job and I found it through a friend. The policy was to take on only uneducated people so I had to pretend. I remember being in the interview and thinking to myself I should act as if I had no education, which is stupid. I should just have acted normal. The interviewer was asking me questions because they were also looking for a supervisor but I didn't want that job.

After three months I couldn't stand it any more and went back to Holland. This time I took control of my life and continued my studies. After I decided to come back here I planned it well, and found out about the UCC course, that sort of thing.

The prices here are mad, while the wages are extremely low. You work really hard and get fuck-all for it. In the job I'm doing now I have to phone people with credit accounts at certain stores to ask them to pay their bills. Irish people have no problem with this. On the other hand, English people hate it when Irish people phone them. I've a bit of a Limerick accent now and when I'm on the phone it's probably stronger. They don't hear the Dutch accent and start abusing me, saying things like, 'Fuck off, you Irish bitch.' They don't know we're phoning from Limerick and they said to a colleague of mine, 'Fuck off back to Ireland and take your bombs with you.' That's terrible, isn't it. She was very upset.

My boyfriend and all his friends are extremely republican and love their country so much. I feel that I love Holland too but that doesn't mean I go on and on about how brilliant it is. If I have to listen to that all day, I get not to like it any more. You're not allowed to say things like: 'I don't think the infrastructure is good, the roads, the fact that all the trucks go through the city.' It's like an insult to the country. And if I say that something is very nice in Holland, they immediately reply that it's the same here.

Everything here is much slower. In Holland, it would be unthinkable for a scheduled bus not to show up. At first, I found this unbelievable. Another thing: when I first came I was wondering if I could get some sort of rent allowance because what I was earning wasn't enough to live on. I was told I wasn't eligible but then friends told me to go back and reapply. I asked why: if the rule is no, then that's it. They said no, go back, go back every day and annoy them and you might get it in the end. They'll give you something to get rid of you. I wouldn't do it but the possibility is there.

I suppose it's kind of romantic here and in general I prefer it to Holland. We go out every other Saturday night. That's not much, is it, but I'm trying to save money for my studies. I love the pubs but they close very early. People from Amsterdam go to Groningen at weekends because there are places that stay open on Saturday nights until ten o'clock Sunday morning, then you can go on somewhere else — twenty-four hours a day.

Here it's the same as in England: the government makes rules for the people, whereas I think people should make rules for themselves. People are getting into trouble with drugs because they haven't a clue. They have this Moroccan hard stuff and they're using it in pubs without knowing how to and it's very dangerous if you do it wrong. So I'm telling them how, even though I don't use it myself. I think that they should put ads in places like buses showing people how to use it: saying that, though it's illegal, we don't want you to kill yourselves.

Another thing: there are no drug-testing facilities in clubs. In Holland, you get your pills and have them tested in the clubs for free. They can tell you then if it's really Ecstasy or some other kind of shit. Here they don't know, so they take it and end up with seizures and all that. They're so ignorant: they don't know that you can't just buy it from anyone.

What I like about Holland is the way you're allowed to make up your own mind about things no matter what you want to do. Actually, I'm originally from a small village in Friesland which was very conservative. I was brought up in the Reformed Church, which is not the same as the Protestant, even though here I'm considered to be Protestant. I don't know if I have a religion now, although I think it's good for kids to think there's an almighty God who's going to make things all right. My father is a very strong Catholic still, with a devotion to Mary.

He'd kill me for saying it, but I find my boyfriend was traumatised by going to a Catholic school, the Christian Brothers. It was some kind of torture, having to kneel down for hours, that sort of thing.

I find women in Ireland extremely strong. I thought they would have been different from Dutch women, less modern. It's not true at all: housewives in Holland have a much more traditional life. Here women have had to put up with a lot, being left to carry the family.

The people look very different. Here I'm tall but in Holland I'd be considered short. You'd get a crick in your neck looking up at everyone there. And when you go out at night here, all the girls are very dressed up, a lot of make-up and their hair is always styled. But in general the crowd in the street isn't well-dressed. My mother noticed this when she was over. I suppose I'm used to the way people look by now. But their skin seems unhealthy, as if they are living on fries and burgers. Irish food I find very greasy. There's oil in everything. And when you ask for a cheese sandwich you get mayonnaise and coleslaw with it. My boyfriend's sister, for example, lives on junk food. Every day she gets a take-away.

Norma Kennedy

Mexican

Norma is a friendly woman in her fifties. She has tanned skin and black hair. A large wedding photograph on the wall indicates that in her youth she was stunningly beautiful. She sits in the drawing-room of the semi-detached house in south Dublin where she lives with her Irish husband, Mel. Charming Mexican artefacts stand on the presses and hang on the walls. Norma still has a strong Mexican accent, despite having lived in the country for many years.

I arrived here in February 1970, after marrying an Irishman, whom I had met in Mexico. At the time, I was working for Avon Cosmetics and Mel came over on a training visit. I was asked to take him around to show him the sights, and the relationship developed from there. It was very romantic.

I didn't visit Ireland before I got married and had no idea what to expect. Everyone told me it would be very cold and I brought over really heavy winter clothes. Come the summer, I had nothing to wear and that gave me the opportunity to buy new outfits.

It was difficult at the beginning. My English was very American and the accent here meant that although I was able to understand one person at a time, when everyone spoke together I was lost.

I still have my accent: I don't dare go to a shop and ask for those things you put on the bed ['*sheets*'] because it comes out sounding wrong. We all laugh about the funny things that have happened to us over language. In Mexico, for example, adhesive tape is called 'durex'! Can you imagine here in the seventies when I went into a shop and asked for it! They all looked at me and said, 'No, we don't sell that sort of thing here.'

The country has changed a lot. When I first arrived, to be foreign here was amazing. Whenever I asked for help, I was taken by the hand. It was fantastic. I go to the same butcher's as at the beginning when I didn't know the names of the cuts of the meat and had to point to parts of my own body, the leg and so on. They still remember this. But they were so helpful then. They even produced a picture of a cow to explain the cuts to me.

Everything was different. I remember going to the supermarket, picking up a tin and hoping that the picture outside was the same as the contents. The other thing was that in Mexico City you can go shopping at three or four in the morning. If you need medicine, the chemist shops are open all night. At that time, everything in Ireland closed at half-past five. I always forgot something or my children got sick. Those little things upset me then more than anything else because it made me realise how different my life was. Coming from the city, I couldn't get used to the countryside. I couldn't touch soil with my hands but had to wear gloves. I didn't like to sit on the grass.

All the same, I never had any regrets. I was very attached to my mother and missed her a lot. But I was spoilt by my mother-in-law. She put me on a pedestal. I could do nothing wrong, and that helped.

I have always been an outgoing person and in the mid-seventies, I set up a Latin-American society as a sort of support group. It continued for several years. Whenever I heard Spanish being spoken, I'd ask the people where they were from and invite them to come along to meetings. Some of them are my friends to this day. And when we moved into this place, I went into the neighbours on one side and then on the other side and invited them in for a cup of tea. They had both been living in their houses for about seven months and met for the first time officially in my house.

In all the years I've been here, no one has ever asked me directly where I come from. They always say, 'You're not Irish, are you?' People say things sideways: it's so funny. A lot of people think because of the language that Spain and Mexico are more or less the same. In general Irish people don't know much about my country. But there are exceptions. Soon after I came here first, I had to get a taxi and when the driver found out I was from Mexico, he started going on about Zapata, one of our revolutionary heroes. He knew more about the man than I did: he had read so much. That made a huge impression on me.

I've seen a lot of changes in Ireland, many for the better. People travel a lot and have become much more adventurous in food. Now they'll try anything. When I came here, there was no way I could get an avocado. Now you even have Mexican restaurants — more Tex-Mex, but still. Theatres, music, movies. After Mexico City I enjoyed very much the peace and quiet here but that's changing. It's got so crowded now. Everything seems to be happening in Dublin. But it has to grow and I think it's nice.

When my eldest boy finished Trinity College four years ago there was no suitable work, so he had to emigrate to America. But now there are opportunities here for my other two children.

There are things that will never change, even if I live here all my life. I always have a kind of fight with my husband over the way I speak English. In Mexico you ask in negatives: 'You haven't done this?' instead of 'Have you done this?' Even my children say to me, 'Are you asking or are you telling?' It seems that after a certain point, your English doesn't continue to improve because you don't make the effort any more. When you start, you're very much aware of mistakes because you know people are finding it hard to understand you. Once you know you are understood, you begin to talk faster so you don't pay attention to what you are saying. In the beginning, you are thinking in your own language and translating. Now I think in English and I just talk. I reckon most of the foreigners I know don't speak English very well. In my own case, I find English very difficult because you don't have strict rules. It's very colloquial.

I still have my Mexican passport. I never wanted to lose my nationality. And I think language is connected to that, too. If I were to speak English perfectly, I would lose my identity — that's how I feel about it. The fact that you speak with an accent is a way of letting people know that you're different. That said, I notice that when I go back to Mexico, I speak Spanish much slower than I used to. I was even told that I have a very Dublin accent.

Recently I went back for three months, and found I missed being here. There's something special about this place. Remember the World Cup, when Ireland played Mexico? In the shopping centre, we were all talking about football. The day after the match, when Mexico beat Ireland, they said to me as a joke, 'Go somewhere else. We aren't selling you meat today.' The last time round, when Ireland was out but Mexico was in, they were all cheering me along. I don't think I'd find that attitude anywhere else.

And at the time of the earthquake in Mexico City, I was trying to get information about my family. My husband sent a fax to the Avon company, but still we couldn't find out anything. Then I rang the newsdesk of *The Irish Times* and explained that I am Mexican, with family in Mexico City. After that they rang me three or four times a day with any information that they had. It was unbelievable. Thank God, my family was all right.

Susie Kennedy

American

Susie, who lives in the village of Kilcoole, County Wicklow, is a small, round, dark-haired woman in her forties, full of energy. For several years she was director of Team Theatre in Education, which brings plays into schools. Since 1999, she has lectured in Theatre Studies at the Dublin Institute of Technology in Rathmines and is just off to spend three months at the Guthrie Theatre in Minneapolis as associate director with Joe Dowling on Brian Friel's Molly Sweeney. *Among many other activities, she is a jazz and blues singer and recently toured in a satirical production based on the Flood and Moriarty Tribunals,* Will we get a Receipt for this? Will we F***!!!? *She speaks softly, with a barely perceptible American accent but frequently breaks into loud, jolly laughter.*

I was born in Peoria, Illinois, which is in the heart of the Midwest, although I lived my teenage years in the suburbs of Chicago. I came here in 1974 but I'd been in England for two years before that, teaching yoga and cooking in a vegetarian restaurant, doing all that whole-food thing. Originally I was going to be an actor, that was my plan, and then I got kind of distracted and was off to India to find my guru, via London. What brought me to Ireland was that I married an Irishman. I didn't know much about the country and had visited just once before I came here to live. By then I had already met Brian in London, but I came over one Easter on my own and stayed with some friends of his. I remember writing back on a card two impressions: one, that it rains all the time, and the other that every-body has blue eyes. I was enchanted by that.

Just before I arrived, I read a newspaper report I found really shocking. Some judge here had dismissed as weirdos the Hare Krishnas for going down Grafton Street playing their music and chanting their chants. I was upset by that, not just because I was on the yoga/Hindu trail, but because I come from a country where all kinds of religions are accepted. Then when I came here to live, I found more of the same on all levels — an intolerance of difference. We're talking about 1974 now, with me coming from the London of Portobello Road. I had this patchwork knitted coat that was brightly coloured with big buttons. I thought I was the bee's knees, you know, dead cool. And remember those Afghan dresses, purple and blue with pink stripes? I had one of those that I'd saved up for. It cost ten quid, which at the time was ex-pensive and I was really proud of it. But when I wore it here, it was like the circus had come to town. I'd be going down College Green and everyone'd be saying, 'Ah God, would you look at your one . . .' The conservatism of the time, in all kinds of ways, I found really restraining. You just had to learn to conform.

At first, I was happy but kind of lonely. I had a new baby, Aoife — she was six months old, born in London. I wasn't used to not working and was going a bit spare. At the time, we were sharing a house with the writer Des Hogan, and one day he said that a few friends of his were going to get a children's theatre company to-gether to visit schools. And I thought, that sounds interesting: I have a kid and I used to do theatre, so maybe I'd be good at that. Through Des I met Jim Sheridan, Neil Jordan, Garret Keogh, David McKenna, Peter Sheridan. I didn't know who they were from Adam. Sure, they didn't know who they were at that stage either; I mean, they weren't famous then. So we started the Children's T Company, which has gone down in the annals of theatre history in Ireland; it was seminal really. It was just fabulous, even though we hardly made any money. I was teaching yoga as well, private classes, which kept us going. My husband was a medical student with three or four more years to do, so I was earning the bread.

I've seen lots of changes over the years. At the beginning, I was ap-palled that there was no contraception. Coming out of America in the sixties, I couldn't believe it. And divorce! I got married here in Kildare Street at the Registry Office. We came over for a weekend from London because it seemed a romantic thing to do. Lovely, I thought, great, real airy-fairy. It wasn't until a couple of years later that I found out there was no divorce. I mean, when you're arrested, they read you your rights. When you get married, nothing! So it was quite a shock really and of course it was more of a shock when we separated, seven or eight years later, and only got divorced after eighteen years. I think I was the first on the list when it became legal.

I'm pure pagan, pure heathen, not religious in any way. I put my foot in it a lot of times, from just not knowing how deep Roman Catholic culture is here. I mean, I'd be very respectful of people's religion, but I was so shocked to discover there was hardly any sex education that I got on my high horse and said, I'm going to go round schools and do that. I didn't, of course. I'd have been arrested as an outside agitator.

I wasn't actively involved in the women's liberation movement but we did a few plays on the subject of women's rights — one I re-member called *Same Sweat, Different Pay* with Team Theatre. The status of women as represented in the plays of the time was very low — and still is, in fact — with few good female characters, so I'd shoot my mouth off about it any time I could. I haven't experienced prejudice against me as a woman in my work, although it's hard to know what I might have achieved if I was a man. But there seem to be more doors open to women in the arts than in other fields. That said, there's only a handful of women directors. And certainly, as I said, there aren't the same number of parts for women, so there's not as much work.

After Brian and I split up, I actually went back to the States with Aoife, to a theatre company in Boston. She was seven then and I found it very difficult. America's not very child-friendly and I had to be on the lookout for her all the time. I didn't have any support system, no family there, and I felt at sea. So after six months I came back and things have been great. I've done remarkably well, actually, being a foreigner.

It's like anywhere. You get work by who you know, who you've worked with, and when you come to a place where you don't know anybody, it's hard. It's not exactly that connections that get you work, but you hear about things through your connections. Like you don't know where's the best place to buy aubergines. Although when I first came, you couldn't buy a green pepper, let alone an aubergine. That's changed all right. It's much more cosmopolitan here now. Then the most exotic place was the Coffee Inn. But what I'm trying to say is, when you don't have a history in a place, everything is harder. It's particularly difficult to get *in* here, when you're a newcomer. I was just lucky, landing in this circle of very talented and lovely people.

It took me two or three years to cop on that I didn't understand what people were saying. There's a big difference between Hiberno-English and American English: literally, words have different meanings. And it took me about seven years more to realise that it's not what people say but what they don't say that's the important part of what's going on here. In every relationship, from getting your plumbing done to a personal relationship, to a contract with somebody, there are things that are kind of understood by Irish people of the same culture that I as a foreigner can't necessarily understand.

The country is definitely improving. I don't believe much in borders. The more people mix, the better. I wouldn't be afraid of losing national culture and identity. That doesn't happen. And if it does — now I'm contradicting myself — I think that international understanding and tolerance are more important. A homo-geneous, closed society is dangerous, verging on fascism. I'm in favour of opening the doors to anyone and everyone. People have always come in to this country. If it's not one group it's another. You used to hear them giving out about Germans buying up property in the West of Ireland. I say, cop on. They bring energy into the country. People come, people go and this keeps it all flowing. But I know there are many here who disagree, vehemently.

I kept my husband's name. Well, it's much nicer than Schmidt, isn't it? You wouldn't get far in Ireland with a name like that.

Anthonia L *

Nigerian

Anthonia is tall and slim. Her black hair is straight and shiny. She is friendly but very quiet in the noisy cafeteria of the Liffey Trust in Dublin's inner city. Her son, thirteen-month-old Victor, stays in the crèche while she attends a course in computer programming. Understandably, she is unwilling to talk too much about the circumstances that brought her as a refugee to Ireland.

I'm from the south-eastern part of Nigeria, from Lagos, and have been in Ireland for about thirteen months. I came as a refugee because I had problems in my country. Now, I have a residence permit. Victor was born in the Rotunda soon after I arrived here and everyone in the hospital was very nice to me. It wasn't good to travel when I was so heavily pregnant, but I had no choice.

At home I studied industrial chemistry. I was doing a Masters' Programme but I was bored with the subject, so when I came here I wanted to study something new. I like the course I am doing and there are good job prospects with computer programming.

I didn't know much about Ireland before I arrived. I knew the capital was Dublin, that's about all [*she laughs*]. It wasn't really a culture shock. One thing though: I am a Catholic but I found the religion very different here. People still make the sign of the cross when they pass a church. In Nigeria, we were taught to do that when we were very small but you don't see it any more. In church in Africa, we clap, we sing, sometimes we even dance. Here it's all very quiet.

Some Irish people are really nice, others not so much, although I have to say I personally have never had any problems. Of course, I've heard about it, how foreigners are treated, particularly the blacks, being called niggers or other names. I've never experienced that sort of thing. I have Irish friends, mostly people I've met because of my baby son, girls calling wanting to mind him or play with him. I've got to know them, their mothers.

I have a flat in the centre of Dublin. I don't go out much because of the baby but then I didn't in Nigeria either. I stay in and watch television and read a lot of novels. One of my favourite writers is Barbara Taylor Bradford.

I'm getting used to the weather. It's very cold compared to Nigeria. I caught flu when I arrived here. That was terrible.

People drink and smoke a lot here. Young girls, too. That's unlike Nigeria where it's not considered respectable for young girls to behave like that.

I'll stay in Dublin for the time being, although I've heard that Galway is nice. I'm OK here, although sometimes I feel lonely, especially at Christmas. This year I was by myself. I did nothing, just sat at home with the baby. That was hard, but it takes time, I suppose.

Harriet Leander

Finnish

Harriet is a broad-faced woman in her fifties, smitten on a winter morning with a bad cold. She sits in her wine bar near the Spanish Arch in Galway city — all rough-hewn wood and comfortable clutter — and sips strong coffee and later fennel tea. It's Monday and the place is quiet except for the cleaners, whistling and singing. Harriet speaks excellent English in a soft voice and has a warm and open manner.

I was born during the war, in 1944, of Swedish-speaking parents. Half my family is Finnish-speaking: that's the way it is there — two official languages. Five years after my birth, my parents moved to Sweden. It was a common thing to do at the time because Finland was very poor and there was more work in Sweden. I finished my studies in Stockholm, a beautiful city. Why I moved from there: that's the first time love comes into the story. I met a Swiss architect. We fell in love and got married and he absolutely wanted to go back home. I was twenty then — very young — so I followed him.

In Sweden I was always out on the Baltic Sea, fishing. And although I lived in Switzerland for twenty-five years, I never got used to being land-locked. I did a lot of alpine climbing and so on but was always homesick for water. That was how my fascination with Ireland started. The first time I came here was in 1971. I was intrigued by the way people treated each other, so friendly compared to the rigours of Switzerland. After a while, you come to recognise the kind of friendliness it is. It's not always deep and sincere. But it's kind of easy-going. It's nice to walk down the street and say hello and see people smiling. And the sea, the sea!

After that, I used to visit on holidays about three times every year. I wasn't taken in for long by dreams of Celtic mists. The first time I was out on Inishmaan, there was no electricity, no running water, no harbour — you had to be rowed in by curragh. I thought it was so romantic. Then I went there in the winter and found that it wasn't romantic at all. We saw what the people were really struggling with, the mould and the damp. Some of the cottages still had earth floors. Women of forty-five full of arthritis. There was no doctor on the island and when one person got sick they all did and took to their beds. A nurse would have to be rowed in to look after them. I was so glad I saw that side of it.

So I came and went and came and went and in the end I was always crying when I was leaving. There's a beautiful story about it. I used to get the bus down to Rosslare, and the boat and the train: it was a very long journey. Sometimes I'd travel three days each way to spend a week here. Anyway, one day, I was sitting in Rosslare with a pint in front of me, wondering when I'd be able to come back, and I started to sob. Near me there was this couple, pensioners from Dublin who'd come down on a free pass to look at the boats. The old man leaned across and tapped me on the arm and said, 'My dear, your pint's not going to improve if you keep spilling those tears in it.' And that was it. I knew I had to come and live here. I wasn't in love with anybody. Only with the country itself. I'd learned my lesson and took control of what I was doing. It was a big move, after all, and I really wasn't ready for it until it happened.

I had a brilliant job in Switzerland at the university, working on contemporary music archives, mainly Stravinsky. That's how I could afford to travel so much. My marriage had broken up after twelve years, so when my son was old enough, I had the choice of going in search of a better quality of life. I have wonderful Swiss friends and there was never any problem about me being a foreigner or anything like that. In fact, I was paid to improve my qualifications. But I just couldn't see myself getting old there. I thought to myself that if I am going to live maybe another thirty years, it has to be beside the sea. To go home is a different thing. I visit Scandinavia to see my mother, but it's like going backwards.

So, aged forty-eight, I sold everything I had and came to Ireland without any thought but that I was sure I could make some kind of living. I have three passports and in fact arrived as a Swiss citizen, but that made it difficult too, because I couldn't work here. Then I found out that if I invested money in some kind of business, I'd be allowed to stay. I had a friend who was running a restaurant and for a time gave him a hand because I was a reasonably good cook, although I soon learned that it's one thing to cook for friends, another to do it professionally. Anyway, my friend then asked me if I wanted to take over the restaurant, and I agreed. I put some money in it, which also prolonged my permit to stay. Now both Sweden and Finland are in the EU, so I have no more passport problems.

In fact, for a long time they continued to stamp in my passport that I was a student and wasn't allowed to work, while all the time I was paying thousands of pounds in taxes. So I complained that this couldn't be right and they said to me, 'Oh it doesn't matter, does it?' I was in my fifties and still being classed as a student! The fact is, they don't care that much, although they're starting to get stricter now.

I don't leave Ireland much. I have friends in Venice and recently spent five days there. My son is a theatre director, so I sometimes go to see his productions — he had a play on in Brussels recently. But always when I come back, I heave a sigh of relief. Now I'm home; now I can relax. My mother has visited me from Stockholm and one time she remarked in amazement that someone had stepped out of her way when she was walking down the street. I said to her, 'But that's normal,' and she replied, 'No, it's not.'

All the same, as a person trying to run a business, it was very frustrating in the beginning: the impossibility of getting an electrician, the frequent flooding, the kitchen going on fire and no one doing anything about it. Now I say, 'OK, we're closed until the problem is dealt with.' I've learnt to live easier here. I don't make a drama out of things any more because I've discovered how to stand back from it all.

I feel that I was born Finnish and will stay that all my life. It's very important to be aware of where you come from. I certainly feel from the way I am treated that I am a part of Galway but certainly not Irish. I live in the Claddagh and have many friends that are old Claddagh families, fishermen. I'd be invited, not for dinner, because Irish people don't generally do that, but for the glass of whiskey at Christmas and so on. I was always dying to go out fishing with them but they'd say, 'Women are useless on boats.' I'd reply, 'Try me.' So finally they took me out mackerel fishing, and who was the first to catch something? Me. They were very impressed and said, 'You can come any time.' This particular family, I know them all. There are twelve siblings from age forty-three to twenty-two, some of them married with families of their own. And they'll tell me, 'You're part of our family.' That conveys responsibilities. It means you have to remember the children at Christmas, at first communion, when someone is getting married.

I'm not a Catholic but I go to church and stand at the very back for some of these ceremonies. There have been a lot of funerals recently. The way they are conducted here, it's specially Irish, a way of saying goodbye. You stay with the dead person for two days almost. For me, that's amazing. In Switzerland they just come out of hospital in coffins and you don't see them as being dead. That's terrible.

Regarding the position of women, I've gathered from my friends that traditionally the woman's power is that she is totally in charge of the family. She constantly gives out to the man for drinking his money, for not working enough, and she's respected by him for that. In the pub he'll call her a bitch but he loves her, even though he won't want to show his emotions. It's breaking down, of course, but here it's still quite a matriarchal society, with the mother controlling her husband, her sons and her daughters. Kind of leading from behind. That would never suit me, but that's because I wasn't brought up to it.

Sometimes I used to think about all I'd given up, the good Swiss pension and so on, and would ask myself if I'd done the right thing. The answer was always the same. I'm very happy here, working hard — harder than I ever thought I'd have to work. I still cook, though I have chefs as well. But we're open seven days a week, so it's impossible for one person to manage that, as well as doing all the books, paying four full-time staff. I love the place, the special atmosphere it has when it's up and running. I don't want to go back.

Brigitte Lennon

German

Brigitte lives in the countryside near Kilkenny city in a large house once owned by an uncle of Jonathan Swift, who spent some years of his youth there. In the late 1980s, her groundbreaking marriage separation made headline news. She claimed half the estate but by law was only entitled to half the house and contents, which she was awarded. Two years later, in 1991, the judgment was overturned by the Supreme Court, on the grounds that there was no legislation to back it up. She then went back to court for unsecured maintenance payments and got the whole house and gardens. After twelve years, she says that she and her husband have a fairly amicable working arrangement.

I've been in Ireland thirty-two years. Originally I came from near Hanover, where my family had a farm. The reason I came was to improve my English before going on to Berlin to study. I never went back. Within a year I'd got married. And even though I'm now separated from my husband, my life is here; my two sons are here. Now, of course, I've lived in Ireland longer than I ever lived in Germany.

When I came first, I stayed on a farm with German friends in New Ross as an au pair. Then a girlfriend invited me to go for a while to Dublin, where I worked as a receptionist in a hotel. I had every intention of going back home in the autumn but one day my husband-to-be came to the hotel for a meal with friends. One of them could speak German and they chatted me up - typically Irish!

We went out together for nine months before going to Germany to get married. Then we lived in Dublin, while my husband finished his studies as a civil engineer. After that we moved down to Carlow — to Borris where my husband came from — and ended up here in this house, which was very run down when we bought it.

I worked part-time, odds and ends fitted round the family. Because I hadn't gone back to study in Germany, I did some interior design courses here, after which I was commissioned to fit out houses for Germans with holiday homes in Ireland. I also did a little journalism for a Catholic newspaper in Bonn — it was just when the troubles were starting in the North, and there was a lot of interest. So we were living here and travelling to Germany three or four times a year, to make sure the children spoke German properly. Then there was the pony club and the hunt — the usual farming life in Ireland, the tennis parties. It was brilliant here in the seventies and eighties, like in the Roaring Twenties. Really it's the only way you can describe it. There was such an upswing after Ireland joined the EEC. You didn't even need a lot of money to live excessively well, though of course you had to have a fairly good job. But at that time, the banks were giving out money quite freely. The lifestyle was fantastic: parties and dinners all the time. And of course, it's very easy here to have access to politicians, and people with influence, which you wouldn't have on the Continent.

We had property in England, so my husband was always going over there. Actually, I'm much more of a farmer than he is; he's more interested in financial dealings. After we separated, the farm was let to a series of people. The neighbour who has it now is into mixed farming. But we still have trouble getting rid of the weeds left by an organic pig farmer; the roots go so deep. We don't want to spray too much too quickly and poison the land.

Both my sons are engineers. I brought them up to be independent, to be actively involved in family life. I know that's definitely not the traditional way of the Irish mammy, but I don't think it's good for boys to have everything done for them. My sons are well able to iron and cook, the lot.

I'm Lutheran. My husband is Catholic. His family is all in the Church, in fact. His brother, who died a few years ago, was a priest and his two sisters are nuns. They were related to a bishop so it was a very strict Catholic family. But they were remarkably relaxed about me. There was never any problem about how my boys were to be brought up and even now I still have close relationships with my former sisters-in-law. I've met a lot of nuns and priests throughout my life and even interior-decorated a number of convents. I've never experienced any bigotry, but perhaps it would have been very different if my husband had wanted to marry an Irish Protestant. You have to realise that in those days, there was this idea that Germans were wonderful people, that they could do things Irish people couldn't, which is stupid. Germans just work a bit harder and talk a little less; that's all it boils down to. Irish people can also be industrious, especially outside Ireland. But I sailed by on those feelings about Germans for a long time: I still do in fact. People have expectations about me — that I always have a spotless house, for example.

I found one thing difficult. After the separation, it took everyone a long time to see me as Brigitte and not as my husband's wife. First of all, you lose a lot of friends. If you make an effort, you can win them back eventually. When I separated, it wasn't exactly a stigma but it wasn't as easily accepted as it is now. Another thing, of course: my separation was huge in Ireland. I set a precedent on property. Every Irishman is afraid of me. Until I took this case in 1987, no housewife had ever claimed half the property from her husband. Originally, when I found that I knew nothing about the legal side of separation and that I was going to be in deep water, I set about informing myself like a typical German. I was gunning for the house because we had bought it together and I had put all my energies into it. It meant much more to me than to my husband.

He wasn't expecting a fight, since I had always been an extremely easy and laid-back wife. For seven years it was sheer hell. The court case was vicious and there was not just one but many.

Of course, I had no family of my own in Ireland, so I was completely alone. In one way, that wasn't a bad thing, for the simple reason
that families always try and influence you to patch things up. My family
just helped out, from a distance, with money because I had no financial
independence whatsoever. My friends too were absolutely fantastic,
supporting me throughout the whole thing. When the results of the Supreme Court judgment were published, everyone was up in arms.
Women hadn't realised they were entitled to half the estate only when
the husband dies, not when they are separating. They got the shock of
their lives. I was invited to address all sorts of women's clubs, which I
did over a two-year period. I found how difficult it really is for women,
especially for farmers' wives, who, having worked all their lives on the
farm, find that if their marriages break up, they can be left with nothing.

A few years ago, my husband came and apologised for everything. He didn't exactly say so in so many words — men don't. But
he conveyed it. He arrived one Good Friday with two legs of lamb.
He had said the most awful things about my mother. She was here
and behaved as if nothing had ever happened; they even drank coffee
together. It was the first time for eight years that he and I had been in
the same house. The way I see it, it's better for the children if the
parents can meet on reasonable terms. His partner and her little girl
even come here occasionally. It's a loose relationship. There are
some of my friends, however, who will never speak to my husband
again.

I don't feel under pressure to get a divorce. I had a relationship a
few years ago but most of the time I am so busy, I don't even think
about it. I think if you are living in a place like Kilkenny, a small town,
you should contribute in some way; even more so if you are not Irish. I
have translated the guidebooks to the castle into German without
charge. I was also involved in fundraising for the roof of St Canice's
Cathedral, that sort of thing.

I don't involve myself in politics. I've had various requests to join
different parties. One group actually wanted to put me up as a candidate
in Kilkenny, when they were looking for women to stand. But it's not
something I'd like to do. You always have to be careful what you say.

And when it comes to the crunch, you have to ask yourself where your loyalties lie.

When I first went back to Germany on holiday, no one had a clue about Ireland. Some of them even thought I was living in Iceland! I had to explain everything about the country any time I went anywhere. Ten people out of a hundred might have had a faint idea. Now they know everything. I only have to say I come from Kilkenny and they know that's where the famous Kilkenny beer is made. Ireland's come a long way.

I still have links with the German embassy. It organises a friendship club where German women in Dublin can meet in each other's houses. Then, of course, there is the Lutheran church, a beautiful little building, with a German pastor; the German school, St Kilian's. We have always celebrated a national day: now it's 3 October, the day the Berlin wall came down. Every year they have a big reception for business people, companies, the German community and guests. Sometimes I feel a little bit lonely for something German, so I go along. It's an opportunity for me to wear my national costume.

Ly Thi Minh Hai

Vietnamese

Minh Hai is doing an MSc in Engineering Hydrology at the National University of Ireland, Galway. She has been checking for e-mails from home on one of the computers in the room, the recreation room of a large prefab where the students also have some of their lectures. Minh Hai is thirty-five, with very long dark hair and a pleasant, if shy, manner. At first she looks uncertain and wary, but soon relaxes and opens up, even though she won't complain on tape about her ex-landlady — who wouldn't let them walk about the house in the evenings, reduced them to talking in whispers and rationed the use of hot water — for fear of angering her.

I am from Hanoi in Vietnam, here to study the hydrology course because at home I work in that field. I want to improve my specialisation and my English. I've been in Ireland for three months, my first time here.

My first day in Dublin I felt anxious and cried a lot. I missed home very much. Previously I was in Belgium, in Brussels, which has a high population density: it was exciting for me. In contrast, I found it empty here, big open spaces. Now I feel better about it because I am kept so busy. When I have nothing to do, I get more anxious. There are very few Vietnamese here and this year only me on this course. I don't really feel too isolated now because my classmates and the teachers here are friendly.

Every day, I check my e-mail and expect to hear from my friends. And every week I speak to my family. I have a seven-year-old daughter but could not afford to bring her with me from Vietnam. It is hard for me to leave her for such a long time.

At first we were two ladies in a house with a landlady. We weren't happy there. My friend, who was from the Philippines, got very depressed: she's sensitive and we had a bad experience with this landlady, who wasn't kind to us. My friend got sick and now she has gone home. I couldn't stay there alone and had to move to the new place, where the landlady is friendly and the facilities much better: television, microwave, everything. There are four other students living there and, though we meet up very little, since we have different timetables, it's a big improvement on what was before. The only trouble is that it's far from here, a long way to walk.

I go shopping every weekend — window shopping, because I don't have much money. With my friends I go to the pub sometimes. I like to see how Irish people live. In one pub they have only Irish music and now I listen to it on the radio. I like it very much and think I will take some recordings back with me.

I'm a Buddhist but here it's impossible to practise the rituals. When we pray, we have to burn something but it's not possible to make a fire in my room. So I ask my Buddha to forgive me.

M *

Middle Eastern (for political reasons she does not wish to be more specific)

M is a woman in her early thirties, with sallow skin and long dark hair. She speaks good English, articulately and with confidence. She sits in a noisy café in the centre of Cork city and occasionally breaks off the interview to chat with the Kurdish waiter, who is a friend of hers.

I grew up in a Muslim environment. I'm not practising and don't be-lieve in religion, but it's an identity. If I'm asked a religious ques-tion, I'll answer it in an Islamic context. Questions you face in a for-eign environment are mostly about your appearance, your religion and your country of origin.

I've been in Ireland permanently for eighteen months. Before that I was here more on holiday — always in Cork. I had about eight months which I call my solitary confinement: going from home to shop and shop to library, a circle, a triangle, a square at the most, perhaps to a poetry reading or a gig. That was the most I did. I can only analyse it a little bit now: normally I'm a very friendly person; I'd talk to anyone. I don't mind personal questions: it's a part of our culture, anyway, to give more information about ourselves in the Middle East than in the West.

One of the problems was that I didn't work — I'm still unem-ployed but I'm doing handcrafts and stuff. And I was very insecure: it was my first experience of living in a small city. I've spent all my life in big cities, so I wasn't sure what the social size of Cork was, whether I was known by everyone or only by people in the bars I would go to. I'm still learning about the pub culture. One of the first things I found in this country was that if I'm friendly with someone in a pub, regardless of their age or sex, we can have a good laugh, have a conversation, but the next day they may not say hello. This was devastating for me. At the end of the eight months I went home. When I came back I started to socialise more, started to go to political meetings. I'm involved with immigrant and refugee groups. I feel much better now. My feelings for Cork are special. Every time I go up to Dublin, I get homesick. It's so intense and much less humble. What I knew about Ireland was from writers or from movies about the IRA. It's almost shocking to find a Wall Street-style Dublin.

My boyfriend is Irish. I met him at a transitional time in my life. I was based in New York and trying to decide whether to go back to my own country. I've no regrets now that I came to Ireland with him. I think I'll stay, but one thing I've learned: no matter what your plans are, they will change. I hope mine won't change any more but you never know.

The position of immigrant women is particularly difficult, especially for refugees, if you don't speak the language well, if you look radically different. I've never experienced violence or verbal abuse in this country but that could be because I look Italian or Spanish. If I were a practising Muslim, if I were veiled and was here with a Muslim husband or boyfriend, I know things would be different. I witnessed something last week in Dublin. I was walking down Grafton Street with a Muslim friend of mine. She was covered from head to toe, though her face was open. She's pretty dark. A group of young men started to tease her. They were making absurd sounds, as if like Arabic. They didn't know her country of origin and were bowing like Chinese people. I was frozen but she just laughed at them and walked on. She's here only temporarily, as a student so she doesn't need this country. She can ignore them but I couldn't. I'm not a refugee but I feel as hopeless as they could. All my life, I've made my living from English. Now here for the first time it's useless. I can't teach here. It's reduced me, at the age of thirty-three, to Leaving Cert level again.

I still have a lot of privileges, compared to many foreign women I've met in this country. Some of them had no say in coming to this country: their husbands decided and they followed them. And still they have to face all the problems of being refugee women. These would be Muslim, Romanian, Nigerian, anything.

I don't think they have a great fear of Islam in this country; they have a greater knowledge here about it than I could have imagined. Quite a few people have been to the Middle East and they have some idea about life there. They have been to Morocco, Egypt, Turkey, Israel.

I find young people much more open than the older ones. And it's changing unbelievably. I was first here in 1996 and even since then, every few months, you can see changes. This is the first time for Irish people that they're having some good times, some confidence in this country, after eight hundred years! They should be left alone to enjoy it. I can easily relate to oppression, conflict, civil war. There are numerous such conflicts going on in the Middle East and very few of them have been acknowledged.

The press plays a remarkable role in determining the feelings of the people about foreigners in this country. I regret the hysterical level of racism generated by elements of the media; the slogans used. I just thank God that I am not a refugee in this country. I am able to work, to write, to get involved in politics.

The group I'm involved with in Cork has a programme, one element of which calls on the granting of the right to work for refugees. It's so important for self-respect. Many of these people aren't prepared to be involved directly in agitation for reasons concerning their own safety and because they don't know the language well enough. Few of them can afford private courses. There's one free school I recently learned about but it couldn't handle all the refugees in Cork. I see more and more here and that's another thing about being a refugee — you're so visible. Most of them are either dark-skinned or dress in a very different way from Irish people. As for me, it's good for my ego. As an Italian-looking woman, I'm being paid attention for the first time in my life.

With regard to Irish women, I was very disappointed when I first came. It's inevitable that you judge people by the way they dress, the way they consume and so on. I call it the Western way: the make-up, the style, the brand names they have to subscribe to in order to get jobs, husbands, on and on and on. And I still see oppression here. Women still have the burden of excessive hard work. I'll tell you a little story. We met an Irish man in my country about a year ago. He and his family — his wife and four children — were on holiday and he was giving out about the men sitting in the coffee shop while the women were doing the work. But here I've seen many cases of men coming home from work, having dinner and going out to the pub or sitting down in front of the television, while mother is dealing with six to eleven children, paying the bills, doing the shopping, doing the laundry, looking after the garden, keeping the house spotless. It's actually very similar to my country, but that man couldn't see it.

Still, I'm overwhelmed here. I love it and really feel that I can make it my home. I'm certain that this society will in time absorb us and we will integrate. There's one thing which is very important here and which may sound strange to anyone who has not been away, but that's peace. It is so important for those of us who come from areas in conflict, who have spent all their lives in a civil war situation. There are many willing to lower their standard of living in order to live in peace. It's a great period anyway, with peace in the North. It's such a privilege to witness this. When I first came to Ireland, the first ceasefire had been broken and the only thing I saw was depression. It's so different now.

When people go on about youth drinking here, I say, why not? They're having fun. If only I could have done it when I was a student back home. We were unable to go out at night: everything was very bleak, everything was banned, party gatherings were banned, clubs were closed and anyway, as a young girl, you weren't allowed go out at night or at weekends. It was such a dull environment. We were supposed to be the lucky ones because we were educated. I only learned to have fun when I was twenty-eight. The first time I got drunk (and enjoyed it) was when I was twenty-seven, which was already too late.

I love the pubs here. The first three months my legs ached from all the standing up, the closeness and intimacy. Now, whenever I go home, I really miss it.

Vesna Malešević

Croatian

Vesna is a tall, pretty woman in her late twenties, with short blonde hair. She is well dressed in a tailored outfit and has just come from her office at the National University of Ireland, Galway, where she is preparing lectures for a course she is teaching this semester. She gives an impression of intelligence and confidence.

I'm from Zagreb in Croatia and have been in Ireland for a little over five years, more by accident than anything else. My husband and I moved out of Croatia in 1994, during the war, although it wasn't the war as such that caused us to leave. Our reasons were more personal in the sense that my husband is a Serb and I am a Croat: not the most fortunate combination in the early nineties. Before, I never knew what my neighbours were. It wasn't an issue. But with the war, my husband started to come under a lot of psychological pressure. It's hard for anyone else to imagine what it feels like constantly to hear all this propaganda against your nation. There were also economic reasons for leaving. We both worked full-time, but still had to take on extra projects in order to make ends meet, and prospects for the future weren't great. So we decided to take a different route and started looking at the Central European University, a kind of Open University which awards scholarships to postgraduates from the former Communist bloc. It was set up by George Soros, an American of Hungarian origin. His idea was to create an intellectual elite to do something about the situation in these countries. That's when my husband got his scholarship to Prague to do an MA in sociology. The following year, I wanted to do the same course but by then the programme had moved to Poland. So while my husband applied to do his PhD in Prague, I went to Warsaw to study, and we were separated for a year, which wasn't very satisfactory. After that, we applied to all sorts of different universities so that we could do our PhDs together. The only place we both got accepted was University College Cork. And that's the not-very-romantic reason why we ended up in Ireland. Actually, I suppose it's romantic in a way, wanting to be together.

Before we came, we only knew general things about the country. The economic boom, for one thing. And we were aware of Irish pubs, which are opening up all over the world. In Central and Eastern Europe you can find them everywhere. But beyond that, I didn't know anything specific.

I was struck by the fact that everyone seemed friendly and helpful. Our programme co-ordinator at UCC has now become our good friend. At the beginning, he helped us find somewhere to live, showed us round the city and so on. It was a nice first impression. And we liked Cork a lot, and stayed there for two years. However, when we first arrived, people didn't like the fact that we kept commenting on how small it is. We didn't mean to insult anybody; it was simply that we were amazed. I personally had never lived in a city of fewer than one million people and it takes time to get use to the different perspective: when you think of the size of these Irish cities in a European context! You could walk round Cork in one hour. Anyway, almost as a punishment for our perceived rudeness, we had to go to Sligo when my husband got a job there teaching Sociology. His students told him that it's the centre of the north-west. For them, it's a metropolis. On the other hand, you wouldn't believe how fast Sligo is developing. In the one year we were there, so many buildings sprang up, so many old places were renovated, so many new coffee shops and restaurants opened. It was great.

We've been a year and a half in Galway now. My husband completed his PhD two years ago and is now employed by NUI Galway in the Department of Sociology and Political Science. I'm still working on my thesis but I start teaching this semester, an optional course on the Sociology of Religion.

The subject of my thesis is 'Civil Society and Church/State Relationships'. I'm basing it on the situation in Croatia but the conclusions will be universal. Like Ireland, Croatia is predominantly Catholic. What's interesting for me here is that while Irish society is turning away from the Catholic Church, in Croatia in the last ten years, through different circumstances, society is turning back towards it. There are a lot of parallels that I can draw. I was brought up as a Catholic although I'm not practising.

With regards to the long term, we have a baby now, Luka, thirteen months old and born here. That changes things. You have to start thinking of him, his opportunities, his future. My husband's position at NUI Galway is permanent and we're in the process of buying a house. Galway's a nice place to live — it reminds me of some of our seaside cities, with tables set on the streets in summer and people eating and drinking outside — and we can see ourselves here for some time. When we first came, we used to talk more about it, whether we'd stay, for how long. Then suddenly we realised that we like it here.

There's also the thing about Ireland being in Europe, as opposed to the States or Australia, far far away. We'd want to be in an English-speaking country.

Luka goes to a crèche for two-and-a-half days a week. We share the time with another couple. He's getting used to it, although he's still sad when I leave him. At home we speak Croat or Serbian. The languages are very similar, like UK English and American English, although now they are trying to emphasise the differences, because of the split and the war and so on. We're planning to rear Luka as bilingual. We've discussed it with some linguists who tell us there is no concept of language among children. It's just another word in their vocabulary. If later on you speak to them in Croatian, they will answer in Croatian and if you speak to them in English, then they will answer in English. It's easy for them. More confusing for adults.

There's nothing major that I don't like here. If I miss anything, it's family and friends, rather than Croatia itself. In fact, the word 'home' to me is already starting to mean Ireland. My mother doesn't like it when I visit and then say something like, 'We'll be going home in ten days.' 'This is your home,' she says. As for me, I can find good and bad things in both places. And the advantage of here is that I'm not emotionally attached in the way I am in Croatia. If there are things I don't like in Ireland, I don't have to care about them. I don't follow politics too much, although I watch the news and try to keep up with what's going on. I notice that most of the reports are about Ireland, which is quite normal. After that you'd have news from the UK and news from the States. And maybe European Union countries. Then maybe you'd have some disturbing item about a violent outbreak somewhere or a disaster. The impression I have is that the news from the rest of the world is filtered. It's not even done on purpose. People are just not that interested. What you see reflects what's happening in society.

The racism that I see reported on here doesn't really shock me. It has to be put in perspective. Ireland is after all an island. And not just in a physical way but in many senses, in a symbolic way too. There's a geographical aspect to the culture and to the behaviour of the people. Because, if you're cut off from the continent, what's the result? People feel alienated; they don't feel that link with other countries. It will take time to adjust. I think the way a foreign person reacts to the country and is received there depends on personal circumstances, whether you have a job, that type of thing.

When I say where I'm from, I never have a negative experience. When the World Cup was on and Croatia came third, that summer and for a couple of months afterwards everyone knew about it. For people who follow soccer, Croatia has a lot of players in teams outside the country, in Spain and the UK, and they would be more aware of us. Other people wouldn't know anything about it, and while at the beginning I'd tried to explain, I soon stopped. If they wanted to know, they'd already have looked it up in the atlas.

I've a lot of Irish friends in Cork. We moved to Galway when I was seven months' pregnant, which made it more difficult for me here. Now we know some of the people in the department, and that's about it. Sometimes I feel a bit lonely simply because I have friends in Ireland but they are not here, in Galway. So it's something of an unfortunate situation, but still we have visitors at least once a month. What I've realised now, after a few years here, is that people are shy, in a nice way. I don't know how to explain it. People are not very direct. There are so many different ways of saying things and it takes time to realise this.

The accents were a shock. The Cork accent, for example, and the counties around. I worked in the accounts department of UCC for a while and it was difficult for me at the beginning. I kept having to ask people to repeat things. But you learn. Your ears grow big and you listen more.

Valeria Martinez
Argentinian

Valeria is a tall slender woman in her early thirties, with short brown hair and an olive complexion. She is shy and diffident in manner as she sits in the noisy café of the Liffey Trust premises in Sheriff Street, in Dublin's inner city. She is taking part in a computer programming course and this is her lunch break.

I come from a city near Buenos Aires, in the middle of the country. It's called Rosario. The north of Argentina is desert and very hot. I lived in the pampas region, fields and open plains. The south is very beautiful, among the Andes. One of my brothers went to live in a very nice city there but couldn't find a good job and had to go back north. It's very difficult in Argentina now, the economy is so unstable. My brothers sometimes have difficulties even paying their mortgages. They can't live the way we are living here. One thing that struck me here is that people in Ireland are always in a good mood. In my country people are anxious and depressed because life is so uncertain.

In Argentina, I studied two years of physics and eight years of music — I play the flute but not much these days. I couldn't get a job in either area and for six years was manager of a stationery shop. Here I'm doing a six-month computer programming course. I like the subject: it's interesting, very challenging.

My boyfriend came here first, two years ago, and found a good job easily, within a week, so he asked me to join him. Since childhood, he has been obsessed with Ireland: the music, the culture, everything. He has always wanted to come here. Me, I knew nothing about it. Everything is very different from what I am used to, the people, the weather. And I miss my family very much. They're so far away, I can't go over often for a holiday and have been back only once, one year ago.

It was easy for us to come here because we have Italian passports. Our grandfathers emigrated from Italy to Argentina. It's common in my country to find people of Italian ancestry, and we are entitled to dual nationality.

At first, because my English was very bad, I couldn't find a job. Then I started to work as a customer service agent for Spain and Italy. All day long I was talking Spanish and Italian and when I arrived home I was speaking Spanish, too, so my English didn't have a chance to improve, especially as we have no Irish friends. I eventually gave up that job because I was overqualified and there were no possibilities for promotion.

It's difficult to integrate. People are quite friendly but it's different from my country. If foreigners come to Argentina, everyone invites them to their home, to dinner. In two years I have never been invited to an Irish person's house.

Dublin is all right but I'd prefer to live in a smaller town. At the moment we are renting a house in Castleknock — it's a quiet enough place but the traffic is very bad. When I get a job, we hope to be able to afford to move south, maybe to Greystones in County Wicklow. That would be nearer where my boyfriend works.

He's a little disappointed with Ireland but is really happy with his job. He doesn't feel his roots are in Argentina, not the way I do. The first year was difficult for me. I was very lonely. We arrived in winter and I was at home all day by myself. Now I'm getting used to it and I think we'll stay.

When I was saying the people in Ireland are friendly, that's true. On the other hand, the children here can be wild. A crowd of ten- and eleven-year-olds hang around our street at night. Where we are living we have a big gate and they have broken it many times, swinging on it. When we ask them not to, they laugh in our faces. There is no respect. The same thing might happen in Argentina among very poor people but they have a reason to be angry: they have no jobs and are hungry. Here it happens in a middle-class suburb. Sometimes I am very afraid. They don't pick on us because we are foreign: they do it to everyone. I haven't complained to their parents or anyone. We don't want them as our enemies. Better to say nothing.

We live a quiet life. We don't go out much, so it's partly our fault that we don't know more people. Sometimes we go to a nice pub near where we live and drink Guinness. I like it very much. But often we are happy just to stay home and watch a film.

Another thing I don't like here is the pension scheme and health service: as a worker you have to pay in full for everything, the doctor, the dentist. That came as a surprise for me. When I was working in Germany, the health service was excellent. Even in Argentina it's better than here.

I worked for nine months in 1997 in a pub restaurant in Germany simply to pay for a nine-month tour of Asia, from India to Europe overland. That was a great adventure. As for Germany, everything is perfect, too perfect. It's very rigid; the people are cold. On balance, I like it better here.

Catriona Mitchell

Australian

Catriona is a very pretty young woman with long curly dark blonde hair. She sits in the café of the Irish Film Centre in central Dublin and drinks tea. Her manner is merry and vivacious.

I call myself Australian, although it's not strictly accurate. My parents live there and my passport's Australian, but my father's Scottish and my mother's German. I was born in Switzerland and spent the first half of my life in Scotland. Before I came to Ireland two years ago, I'd been travelling around Europe. I taught English in Paris for a year and then stayed in Germany for a short while, to get to know my German family. After that I was living in Edinburgh, which is when I met an Irish man. He came to Australia with me for a while but felt himself too far from his Celtic roots. So we agreed to come back here together. I'd always been attracted to Ireland, although I'd never been here. Coincidentally, some Buddhists I knew in Australia were moving over to do some teaching, so we came with them, which actually proved a bit disastrous. That was when I found out that I'm definitely not a Buddhist — I don't want to live that kind of lifestyle, even though aspects of the philosophy appeal to me a lot. And then I broke up with the man as well. So nothing is as it seems and the reasons I thought I was coming for, I wasn't here for at all. But I felt an instant connection with the place which hasn't died off, and I think I'm going to stay. I have a British passport, too, so I'm legal.

In hindsight, what I think immediately attracted me was the nature of the culture here. It's very oral. People love to talk and I really like that. And it's relaxed and laid back. I've lived in other cities where the emphasis is on money-making: your social status is defined by your wealth. Ireland's still rooted in a rural culture, although Dublin has changed a lot, even over the last months. Camden Street, where I work, is an old part of the city, full of fruit-sellers, charity shops, generations of women who've done the same thing. Now trendy cafés and bars are opening up everywhere. They're even talking of putting trees in the street. It's great so long as it doesn't destroy the character of the place.

When I moved here with my partner, he'd been studying in London for five years and he found it tremendously parochial, having fled from Ireland in his teens. For me it was more charming because it was a novelty. All the same, there's the racism that goes with the fact that it's still not truly multicultural here yet. On the other hand, in Melbourne there's a big Asian population, as well as the biggest Greek population outside Athens. It's very multicultural but there's a lot of racism there too.

I also find it a bit rough here. It doesn't help that I do most of my shopping in Thomas Street, near where I live, and there are a lot of drug problems there. I find it quite dirty as well. Then there's drink. The culture centres so much on alcohol. The thing that would really make me aware of that would be walking to work on a Monday morning and looking at the state of the pavements. They're disgusting. On the other hand, Dublin is so easy to get out of. That's an amazing feature.

It's not really a place that's very visually oriented, at least not yet, particularly with regard to the architecture. Other cities are a lot more beautiful — Edinburgh, for example, is spectacular. Here the magic lies in the people. I find the Irish much more open and humorous, and it's a slightly gentler culture than Scotland in terms of the landscape; the climate's that bit milder. And I feel freer here for some reason. Edinburgh's quite a conservative city. Perhaps that's where religion comes in. I wasn't brought up with any particular religion, so I'm not aware of the nuances. Irish people are always quite shocked about that.

Mostly the reaction of the Irish of my generation is that they can't believe my luck — that I haven't got all this guilt.

Now many Irish people are looking for an alternative spirituality to the Catholic Church. Since I arrived, I've been running a healing centre. There are lots of different therapists operating from the building, with massage, meditation classes, t'ai chi and so on. For a while I was studying Chinese medicine and in the course of that came across a book called *The Artist's Way*, which made me think that while I'm still young enough I want to have a creative life. So that's where I am at the moment. My mother's a painter, and I would have grown up with that awareness. In fact, at one time I thought visual art was my creative outlet but I'm more attracted to writing now. I feel it's a deeper form of expression for me.

I'd like to write fiction, probably short stories. I've attended several workshops, and find the teaching levels here amazing. I did an English degree in Melbourne and the standards here are much higher. Sorry to all those professors back home!

All the same, I miss Australia, especially at this time of year, January, February. The light and the colour. And the food's another thing. The quality. I think I'm probably spoiled from Australia, which is so incredibly abundant, especially with fresh fruit and vegetables. Over there, I'd live almost entirely on fruit and here I don't even like to eat it, it's so full of chemicals. There isn't much emphasis on health here either. If you're not a fan of the batter burger, then you're in trouble.

All the same, things are improving all the time. I love the Temple Bar market: oysters and wine first thing on a Saturday morning. There's a man who brings his shellfish straight from Clare and they're wonderful. I like pubs, especially Grogan's in South William Street. It's got paintings on the walls and it's full of eccentrics, woolly poets in khaki trousers.

I've travelled around the country a bit, probably not enough. I'm really enamoured of West Cork, which is wonderfully wild and clean. I try to go walking in Wicklow at the weekends if I can. I like dancing, any time, anywhere, to anything. And I used to enjoy going to the horse market in Smithfield. It's absolutely amazing. I think it may have closed down now.

With regard to Irish men, I have an ideal in my head but I've yet to meet him. I was in a pub recently in Roundwood, and on the wall was painted, 'An Irishman's heart is nothing but his imagination.' I thought that was lovely. I've met a couple of men here who are interesting but on the whole they don't feature as one of the attractions of Irish life — unfortunately. The Irish women I know complain an awful lot about the men. They'd rather have anybody else on earth. I went to a comedy night at the International Bar and a woman there was doing a skit and she said, 'There's good sex and there's bad sex, there's foreign sex and there's Irish sex.' All the Irish men started putting on foreign accents immediately.

People here believe in the soul, the spiritual side of things, quite openly. I work with two people and we found an old mill just outside Dublin, which would be ideal for a holistic centre. They took a look round and said, 'We're buying it.' The asking price was one million pounds and they had nothing at all, but they said, 'The money will appear.' Within a week someone offered to buy it for us as a gift. I really believe there's a certain magic here that can make things happen. On the other hand, the whole project has ground to a halt, not because the money isn't there, but because of in-house politics, another feature of Irish life.

When I first started working here, I felt that Irish people were very suspicious of me, as a foreigner in their midst, telling them what to do. That took a while to change. But now I find people very open, certainly within the work context. Now they tell me straight out that they hated me at first. They thought, 'Who is this upstart?'

Igbal Salah Mohammed Ali

Sudanese

Igbal is small and bespectacled, and in her late twenties. Her head is covered and she wears long clothes in the Muslim style, but her face is unveiled. She is beaming with smiles at the prospect of an imminent return home, having just completed a fifteen-month MSc course in the Department of Engineering Hydrology at NUI Galway. She sits at a computer in a study room, with a view of the river and the cathedral out of the window. She had been described as shy by her professor, but comes across as chatty and charming. Her slightly earnest manner is frequently offset by peals of giggles.

I am from the capital of Sudan, Khartoum. This is the first time I have been out of my country. The fellowship is a good opportunity to do postgraduate studies, especially for women in Sudan. We haven't so much of a chance in our country because it's expensive, and so it's always the men who get to do it there, the PhDs, the good degrees.

I found many things different here: the weather especially. In Sudan it's very hot — often more than 40° centigrade — and it rains only for three months. I knew it would be cold here but until you experience it, you can't imagine it. Also, as Muslims we find it strange. There is a mosque in Galway but it is very far away so we have to do our praying at home.

It is nice to meet so many nationalities, especially on our course. There are people from Pakistan, Bangladesh and India. Also, for me it's the first time to speak English. I've improved a little. There's no problem reading or writing in English, because we study it at home, but speaking is another matter. The accent here in Galway was a problem at the beginning but now we're used to it.

I'm living in a house with other students: many girls come, for example, from Poland as tourists and stay in our house, so that's very interesting for me. We have lots of discussions with these people and find out what they are thinking.

We have made friends in Ireland, too. Our neighbour is a very kind woman; she often calls to our house and wants to help us with our English. There's also an Irish family who lived for fifteen years in Sudan and they've taken us around to many places: to the Cliffs of Moher, to Connemara. And we've been to Dublin a few times, shopping. I like Galway better, though; Dublin's too crowded.

With regard to food, we brought our own spices and cook for ourselves. We like hot food, chillies, other special spices. Our food is very different from what people eat here.

In the evenings we might go to the cinema. Not to pubs because as Muslims we aren't allowed to drink. Our friends invited us many times, just to go and see what it's like. We have parties maybe three times a month in college and have music from all the different countries, including Ireland.

I'll miss it here when I go back but I think everyone wants to return to their own country. It would be difficult for me to stay longer: I've been quite homesick. In Sudan, we have big families and everyone lives together. I have six sisters and two brothers. Some of them are married and have children. It's nice to live with them all.

At home I am employed in the Ministry of Irrigation. My MSc is related to my work with the flood warning system and when I return I will apply everything I have learned here.

Because there is war in the south of our country, many people leave and come up to the capital. It's difficult to live in Khartoum because it is crowded and hot even for us. On the Irish news, they report on the bad harvest in my country, but that is only in the south. Sudan is very big and what is happening down there doesn't affect our everyday lives so much. The people are nice; everyone cares for everyone else. Preparations for a wedding, for example, take a long time, a month. We don't have arranged marriages any more; the women can choose. My younger sisters are all married because, unlike me, they didn't enter university after school. Now they have had their children, they are able to continue their studies. For me, now I am twenty-eight, it is time to think about getting married too.

Gisele Heike Müller

German

Heike's bungalow is perched on a cliffside with a stunning view across Mulroy Bay in north County Donegal. The room is crowded with heavy, carved furniture, each piece, as she says, with a history. There is no sign of any of her ten cats and two dogs: apparently they are not allowed in this room. Heike serves vanilla-flavoured coffee, especially imported from north Germany. Small and pretty, though initially intimidating, with searching eyes, she amazingly admits to having just turned sixty. She has a strong accent, imperfect grammar — for which she apologises.

I was born in Kiel, in north Germany, though I didn't always live there. I come from an old navy family — my father was fourth generation — and my husband was a naval officer. He died sixteen years ago. And that's the reason I am here: over the last twenty-five years I lost my whole family, apart from my daughter who is living in Frankfurt, married with two children.

The story is that after all these troubles I wanted to go to Finland. I studied the language and I have a lot of friends there. However, another good friend, a herbalist who can look into the past and into the future, told me two years before I came here that I wouldn't go to Finland, but to Ireland. And I said, 'Ireland? No, never!' But she said there were many people here waiting for me. I was born with the gift of healing hands, a special child. My great-grandfather was the same. He was

Russian, with a long beard down to his feet, and he travelled all around Russia and Poland doing cures.

Anyway, I still planned to go to Finland but in the meantime I met a guy with friends in Letterkenny. They came over one summer to Germany and lived with me in my apartment and invited me to visit Ireland. I told them that I had learned in school that Ireland is very flat — I think my teacher must never have seen the country! So they said, 'No, no, there are some hills there.' Anyway, in January 1993 there was this special offer on flights to Ireland with Lufthansa, so I wrote to tell them that I would be coming over. And they said, 'God help us. It's the worst time. It will rain, rain, rain.'

But the sun was shining when we arrived. I only wanted to see the country; I had no plans to live here. The guy I was with said that when he was older, he would like to have a little cottage and some sheep in Ireland, but they told him, 'No, not when you are older. Now is the time to come.' We looked at a house in Kerrykeel but I had a bad feeling about it. And then we saw this place, with its very wild-looking garden. 'That's the house for you,' the auctioneer said. I stood in the hall of the house and looked across Mulroy Bay — the sun was still shining — and I knew it was right. I can't tell you why, but I always have such feelings.

I like the weather here. In Germany you have so much up and down. If you are getting older, you like it more on one level. And now I'm not so fond of strong sun. I think it's not good for the skin.

I don't practise healing too much here. I want to write a book for children about animals. People here are so cruel to cats — sometimes they even drive over cats sitting in the road. I saved some kittens that were going to be put in the river. There were six of them, two-and-a-half weeks old; I don't know what happened to the mother. So I fed the kittens with a bottle till they were six weeks old and then gave three of them away. They are like my children. But of course I also do some healing. There's a man living up at Fanad, a German physiotherapist; he knew about me and rang me one day to tell me about a child in his neighbourhood who couldn't walk properly: he has severe Down's syndrome. I said I would try and help him. They brought him here every second day for six weeks and now the little boy is running up and down hills.

When people want to see me, they ring and fix an appointment. I am very concerned about little children with asthma: I cured a boy from Belfast who was visiting the area with his parents. Shingles is one of my specialities. I have treated this in Germany where there's a different attitude, an acceptance of the practice. They know that there's no medicine for shingles once it has reached a certain stage, so they ask people like me with healing hands to come to the hospital and, if the person is healed, then the insurance will pay us. They take us seriously.

The healing has nothing to do with religion. My grandmother was Russian Orthodox. She wanted to marry a Catholic but this wasn't allowed, so they married as Lutherans. My mother grew up a Catholic. She married a Protestant. After my husband died, I went back to Russian Orthodoxy — this gives me more than any of the other religions. We believe all things have a soul, even plants and animals, and that it's all coming from the same man, call him Allah or Buddha or whoever. The people around here say to me, 'If we see you working in the garden on Sunday, you are nearer God than we in the church.'

My feeling is that all illnesses begin in the head and it's the soul that is ill: when people are angry about things, when they worry too much. It can begin years and years before and then one day it comes out. I will tell you a story about a good friend of mine in Derry. A few days before Christmas her sister and brother-in-law were killed in a car crash. Six weeks later, my friend rings me and tells me she has cancer, a lump in the breast. She had a small operation to remove the lump but the doctors were saying that really she should have a mastectomy and a course of chemo-therapy. I said, 'No. I will put you on a diet of brown rice and raw vegetables for six weeks.' After one week, she rang me and said, 'Heike, the rice is coming out of my ears, I can't do this.' I said firmly, 'You can.' After six weeks she went back to the hospital and the doctors were puzzled. One older doctor still thought she should have chemotherapy, but I thank God for the younger doctor who said that there was no need — there was nothing there. And since then, my friend has had no problems and is still very much alive. Now she even likes brown rice. So eat rice and rice cakes and butter. No low fat spread — it's so full of chemicals. Wear cotton, not synthetic fibres — it causes eczema, all sorts of troubles. Changes are coming: young people are more aware now. We went through this in Germany twenty years ago. It's coming a little bit later to Ireland.

I get on well with the people here. OK, some people like you, some don't — that's always the way. Very quickly I got a five-year permit to stay and this is my house now. I don't want to go back to Germany. I like it here — the nature in particular. I have a lot of friends. And I think maybe I lived here in another life: I've always been interested in Celtic things. I have an old Irish rocking chair, a woman's chair, and I like to sit in it and think of all the other women who have sat in it over the years, knitting, nursing their babies.

When I go out, I go to concerts, to the opera in Belfast — last year I saw my favourite opera, *Madame Butterfly*. I have no TV, only a radio, and I like to listen to music — Beethoven, Sibelius, Tchaikovsky and all the Russians. No, I am happy here. I miss nothing.

Nkem N *

Nigerian

Nkem is a tall and very beautiful woman of thirty-five. She wears a knitted hat over her hair to protect it from her six-month old baby son, who is intent on pulling at it throughout the conversation until she starts to breast-feed him, at which point he becomes fully absorbed in the new occupation. She has a pleasant and intelligent manner but seems shy and self-effacing; also a little lost and sad. She sits in the Parents' Room of her older son's school, where she and other mothers have been baking cakes and buns.

I'm from Nigeria, an Ibo from the east of the country. I've been in Ireland just over a year, with my husband and two children. We are refugees. Ola was born here but even so all our residency applications have been denied. The first time was the third week after we arrived. We don't know exactly what our position is here now; we're just waiting for them to answer us. Sometimes they say no, sometimes they say maybe. I don't understand the government's approach.

I knew nothing about the country before coming here. In fact, I thought we were coming to an 'island', a place in a river. When you're in a difficult situation, you just want to get out. You don't ask questions. It was my husband's brother who helped us and the plan was initially, I think, to go to France. But then we were told that we'd be better off here. We came by road, by air, by sea and arrived off the ferry in Dun Laoghaire. At that point we didn't know where we were.

We just followed the man who brought us. I think he was from the Ivory Coast. He took us down to the office to apply for political asylum. He organised everything.

At first we were put in a hostel and a week later we got a letter asking us to come for an interview. It was after that we heard for the first time that our application had been rejected. The Department of Justice offered us the services of a lawyer, who has been working on our behalf ever since.

I'm trying to be positive about things. I'm alive and well and in good health. All the same, I'm not used to sitting doing nothing. I studied fashion and textile design at school and before I left I was running my own business, similar to what here you'd call a café, except that I didn't serve coffee. I bought in bulk from suppliers to resell in my shop, which was situated at the back of a club. I sold children's confectionery, too. I also sewed and designed clothes and if people wanted to decorate their offices or their houses I would give them advice. I'm big into sports too; I used to be an active sportswoman. After the shop closed in the evenings, I'd coach squash in the club and teach swimming at weekends to kids from about eight to fourteen or fifteen years old.

I had a very full life there and wish I could go back. I miss everything. I want to see everyone again. If things change there in the future, maybe it will be possible. I keep in touch as much as I can but it's very expensive to phone. As for letters, they don't seem to arrive, I don't know why.

I attend the Redeemed Christian Church — it's a Pentecostal church — and do voluntary work there, typing and so on. I know how to use a computer. I can't just sit around. The first three months, that's what I did but I couldn't stand it. It was so boring, watching TV all day, every day.

I also do voluntary work in a place called Spirasi at the Spiritan House, which provides a service for refugees, teaching them English, running courses and so on. They offer advice when necessary. I'm a member of the women's group there. It's amazing what they achieve. I've seen people who arrive here with no English able to chat after a few lessons. It's the same with computers. And many of the refugees already come with special skills. What I can't understand is that I read every day that there is a shortage of workers in this country and I wonder why the government doesn't use this pool of people instead of leaving them with nothing to do. There was one Chinese man in particular who had very specialised knowledge of computer languages, Java and so on, and he couldn't get a job here, so now he's gone to India, where they were delighted to welcome him.

I had my baby here [*Dublin*] in the Rotunda. It was very different from the time I gave birth to my first child in Nigeria. Then I was at home with my family around me. In my place they treat the mother as a person, and for the delivery I was surrounded by nurses and doctors. The antenatal classes I attended were fun. Here it's more impersonal, even if the equipment is better. And I never saw a doctor. It's a principle in my country that there must be a doctor, a midwife and nurses in attendance at a birth. And back home a new mother gets more attention from the older women — in fact, too much attention. They didn't let me take care of my first child until he was about five or six months old. They wanted to take over and play with him all the time. I just fed him and then they took him off me until the next feeding time. In some ways it was great. I was actually very surprised in the antenatal class here when more than two-thirds of the women said that they didn't want to breast-feed their babies. That's another big difference.

My eldest son is now seven. He quite likes it here. What he enjoys most is school. And he has good friends where we're living now but he doesn't like to go out and play in the cold. Back home there were lots of open spaces where the children could play safely. Now we're living in a two-room apartment in the city centre. Most times we walk to the school. Sometimes we get a bus.

I have two very lovely Irish neighbours. One, Auntie Jo, is especially nice. She's done everything to make us comfortable. I don't want to be rude but when we moved into the new area most people initially avoided us like we had a disease. It makes you feel terrible. Auntie Jo was the first to come to my door and knock and introduce herself. She said I was welcome any time to call in. She's a middle-aged woman, very nice and kind. And then the neighbour opposite saw my son out playing and her son came over and started playing with him, and she became friendly too. But I've also experienced a lot of racial abuse. When I was pregnant, I was punched the ground by a man who came up behind me. And there are two people in particular where we live, an elderly man and a middle-aged man, who try to make life difficult for us: one cycles up and down the road all the time and whenever he sees us he curses.

What do I like here? I love this cooking class. It's not a class as such. We share recipes, we share experiences. And the people in the school who set this in motion — they are the ones who have made life here bearable for me.

Nenu Navarro *

Spanish

Nenu is a striking woman in her mid-twenties, with long dark hair. She sits unconcernedly in the very messy sitting-room of the small redbrick house in Fairview on the northside of Dublin city which she shares with several other Spanish women. She smiles a lot and has a deep chuckle. Her English is fluent.

I came to Ireland to learn English. I finished university in Spain three years ago with a degree in sociology and decided to find a job over here. At first it was quite difficult because my English was so poor. I started to work in a factory making sandwiches but after six months I left there. That was in Dunshaughlin. I was living with a load of Polish people and had a very nice time. But we were kicked out of the house and had to move here to Dublin.

Now I work in a crèche. I've been doing a Montessori course for a year and love working with kids. The children are between one and four years old and are brilliant, wild. Everyday I learn something different from them. I really enjoy it. I'm hoping to get an extension because I want to stay on at least for a few years. I'm really happy here, the style of life here.

I'm from Madrid and for me Dublin is like a village. Everybody knows everybody. I've Spanish friends, Catalan friends, French friends, even refugees. I know Irish people as well but I think it is really difficult to make good friends with them.

What really surprised me was seeing all the girls — fifteen, sixteen years old — with small babies. At first I thought they were older sisters but then I found out they were mothers. It was incredible. It's society's fault: the fact that the religion forbids abortion. But if you are sixteen with a baby, the government gives you money, a place to stay. That's not right. These girls aren't ready to have babies.

I'm interested in women's studies. There's a course at Trinity College I'd like to do because I'm interested in working with women in prison. I want to continue working in the crèche but do something else as well.

There's very little information here about the rest of the world. The media just don't cover important events properly. It's a kind of tabloid mentality.

The racism in Ireland is incredible. One day I was in the GPO with some friends and this old man came up and said, 'You fucking Romanians! Why don't you fuck off!' If I had really been a Romanian I would have killed him. It was very shocking. And if you are Catholic, you shouldn't be like that. The government should be educating people.

Aileen Niven

Scottish

Aileen is in her early thirties with blonde hair tightly tied back in a ponytail. She sits in the kitchen of her rented modern detached house in a pleasant suburb of Limerick city. Two small children disrupt the conversation periodically, with demands and screams, and Aileen, who is a few months' pregnant, deals with them wearily. She has a chatty, friendly manner and speaks with a strong Glaswegian accent. When she describes the loss of a house she and her husband were having built, she breaks down in tears.

We've been in Ireland a year and nine months now. It was my husband's job that brought us here. I'd never been to Ireland before we came over for his interview. We spent a few days at that time looking round the area, at house prices, general things, to see if we wanted to move here.

My husband loves his work but for me it was very difficult to begin with. The first six months, I was miserable and just wanted to go home. It was the middle of winter; the house we were in was cold and damp and our second child was only eleven weeks old at the time. But then summer came; we moved into this house, which I really like, and anyway you get used to things, you start to make friends and build up a life for yourself. At least we're not too far from the family. It's only a short hop home by plane and we try to go back twice a year.

Before I came, I thought people here would be very friendly and easy-going and that's partly been borne out. Actually, I don't know very many Irish people, though the few I do know are lovely. Most of my friends here are foreigners I met through the International Women's Organisation, set up mainly for the wives of men who've come here to work. They arrange all sorts of activities: meetings, lunches, craft mornings, bridge, golf, walks, but because of the children I can't really get to much except the mother and toddler group, which I'm helping to run. The IWO was set up to give isolated women company and is really great. I think it has saved the sanity of a lot of us.

Many of the Americans and Canadians who come here would like jobs but can't get permits. As a UK citizen, I'm not in that position and would love some day to go back to work. I'm a staff nurse with fifteen years' experience. That was another problem for me when I came here: not working, missing the sense of independence.

What I found surprising was that for a country with such large families, they don't provide for children. There are no facilities, no swimming pools, no ice rinks, no sports centres, at least not in this town. I find that very frustrating after Glasgow.

People keep asking if I support Rangers or Celtic, which is a way of finding out whether you're Protestant or Catholic. I just say I don't follow football, which is a way of saying, *mind your own business*. I was brought up a Catholic and will send the children to the local Catholic school, so that they are the same as everyone else — I want them raised with some sort of religious belief, but wish there was more choice. I'm sorry, I don't like Catholicism any more. It gives me the creeps.

I find business people here hard to deal with sometimes. Yesterday we lost the house we've been having built for the past year. We discovered a problem — actually, the house was being used as a lavatory — and when we complained, the builder just didn't want to know. I don't think I should say on tape exactly what he said to us. But the jist of it was that we should go back to Scotland, that we aren't welcome in Ireland. He added that he wouldn't deal with us any more and that if we wanted to make a fuss, we could take him to court. We can't afford that. It's just bricks and mortar and I'd rather let it go. But it's very up-setting. I know some other foreign women have had similar experiences — it's hard enough trying to settle without that sort of thing. That said, it was just one incident and any Irish people I've told about it have been horrified. They said, please don't think we all feel that way. I know they don't. I just have to try and keep it in perspective.

I think we'll settle here all right. It's just the business with the house that upset us because we're now back at square one and can't afford to buy a place in this estate, the prices have gone so high.

I'll be having the baby here. The hospital is all right but it's like stepping back maybe twenty years. There's none of that routine pre-natal screening for Down's syndrome and stuff, the scans that you get in the UK. I've had tests done but it cost me £100. I suppose be-cause there's no abortion in Ireland, it's considered that there's no point running the tests. It's just a shame that you don't have a choice.

What I don't understand about here is that there's such a high rate of tax but you have to pay for all the GP visits, medicines, and so on. And the roads are awful. I wonder sometimes: where does all the money go?

Waltroud Nohava

German

Waltroud is a small, quiet woman in her late fifties. Her bungalow, set in picturesque countryside near Ballyragget, County Kilkenny, is filled with furniture and items collected by herself and her second husband, Franz, in the course of many travels — to Mexico, China and Israel. Her own paintings crowd the walls, including one of a mountain range in New Zealand, which she has also visited. An eleven-year-old boy from a troubled family in Germany is spending a year with them as part of a programme to try and help children at risk. He is very lively and attention-seeking and looks in from time to time.

I was born in Bavaria but went to school in Stuttgart. I came over here in the autumn of 1960 just to get away and live somewhere else for a while. I'd heard the best English was spoken in Dublin — that was what we were told at school. I got a job with a company that did a lot of business with Germany and had to learn shorthand because I couldn't work with Dictaphones— I could understand when people were talking to me but not on tape. In that first job I earned £11 per week, which was a fortune then. I did up the wages as well and saw that I got the top money there. In general, people were poor at that stage; they had to work hard and save to be able to afford something. And accommodation was always so awful, with no central heating. Now it's got very materialistic. The Irish appear friendly but it's no longer from the heart.

Every year before I got married I had to go to the Aliens Office in Dublin Castle and sign on and get a stamp. Each time you moved, you had to report there with your book, and the new address was entered. There was never any prejudice against me but they were against coloureds. I don't think it's changed that much. It's such a pity: a bit of cosmopolitanism can change the life of the country. My first husband was Irish, so I had no problems meeting people then. In fact, we had a great life at first. We had one child and sent her to the German school. She died, and that was when our marriage broke up, after seventeen years.

I got married here and divorced here. That is to say, we tried first for an annulment, but it didn't go through. I didn't really understand what it was about. I couldn't have cared less about any annulment; I just wanted a divorce. Eventually the marriage was annulled in the States and I finally got a divorce in Germany. I remarried there, but my ex-husband remarried here. In fact, the Revenue Commissioners did not recognise his second marriage and I had to accompany him to the High Court over this. I said at the time, 'What'll happen if they don't recognise it? I'll be a bigamist.' My domicile at that time was in Germany, so there were no problems in the end. Now that divorce is legal here, from what I read, not that many are bothering with it.

I was reared a Catholic but in a mixed marriage. And religion was anyway very different here from Germany. In Ireland they really all went to church and not on Saturdays like they do now, so they don't have to go on Sundays. If you feel that way about it, I think you're better off staying at home.

I met my present husband, who is Austrian, when I came back to Ireland. He was working in Castlecomer, in fact, just over the hill from here. Then his contract finished and he was to be sent to Israel so I went with him. Why we chose to come back here to live: we wanted to be in the countryside, not too far from Dublin. First we tried around Wicklow but couldn't find anything. So then we settled on the Kilkenny area. If I get up in the morning and feel like going to Dublin, I can be there within two hours — although recently, the traffic has got so bad . . .

When I came back here with Franz, it was different. I still had the friends from before. But it's more difficult to make new friends as you get older: age is against you. That said, I'm not lonely at all. I wouldn't want people dropping in all the time and once your husband is retired, everything changes anyway.

We've been five years in this house. Before that, we were travelling the world. The best time of my life was when we were in Israel. They are the friendliest people I have ever met and there was no prejudice because we were German. If things had been different, we would have retired there, but we left just in time, before the Intifada started.

Now I'm a lady of leisure. I paint, I do gardening, I read, I knit. The days are too short. I don't think we'll move again. If I did, I'd just take a couple of suitcases. We're getting too old for all that packing.

I like Ireland. I didn't want to settle in Germany; I've been away too long and find it all too regimented. That's why we came back here. And then all the big changes started — some but not all for the good. It's rush, rush, rush now, and reminds me of what it was like in Germany a long time ago. And there are lots of other things I'm not happy with. The way they're cutting down the hedges, for example. There was a protest against excessive pig farming in the area a while ago, but nothing came of it. There are too many people related to each other down here. We pay our taxes, so I feel entitled to voice my opinion. No one expresses resentment about this openly; only sometimes in a roundabout way.

Regarding the position of women here, it's improving but it's got a way to go. If I want to get a workman or a tradesman in, I'll still ask Franz to call them up. As a man, he gets a better response.

When you live abroad, you change. I've noticed that now when I go back to Germany and mix with old school friends, I find I've nothing in common with them any more. They can't understand why you wouldn't want to live in the same place all your life.

Yuki O *

Japanese

Yuki is tiny, with short black hair. She is in her early thirties and dressed casually in jeans. She sits in the comfortably untidy kitchen of a modern house in Clontarf, a suburb of Dublin. She has just completed an MA in Women's Studies at University College Dublin and is awaiting the results. Her English is good, spoken softly with a slight accent, and she is very articulate.

I'm from Osaka, a big city, and have been living in Ireland for three years. I came because my partner was transferred here. In Japan I had been working for a time in the same company, in the overseas section, translating documents and working as an interpreter with Irish trainees. From them I'd heard lots of stories about life here. So when they established a factory in Dublin, I was very interested to come over, even though by then I had left the company because of limited job opportunities. For women in Japan it's difficult, especially as they get older. There are a few in high managerial positions, even company presidents, but not in the mainstream.

At the time we came to Ireland, I was working in different jobs: I was teaching English; I was also involved with a bilingual magazine translating articles and writing about women's experiences. I had also joined a group involving itself with women's issues.

An Irish woman I knew told me about the course at UCD, that it was very good, so I applied from Japan. After coming here, I had to wait a year before starting my studies, partly because of the language. I had graduated from university in Japan majoring in English, but had never used it in daily life and found it as spoken here in Ireland very different from what I knew. Sometimes I still don't catch everything. I can listen and understand the lectures but a women's studies course is so exciting — with a lot of people talking at the same time — that at the beginning I was overwhelmed by the amount of information and the different style of communication. In Japan it's much quieter: the teacher talks and the students listen. We don't have lively discussions. I wasn't used to asking questions and making points, so it was a big challenge for me. I still have a lot of difficulty with that.

What struck me first when I came here was the difference in the pace of life. It's very slow in Dublin compared to Osaka. Japanese people work hard and expect efficiency. It was my first time in Western Europe and at the beginning I felt frustrated but gradually I'm getting used to it.

Ireland is very interesting for me. Once I got to know people, to make friends, it gave me a different perspective. At the same time, I see a lot of similarities between Japan and here. Both are islands, with the mentality that goes with that. Regarding the acceptance of other nationalities, regarding racism, I see that Ireland faces many challenges. It is the same in Japan, where there are now a lot of returnees, especially students, who have difficulties adapting back to the very restrictive Japanese system. For example, high school and university education is much harder in Japan and children have to attend additional classes on Saturdays so that they won't get left behind when they go back.

Relatively speaking, quite a few Japanese people live in this country. About 750 or 800 have registered, but students who only stay up to three months don't have to do this, so there are about 1,000 resident at any one time.

I had a lot of problems making friends at first. Most of the Irish people I know through the course, and they were kind and helpful from the start. However, I sometimes have difficulty understanding what they really think. Sometimes I feel they are not honest about their feelings. It's easy to establish a basic friendship with them but it's difficult to deepen the relationship. In Japan, people at the beginning keep a kind of distance — it takes time to get to know them — but once they are friends they become completely open with each other. In that sense, sometimes I wonder if I can ever make real friends here.

I think my partner is happy enough but his life is work-centred and, in the evenings and at weekends, he is very tired. Women in the home have an advantage in that they have more of an opportunity to broaden their lives. It depends on the circumstances, of course. Some of my Japanese friends who live around here — the wives of my husband's colleagues from work — don't speak much English and have to take care of small children, so they are restricted in what they can do. But still they have more time than their husbands to expand their world. However, I find that in general Irish people aren't ready to give space to foreigners to express themselves. Sometimes I am able to break into a conversation but still find it very difficult. Japanese women especially don't have the assertiveness for that.

In many ways, through my course, I see similarities between Irish and Japanese women. They are expected to fill the role of mother and wife. That's heavily emphasised here through Catholic morality, especially in rural areas. Of course, it's gradually changing in both countries. In Japan, men tend not to want to change, so there's a big difference between what men think and what women think, although the younger men tend to be more open to new ideas. Japanese women married to Irishmen find a strong bond between mothers and sons, which can create difficulties. In addition, the power of Catholicism here comes as a culture shock to most Japanese. Religion isn't strong in my country, where most people are Buddhist but don't practise.

Irish society is changing very rapidly and becoming more diverse. It's important for Irish people to listen to foreigners but I'm not sure whether they are willing to do this. Sometimes I've felt that because I'm obviously foreign I'm treated differently — by officials or service providers. Also, it's a small thing but when people ask where you're from, they always add, '. . . and do you like Ireland?' I didn't think too much about it but one of my friends said that they ask that because they want to confirm that Ireland is accepted: to confirm that Irish people are very kind and hospitable to people from outside — and therefore can't be racist. Of course, even if we have any reservations, we have to be polite and can't be completely honest in our replies. We have to say nice things.

Benny Oburu

Kenyan

Benny lives in a light and airy modern bungalow in the countryside near Fermoy, County Cork. A Bible lies open prominently in view. She appears confident and colourful: the bright red of her lipstick and nails is picked out in the occasional red streaks of her light green dress. She speaks flawless English in a soft voice, with a very slight Yorkshire accent, although her four children have acquired a north Cork lilt. Her manner is slightly didactic and she follows points through, giving away the fact that she is a teacher. Her mother, Rosemary Karuga, is a prominent artist, working mostly in the medium of collage. Benny proudly displays some of her work on the walls.

I've been in Fermoy for six years. Why I'm here is a long story. When I got married, nineteen years ago, we emigrated, first to Scotland, then to Leeds. That's where I did a diploma course to become a nursery nurse. We lived on a large council estate that was very rough, rife with joyriders and crack and everything. It was no place for a young family. A friend then started telling us how lovely it is to bring children up in Ireland. To me there was even more to it than that. I was taught by Irish nuns in Kenya and my mother was taught by Irish nuns as well, in Uganda.

It may interest you to hear about my family. My father had a very good job as a senior clerk with the East African Railways. We lived in a company house with servants and we children went to a fee-paying school run by the Mercy nuns. But when I was about eleven, my father lost his job. In Kenya it's not like in Western countries where you can turn to social services. Overnight, we lost everything. My mother wasn't a trained teacher, but because of her qualifications in art and music she was taken on, although at the lowest rate of pay. She was sent to a rural school in the back of beyond and we ended up living in a mud hut. The nuns recognised that if my education stopped at that point, I would end up with no future so, very kindly, they let me carry on without paying. I had to leave our house at six in the morning and walk for one hour to reach the city border where I could get a bus. Now when I think of it, I don't know how I did it. The path went through high grass infested with snakes and over a river. Sometimes the bridge was washed away and I couldn't go to school at all. It was a hard four years, but I'm always grateful to those Irish nuns for letting me do it. And so when we came here, it was like returning home.

When I was a small child, my mother taught us a song she had learnt at school, *It's a long way to Tipperary*. So when a friend took us to a beautiful place called Clogheen, in County Tipperary, I sent my mother a postcard to tell her that it wasn't a long way any more! Also, the way the Irish talk gave me a comfortable feeling, like reverting to my childhood. In my own children's school, some of the old books are the ones I used myself: Angus McIvor's *First Aid to English*, for example. I never felt the same about my children's school in England.

I was brought up a Catholic and even used to sing the Mass in Latin. But when we lost everything, we went to live on a coffee estate among extremely poor people. They didn't even have a church, and the priest had to come to the schoolhouse to say mass. One day this priest — he was Irish — stopped mass to complain at the small size of the offerings, saying it wouldn't even pay for his breakfast or petrol. He added that he wouldn't come back unless they gave him more. The coffee labourers were in fear and awe of him and hung their heads. I was only fourteen but I spoke up and said that Jesus would have done it for nothing. He abused me verbally and tried to take a swipe at me. I never had anything to do with the Catholic Church after that.

Much later on, I met some Jehovah's Witnesses. I was very suspicious of them at first — these people who didn't ask to be paid — but when I was nineteen, I joined them. In Fermoy, there's a community of about sixty adults, although there might be ninety or more at any service, if you count children and visitors. It's a wonderful support group. Everyone helps. Recently I was in hospital and they made a rota to look after my children.

Getting on to what I do now: I'm what's called a facilitator in Development Education. It's a position that was created specially for me and I'll explain how this came about. When I first arrived here, I desperately needed a job. My sister had died, leaving six children; their father had gone off and it was up to me to support them. At that time, my own children were attending a two-teacher Church of Ireland primary school. We were made welcome and the head teacher, Hazel Baylor, asked me to talk to the senior class about Kenya. It was very successful and Hazel then put me in touch with a lecturer from Trinity College, Dublin, interested in developing education about other cultures in Ireland. This woman, Bet Aalen, came to Fermoy to see what I was doing, so we put on a concert for her with instruments made by the children out of recycled materials, and we prepared *mandazi*, which are Kenyan doughnuts. It all started from that. Myself, Bet, Hazel, Heather Smith, the other teacher in my children's school, and others formed a voluntary organisation called 'Cultural Links' to promote multicultural understanding. Now I go around schools all over Ireland and teach them about Kenya. I'm still unofficial as far as the Department of Education is concerned, for the simple reason that I don't have fluent Irish, so can't be employed by them as a teacher. I come under the Department of Foreign Affairs, through the National Committee for Development Education, which also part-funds us.

When I first arrive in the school and tell them who I am, depending on where I am, I can see that sometimes they aren't sure of me. There was this little boy in Sligo who was looking at me all the time wide-eyed. At the end of the week, his mother confessed that the boy had said that he thought black people were only on the television, like cartoons.

I wouldn't say I have come up against racism. The children I teach have the idea that every African child is starving, to be pitied. But that's not prejudice. Personally, I have found Irish people to be very tolerant. I often think that what people call racism is just one's perception or reaction to a situation. Perhaps my attitude comes from my childhood. For my father's generation, it was not usual to marry out of your tribe. but he even married out of his country and, as a result, my mother, who was from Uganda, experienced a lot of prejudice from his relatives. So I grew up with it. I didn't have to come abroad to see it.

That said, maybe I'm protected here by my circle of good friends. I know that there is racism but it seems to me that those people fall into two groups: uninformed people who don't understand the issues, and troublemakers. With the first group, the minute you explain to them that their jobs aren't under threat and so on, they start to come round. As for the troublemakers, nothing can be done about them. They're always going to pick on one group or another.

Recently I was asked to give a talk in Westport by the St Vincent de Paul organisation on how Irish people could help refugees adjust to life here. As an African woman, I was thought to be able to offer a good insight into this. In the question-and-answer session, a woman from Sligo said that the refugees there often complain about being bored, but when activities are organised for them, the refugees aren't interested. It seemed they thought that if they didn't co-operate, they would be sent back to Dublin where the rest of their friends were living. I said this was simple bad manners. That it's like inviting someone to your home: if you offer them food and shelter, the least they can do is to do things your way. As I see it — and I can talk about it because I myself did this — refugees and immigrants must also be prepared to make concessions; they need to make an active attempt to fit in. When I came, I tried to do things the way they were done in Fermoy. And I don't take offence because everyone there knows me as 'the black lady'. In my own country, if a white person appeared, the children would all come running, shouting in Swahili, 'A white man is coming!' As a child, I myself was part of that entourage.

When I started on the teaching, it was just a nice idea. But now with all the changes in Ireland it's become a necessity. And I've become much more structured in my approach. I started in national schools but now go more into secondary schools, particularly in transition year. What I tend to focus on is the inter-dependence of the developed and developing worlds. For example, I get the students to check the labels on their clothes. More times than not, what they're wearing is imported. Or we'll discuss what they had for breakfast: orange juice, tea, coffee, none of them produced in Ireland. I like to address similarity rather than difference. Enough people are out there talking about differences.

I've applied for an Irish passport now and am learning the language. I hope to conduct my citizenship interview in Irish. Then I dare them to turn me down!

I went back to Kenya last year. It was wonderful to visit my family but sad to see the state that the country is in. Big business is flourishing, high buildings, signs of great wealth — in fact, when I show pictures of the city to students here and ask where they think it is, they'll say New York, San Francisco, Paris, London. Never Nairobi! But there's another side to it. When I left Kenya there were beggars in the streets but they were adults. Now we have three- and four-year-olds, AIDS orphans. It's really heart-breaking.

Development Education now is just so exciting. We need to know about the rest of the world — do you hear that I am already saying 'we'? At the moment, my life is the best it has ever been. I've never been happier. I've built up my self-confidence. When I think of the quiet little African girl I once was, I've come a long way.

A few years ago, I went to Scotland on a holiday to meet old friends. We went out for a meal and they asked if I remembered when I first arrived from Kenya. I'd never seen an electric kettle. I didn't know what a washing machine was. We laughed and laughed.

Candélas Peñalosa O'Callaghan

Spanish

Candélas is in her mid-sixties. She is small but elegant-looking, very Spanish, with black hair pulled back from an aristocratic face. An oil painting on the wall depicts her as she was in the 1950s, a lovely young woman with short, wavy hair and high cheekbones. She sits in the living room of her bungalow, with its stunning view across an inlet of Bantry Bay to mountains beyond. Her English is impeccable, with a West Cork turn of phrase and very slight Spanish intonation. Candélas is now a widow, but during the interview her daughter-in-law and two very active grandchildren arrive.

When I was about fifteen years old, I came to boarding school in Arklow. I stayed there two or three years and loved it. My sister wanted to come over to improve her English but, as she was too old for school, she visited me during the holidays. I was staying with a past pupil and it was there that my sister met the man she would marry. He was an Irishman, a dentist. The wedding was to be in Madrid and the husband-to-be turned up with a friend — not his best man, because we don't have them in Spain, but a witness. This was Peter, whom I myself was later to marry. He was a dentist, too. That sister is now living in Dublin. I have another sister in the States and one back in Spain. My only brother died.

When I was at school I wanted to learn languages. They came easily to me, perhaps because anyway I am bilingual. My mother was born in France and I went to a French-speaking school. Originally I was to go to England to study the language there, but my family was strait-laced and insisted on a convent school. When the nuns in England sent a long list of the things I needed, they included eveningwear, which my father didn't feel was appropriate for a young girl. So I went to Ireland, to the Mercy nuns. This was in 1948 and although it was very depressed here at the time, I didn't notice. I thought it was beautiful. It was pleasant to walk around Dublin then because there were so few cars. O'Connell Street, up past Nelson's Pillar, would be chock-a-block with bicycles. As for the countryside, there were still horses and carts everywhere. This amazed me, after Madrid. I also learned history from the Irish point of view and as a child became very anti-British.

My husband was from Dublin, although his father was a Cork man. At the time, I had never been to this part of the country. I thought there was no place like Wicklow. However, when I first got married, my husband was working in London. We used to visit the National University of Ireland Club, in preference to the Irish Club, which had general membership. The NUI club members consisted of graduates, doctors, teachers, dentists — people who had all been pals at college. When the children came, we wanted to get out of the city, so we moved to Sevenoaks in Kent, but even then my husband would go up to the club periodically, as he said, to recharge his batteries. For Irish people who emigrate, the yen is strong to go back home. On St Patrick's Day, for example, you could see grown-up people crying, singing all the Irish songs.

Finally we came back to Ireland and at first lived in Dublin where my husband was in private practice. Then one day he saw an ad for a post with the Southern Heath Board. He kept saying how much he would love it and quite frankly drove me mad, so in the end I told him to go for it. He explained that it would mean a reduction in salary but I said, 'It's enough. As long as we're happy.' So that's what we did. This was thirty-two years ago, when the youngest of my five children was aged four.

My husband was attached to Bantry Hospital. From the start, I wanted to live here in Glengariff but at that time there was a rule that he had to live within a radius of six miles of the hospital. It was difficult to find a suitable place because that was when the Whiddy Oil Refinery was attracting lots of workers and house prices were high. It happened that we owned a very fancy caravan with separate rooms, so we drove it down to a site in Ballylickey and stayed there until we found a place to live. I loved it but my sister in Dublin was horrified.

How we got the caravan in the first place is a nice story. Peter's plan when we came to Ireland first was to buy a boat to go fishing and that's what he did. He often went to Cavan, to Lough Sheelin, when it was still possible to fish there. It was a beautiful place then, before the pollution. We used to go with him and stay in a local hotel, until one time he said that what we needed was a caravan. 'Over my dead body,' I told him, envisaging something very basic. Then one day he lured me to a sale in Foxrock where we were living, and I couldn't believe what I saw. For those days, it was luxury, but what sold it to me was the dividing door and separate rooms. We used to take it to Brittas Bay for the summer. The children and I would stay there, with Peter coming down to us from Dublin at the weekends. The summers in those days were absolutely beautiful, believe you me. It was very unusual that the weather would be too bad for us to go out.

So Peter went down to West Cork before us and was living in the caravan for about two months or so. Then we joined him. The Eagle Point site at Ballylickey is magnificent. It was very primitive in those days, of course, but the children had a ball. Nevertheless, we had to find a house for the winter and ended up in a housing estate in Bantry. I didn't like it. It reminded me of *Coronation Street* — houses pressing in, front and back. Eventually, the six-mile rule was done away with and we were able to move here. The house itself isn't much but the view, as you can see, is magnificent.

Do the children feel Spanish in any way? Yes and no. They all speak Spanish except for the youngest: he's not so fluent. You see, when we were living in London we had a Spanish maid and spoke it all the time at home, even my husband. But then the children had difficulties at school with English, so I had to put a stop to it. My daughter, Maria Theresa, is the only one who ever felt really strongly about her roots. Because she couldn't get to be a nurse here, she became very anti-establishment and one day announced that she was going to Spain. She stayed there a year, went to university in Madrid and got a diploma in Spanish. Then she started teaching English to pilots with Iberia Airlines, which was a strange coincidence because, before my marriage, I had worked as an air hostess with the same company. I wanted her to do more with her life, so I made her come back, and in fact my family in Spain didn't talk to me for a year after that. But then she told me that she wanted to obtain a Spanish passport. For that she would have needed to produce my Spanish passport, which was a problem because when I got married the law was that any woman marrying a foreigner had to lose her citizenship. That of course has changed now and I am entitled to a Spanish passport, but there's another obstacle. I have no birth certificate. I don't officially exist. The archives of the town where I was born were burnt during the Civil War. I pursued the matter for a while but then gave up, and by then my daughter had lost interest, too. Don't get me wrong. I love Ireland but I am Spanish, passport or no passport.

I work now as a translator for a pharmaceutical company in Bantry, mostly translating from Spanish, a little French. I only started this a few years ago. My husband was against it when the children were younger. It was of course very difficult in those days for wives to work outside the home. Ireland has come a long way, but there's much further to go. My heart breaks when I see all these poor people, these homeless children. There shouldn't be such things here. Ireland always gives generously to foreign countries when there are disasters, but surely charity should begin at home. In Spain before the Civil War there was a similar divide between the very rich and the very poor, who in fact were often illiterate. As a small child, I must have heard my family, Franco supporters, giving out about the Reds. I remember I got a slap for saying that if I was hungry and someone, anyone, came up to me and offered me food if I would take a gun, then I would take it. Of course, I didn't understand anything. Still, I could see that some of my friends were scandalously rich. And now in Ireland there is a similar trend. Now even the middle class is getting poor.

There was more pride in the old days. Thirty-two, thirty-three years ago, my husband had a surgery in Dublin, near the Castle. There were a lot of people living in flats around there. For a while I worked for him in reception and remember many times asking someone who was evidently very poor whether they had a blue card (the equivalent of today's medical card). They would be shocked at the suggestion. They would have too much pride to accept what they saw as charity and would insist on paying something, even if it was only a shilling. My husband would laugh and say, 'We'll never get rich this way.' And look at it all now. People who are loaded actually boast that their children get grants to go to college. There's a law here for the rich and another for the poor.

Michael Collins has always been my hero and I often say that if Michael Collins came back today, he'd open one eye and then quickly close it again at what has become of the country he fought for.

Catherine Kollefrath O'Leanacháin

French

Catherine has described herself as looking very French and indeed is unmistakably so, entering the Bridge Mill Café in Galway city, with her Mediterranean features, her dark curly hair pulled back in a ponytail. Aged about fifty, she is one of the prime movers behind the Artspace studios, the first artists' collective in Galway, and is currently chairperson. Recently they have moved to a new space in an industrial estate on the outskirts of the city, where later she shows some of the paintings she is currently working on, swirling goddess shapes — she takes inspiration from primitive statuary — in vivid colours. Her manner is very warm, chatty and friendly and she appears full of boundless energy and enthusiasm.

What brought me to Ireland was that I met Seán while I was studying in Paris, and we fell in love. He was working with Kodak but was homesick after three and a half years there. At the time I was looking for an architectural project for my diploma. So I said that I would come with him to do it here. And that's what we did. We arrived in Cork and searched along the west coast for a place to stay. In a pub in Skibbereen we met someone who knew of someone else who was letting a house in Baltimore. We went to see it, loved the place and stayed. I finished my diploma there: the subject was 'The Human

Landscape in the West of Ireland'. It taught me a lot about the history and sociology of the country.

In the meantime we got married in France and Seán got a job at University College Galway. That was twenty-two years ago. Sometimes I feel I've got lost in the Galway triangle: it's a very welcoming little city. At least, it was then, with a lot of charm, before all the developments. What I particularly liked was that it wasn't anonymous, like Lyon. You always meet people you know. It is a university town, so there are lots of people here interested in the arts, literature and so on. It was in fact people from the university who first got the Arts Festival going. I suppose they had this edge. And being so far from Dublin, if they wanted something done, there was nothing for it but to organise it themselves.

When we first arrived here, I started looking for a job teaching art history, but without the Irish language it was impossible to get into the public sector. For a few years then I worked in an architect's office. At home Seán and I were speaking English and suddenly I realised he was losing his beautiful French. And for my own sake, I liked to speak French with him. When you speak in another language your personality is slightly different: I can't really explain. It's something very subtle. Anyway, Maev was born in 1979 and we decided to speak French at home so that she should be fluent. I stopped working, even though I always said I would go back. But I couldn't find anyone to mind her because we had no family around and there wasn't anyone else appropriate. I've always been very particular about that and in fact I never went back to work full-time in architecture.

All the same, I found it difficult to stay at home, so I was lucky enough to meet some like-minded people from the La Leche League.[*] Together we founded a Mother and Toddler group. This was my first social contact in Galway and it was fantastic both for me and for Maev. I had always wanted to paint and at school my teacher had encouraged me. Through the group, I met a woman artist and we set up a morning painting session, while the children were in a crèche. That's how I started. I showed some work in local exhibitions and after one of these

---

[*] An organisation that promotes breast-feeding.

I was approached by an artist who wanted to know if I'd be interested in looking for studio space with several others. That was the beginning of my involvement with Artspace, which still isn't finished. It gets stronger and stronger and bigger and bigger.

There were a lot of derelict buildings in the city and eventually we found a warehouse near the railway station — space for eight of us. Because it was a large open area, we could share practices. It was very stimulating. And it was great for me because, although as an art historian I had all the theory I needed, what I lacked was techniques like printing or etching that would have been taught in art college.

Our big problem was funding. We organised a FÁS* scheme which, as a married woman, I wasn't entitled to take part in. At that time, my economic status wasn't even taken into account — I had after all been working full-time for three years. Marriage alone debarred me from these schemes and I felt discriminated against. The attitude here was that a wife should stay home and, after France where things are completely different, this was a shock to me. But eventually it was sorted out — I came to be employed within our scheme as a supervisor.

After a few years we couldn't renew the lease and moved to premises in Dominick Street, where we stayed for seven years, funded with a small grant from the Arts Council — and I should like to say that I think we are fortunate here in Ireland to have such an active Arts Council. Our studio wouldn't exist without it. Anyway, we were very active as a collective with a few exhibitions every year. At the same time, I wanted to broaden out and was also a member of a Dublin-based group, WAAG (Women Artists' Action Group). We had meetings all over the country and even had an exhibition in the Irish Museum of Modern Art. It was fantastic. The group finally disbanded for lack of funds but many of these women are still active in their various fields.

Anyway, what I was feeling in Galway was a lack of exposure. It was difficult enough even to break into the Dublin scene. Then I read

---

* Government employment and training agency.

that there was to be a festival of Irish culture in France in 1996, *L'Imaginaire Irlandais*. I felt I wanted to be involved with that. I went to Lyon to look for exhibition space and found this wonderful place called L'Embarcadère. It was an old warehouse by the river that had been transformed into a cultural centre. They were very interested in taking part in the festival, so then it was just a question of my contacting the organisers in Dublin, who were acting as facilitators and who were only too pleased to agree. L'Embarcadère comprised a huge space, so we were able to bring over large canvasses. It was quite an adventure but it was very difficult at the same time, because it was our first big project. We had to arrange transport, sponsorship money, over and above what we got from the Arts Council, for postcards, that sort of thing. Three of us went over to organise the exhibition and had one smashing week.

Now we also do exchanges with artists in Lorient in Brittany, which is twinned with Galway and, as an extension of that, with artists in Ludwigschafen in Germany, which is twinned with Lorient. What's nice is that our three cities are all away from the main cultural centres of their respective countries. Last year, it was our turn to act as host and we invited a group over. We took them around Connemara, along the little winding roads to Killary Harbour and places like that. They also painted with us. It was a great success.

We had to leave the premises in Dominick Street when it received a tax incentive to be developed into flats. For a time we were expecting to move into new premises in the Black Box complex, alongside Macnas and other arts' groups. But it was unclear how much space there would be for us. There were also delays, so, without a home over many months, we were faced with no alternative but to look for space ourselves. We found an empty shell of a warehouse in an industrial estate with space for eight studios. I designed the layout and got a certified architect to draw up the plans. Then we organised builders and carpenters to come in and do the work for us. It was very time-consuming but now we are delighted with the result. Again, we have to thank the Arts Council for its support.

Eventually we secured another five studios in the Black Box complex and now have thirteen studios for the eighteen members of Artspace, which is fine, as some of us can share.

There's an administrator who does the routine work but we still have a lot to do. A few years ago we changed from a collective to a company and have to be more organised, with audits and so on. It's becoming a serious business. There's a price to pay, which some found too heavy, so they left. There's a problem too for artists in that, unless they have a partner who is working, they need to have a second job or go on the dole, just to live. I have just completed a course in Marketing for Small Businesses, to try to develop schemes to employ artists in the community, and so on.

There is another scheme whereby one per cent of the cost of a building is set aside for art work, and that seems to work well for artists in Dublin. But in smaller places like Galway, they are slow to realise the potential. I think we have to market ourselves but without the pressure of having to respond to purely commercial considerations. It's a big question: what is the position of the artist in contemporary society? It's very ambiguous.

The charm of Galway is disappearing architecturally. I'm concerned that several important buildings around the city have disappeared. And the atmosphere has changed since the new architectural developments. That's all due to urban renewal, the tax incentives, that brought down the old shops, the old pubs where you had a one-to-one relationship with people, a sense of folklore. I am worried about the way society is going. It's becoming much more materialistic. There's more to life than washing machines and houses. You have a house — so what?! People love houses here. It's a culture of houses. In France we've a lot of rented flats, even though the dream is to own your own place. Of course, it's important to have your own space but ownership brings other problems. I see that in the new estates where there is no village structure, nowhere for people to congregate now that the role of the church is diminishing. People are becoming increasingly isolated; the sense of community is eroding.

I have always made an effort to balance family life and my commitments to work. Between all this I feel that I have lost opportunities to have my own shows — I didn't mind because it was a case of sharing. But now I want to start concentrating more on my own work. It's not easy as a woman artist, a married person. You have to juggle so many things, which is difficult when you need time not to be interrupted. Now that my daughter is leaving home, I have more time to think about it.

I have loads of ideas and I'm still experimenting. And I still don't know how to pronounce my last name properly. I intend to learn Irish some day but I'm always too busy with other things.

Sophia P *

Mexican

Sophia is small, slightly plump and tanned, with long brown hair and bright eyes. She is in her early forties and has a vivacious manner and a quick smile. The bungalow, just outside a town in the south-east where she lives with her Irish husband and children, is filled with Mexican artefacts, pots, wall hangings and paper flowers. There is a view from the conservatory where she sits, over a flower-filled back garden to mountains beyond. She speaks fluent English with a quaint turn of phrase and a strong Spanish accent. Her voice is light and high, and she frequently claps her hands sharply together to emphasise a point.

My parents now live in Mexico City but I come from the south of the country, a nice place by the sea. I have two children, both born in Ireland — the first in 1979 when my husband was over doing a course; the second a few years later when we came back permanently.

The first time I visited here was twenty-three years ago. At that time, Ireland hadn't a lot going for it. It was very peaceful but not a place for someone twenty-one years old, so we went back to my country. I'm a qualified dentist in Mexico. It was so funny, because I couldn't get a job here even though they were crying out for dentists. There was even an article about it in the *Irish Independent* when Charlie Haughey was Minister for Health. They changed the legislation but still I couldn't work here. So I practised dentistry in Mexico until twelve years ago when my husband was moved back. You know how we women follow husband and family — we're the last on the list to be consulted!

I found it very hard to adjust. The weather! Dark and cold. Wet. I've got used to it now, like everything else. To make it worse, I was living in a small village where the neighbours were checking everything I was doing, out of curiosity. At the beginning what I needed was a good friend. I found it very lonely and couldn't connect, even though I tried hard. I'm very direct and say what I think and people couldn't cope with it. Later, I learned how to deal with the Irish personality and way of life, which is completely different from the Mexican. We are much more open.

I have nothing in common with Irish women who just want to be housewives, and I was depressed at first because I wasn't working. It's a shock moving house and even more giving up a career. In Mexico I had a girl who did everything for me in the home but here I learned a lot by myself: to build, to sew, to cook. I went crazy knitting cardigans for everyone. I designed this house; studied philosophy; did a film-making course.

Most of the interesting people I have met are foreigners, artists, designers. I myself paint. I love it. That's one thing about Ireland: there's not a lot to distract you. Mexico is very lively and exuberant; it blows your mind. You'd have no time to do anything artistic. You wouldn't even want to, you'd be having such a good time. Here, you have no choice: you have to do something to amuse yourself.

I don't think I'll go back to dentistry. I've moved on. Now I've started this company. It involves a lot of work, a lot of travelling. I import pots from Mexico as ornaments which I sell to garden centres. Ireland is such a great country but when you start something, they're on top of you straight away. You spend more time organising your taxes than you do working. It's crazy! But I enjoy it.

I don't know if I'll be doing the same thing as now in five years' time. I don't even see myself staying here for the rest of my life. It's nice now that the kids are growing up, because I can move on. My husband is supportive — he has to be! I think in marriage you have to have freedom to do what you really want to do, to lead your own life. Sometimes we go on holiday together, sometimes I go on my own or with a friend and he minds the children. I get in the dog food, the cat food, leave a menu and say 'Goodbye'.

There was this Irish woman in Los Angeles who said to me, 'You're lucky to have married an Irishman.' I replied that, on the contrary, he was lucky to have married me. I had to say something. I don't like to judge people by where they come from. I wouldn't have married a Mexican anyway: I don't think any of them would have liked me. In my time, Mexican men were awful, so macho, immature. I found them very boring. My husband was only two years older than me and working — but he saw me as an equal. Perhaps he's not the usual sort of Irishman: he doesn't drink, he doesn't smoke, he's extremely quiet and gentle and minds his own business. I never had any other Irish boyfriends, so I don't know what they're like.

The tradition in Mexico was to marry within your circle. I was lucky that my father said to me, 'It's your life. Whatever you decide, it's up to you.' And you know something, it's very funny: I only met my husband for a week. Then he went away for a year and came back to marry me. It was so romantic. I don't know, if he had stayed, whether or not we would ever have got married. I always wonder about that.

Anne Payne

American

Anne is in her mid-thirties, slim and dark-haired. She lives in a semi-detached house in a landscaped estate in Lucan, County Dublin, with her Irish husband, Adrian, eight-year-old son, Dylan, and two lively dogs. She is particularly proud of her garden — it's the first time she has ever owned one — and has just returned from the Chelsea Flower Show full of ideas. She is from a suburb of Boston, has a light American accent and a pleasant if somewhat nervy manner.

We married in the States and lived there for a few years. In 1991, we agreed to try living in Ireland for five years. We're still here, so obviously it's going well, though there were big problems at first. I had started dating Adrian in 1980, and had come over for three weeks in 1981 and a few times after that. But holidays are much different from living here. I can't say it was a huge culture shock. It doesn't really hit you in the face: it sort of kicks you in the behind. Just when you think you have it sussed, you realise you don't. Like the first week I was here, I couldn't get the devices to work because in the States we don't have switches on our sockets. So I'd forget to turn on the cooker at the wall and I'd be waiting forever for the kettle to boil. I was living with my mother-in-law at the time. She'd go off to work and it would take me all morning just to figure out how to get breakfast. I remember I wanted to make Dylan a chocolate cake for his first birthday but couldn't find the ingredients. The shop assistants didn't know what I was asking for — everything here has a different name. In the end I had to buy a cake mix and put chocolate into it.

There were of course more drastic changes: my entire family is in the States, all my friends. I'd left a job that I absolutely loved. After I was eighteen I had my own car. I had always been very independent but when we moved here I was a new mother and the first year was horrendous. I felt victimised and for a time even developed a strong dislike for my husband for bringing me here. If I did the housework for my mother-in-law, she thought it was because she was a bad housekeeper and if I didn't do it I was skiving. So it was a no-win situation. It must have been very difficult for her when we moved in with a two-month-old baby because she had been on her own for ten years and I really appreciate what she did for us. But for me it was very hard living in another woman's house.

All the people I knew here were friends of Adrian's. There was no one I had a history with, no one to discuss my problems with over coffee. I felt invisible: when I was walking down the road, it seemed I could disappear from the face of the planet and no one would even notice I was gone.

The major breakthough came after six months when we moved in with my brother-in-law and his wife. They were laid back and also out during the day, so Monday to Friday I would do their housework and have the dinner ready for them when they came home. I would feel that I had a purpose.

In the States I was working with acute rehabilitation patients, but when I wanted to take up nursing again here, I had to work seven weeks unpaid to prove that I knew what I was doing. I was doing that voluntary training when we bought this house. Then I started working as a relief nurse around my husband's schedule. I saw a permanent post offered as a staff nurse and now I'm a sister in a ward for the physically disabled within geriatric facilities. It's a long-stay ward and very different from what I was doing in the States.

I was born a Catholic, though I'm non-practising. I went to school for twelve years with Irish nuns. I always thought that something happened to you when you became a nun — that your accent went funny.

Then when I met my cousin's boyfriend, Adrian's eldest brother, I thought there was something wrong with him because he talked like a nun. I didn't know at age seven that there was a whole country where people spoke like that. All my relatives had French accents because they were from French-speaking Canada.

We had Dylan baptised in the States. We discussed our problems about religion with the priest and were able to turn the baptism into a celebration of birth. It was a college town and the priest was very free-thinking. His idea was that the more adapted you are to people's needs, the more people will be drawn to the Catholic faith. We had a beautiful ceremony and I'm really glad that we did it. We've decided that here we'll bring Dylan up as a Catholic. He can make his own choices when the time comes. Sometime I'll have to take him to the inside of a church. The other day he said to me, 'What do they do in there?'

The first thing that came through our letterbox when we moved here was a form for a direct debit to the local Catholic Church account. The priest didn't even come around to introduce himself. I think that's sad. But the focus on religion in Ireland hasn't affected me directly. The first time one of our patients died, I was told to prepare him for the removal and I said, 'Great, but could you tell me what it is?' We don't have them in the States. But I've learnt: now I know how to set up a bedside altar when a patient is dying.

It's a misconception that the pace of life here is slow. It's madness. I've never worked harder in my life: of course, I was never a working mom in the States. And there are issues here that really surprised me. We didn't send Dylan to the local school because of the bullying problem. And then the break-ins: our house was broken into once and there have been two other attempts. Our car was broken into twice and Dylan's baby buggy was stolen from the porch of my brother-in-law's house, his new bike from the shed. The level of petty crime is horrendous in this country: there have been times here when I felt we were under siege. One night we were in bed and I heard the back window being smashed. I was terrified and ran into the baby's room. Often of course it's just general devilment: the breaking of trees — the trees in the front of our estate have been replaced four times — the littering. This disregard for other people's environment is something I would never have thought of in the Irish. The general perception of them in the world is that they're gregarious, fun-loving, have a beautiful country. But they treat their country like a rubbish tip. I painted that picture there [*a rural scene with a stream flowing over rocks*] and my brother-in-law said that it's not realistic: there's no shopping trolley in the river.

It's also frustrating when you want to get something done. Like when I went into a shop to get a vacuum cleaner fixed a few weeks ago. The woman behind the counter said, 'I don't think we do that.' I told her that it said they did over the door. 'Oh, does it?' she said, 'Well, he's not here till next Tuesday. You'll have to come back.' I thought to myself: who is this woman and why did he leave her in charge of the shop? And when they go out of business next year, I'll understand why. In general, though, customer service has really improved since I came here first in 1981. I used to run out of shops screaming because the assistants were so rude. I couldn't understand it because people are usually so nice here.

Every time something bad happens, I start to say I hate this country. It's a knee-jerk reaction and I don't mean it. I'm very happy. A lot of bad things could happen to me in the States as well, but I'm not in the States right now.

I still don't see myself as having close friends here. Most of the people I know are colleagues from work but when people leave, we don't keep in touch. I stay in contact with my friends in the States and when I go home we always go out together. So I have good friends but they're three thousand miles away across the ocean.

Regarding the position of women: when I came over on holiday, my sister-in-law, who had just had her first baby, invited us over for dinner with another American couple. After dinner, the guys got up and went off to the pub, leaving the women behind with the baby. There was no talk of can we — the men — do the dishes or should we have drinks here? Nobody batted an eyelid, except my American friends. But now women are becoming more willing to stand up for themselves, going out to work and having their own income. Even the junior nurses: in the good old days, they were treated like dogsbodies. Now they'll speak up; they're demanding to be educated, and even going on strike. It's great.

Edith Pieperhoff

German

Edith lives in a tiny house in the Claddagh area of Galway city. She is in her thirties with short dark hair. A maker of animated films, at a certain point in the interview she opens a large wooden box in her living room, to reveal Spitting Image *style puppets of Ian Paisley and Michael D. Higgins, squashed in together. Albert Reynolds is brought in from the kitchen. Edith is very quietly spoken, but at the same time laughs a lot and can be quite acerbic in her comments.*

I'm from the industrial heartland of Germany, from Duisburg, where the only green patch is a football pitch, so it's quite a difference, living here. I've been in Ireland for about fifteen years and don't really know why I came. There was no one single reason. I was studying to be a teacher but was at rather a loose end in Germany, where there was a strange climate at the time: the Cold War; demos against nuclear power; living in squats. There was a very negative atmosphere: you couldn't get a teaching job if you were found to be a radical. I didn't want to stay there with that shadow hanging over me. Also, I thought the world would end soon: that makes me sound like a religious nut, or rather, a political nut. But it wasn't all that unrealistic either. So coming to Ireland was like a time warp. Ireland wasn't touched by the last war. They called it the 'Emergency' — how cute! Fifteen years ago NATO wasn't an issue here, atomic power wasn't an issue; people had their own issues. Maybe the Troubles concerned people, but even that they didn't want to talk about. The landscape just knocked me out: so much nature and nobody in it. People were friendly, and speaking English was a help, so I just drifted into staying.

Now I make animated films. In Germany I'd studied history and fine art with a view to becoming a teacher but I came here instead and became a hippie, a drop-out. I was living in Donegal for a while, for two years in a thatched cottage that the rain came through, doing FÁS schemes in hand-weaving, spinning. After two years I had enough of that lifestyle. I came to Galway and started back with what I knew I could do: drawing. I did an art foundation course at the Regional Technical College and then had to go to Dun Laoghaire College of Art to study further for three years. Unfortunately I couldn't do it in Galway. Anyway, I did a module in animation and got completely hooked on it.

My graduation film was on the facts of life for kids. I would have been working on it in the late eighties and needed to check out references. So I went to the library and asked for books on the subject, as I couldn't find any on the shelves. They had stacks of them under the counter! Books that were written for five- and six-year-olds, with cute little drawings. When I asked why they were hidden away, they told me that some parents had complained. I couldn't believe it. I took them out on the counter and started looking through them all really slowly, just to make a point. My own film was never shown to kids, although the other day a friend asked if she could borrow it for her own child, which was really nice. To think that it'll be put to some use.

After the film was shown at the Galway *fleadh*, I was offered a job in a small animation company — still in Dublin, unfortunately. I don't like it there. I come from a big city, but actually find Galway much more cosmopolitan than Dublin. In Dublin, for example, I'd be asked where I was from and when I replied, 'From Germany,' they'd say, 'Get away!' They'd have thought I was from Kerry, Cork, Belfast, the Midlands, Offaly, anywhere but Dublin. Here in Galway when they asked the question and I'd reply, 'From Germany,' they'd say, 'Yes, we know that. What part of Germany?' They'd be much more clued in to accents.

Anyway, after two years with the animation company, myself and another woman set up on our own to make these kind of Spitting Image puppets. We displayed them on *The Late Late Show* — we had a lovely little Gay Byrne as well. But we never really capitalised on it. We were hoping to get a slot on a comedy programme called *Nighthawks*, but it was taken off. We had no money and were walking around with plastic bags inside our shoes and asking each other what we'd do when we got money — get a haircut at last. The other thing is that in Ireland people weren't prepared to pay any sort of decent money for artistic work.

Then we were approached by some guy who wanted us to make a ten-minute animated film about a *sean nós* song, which we did. It took about two years and was great fun. Finally, I came back to Galway in 1996. I was very lucky that I bought this house just before the boom. That's my dream come true: my house in Galway. It's the best thing that's happened to me.

I made another film then with funding from the Film Board. Again, it took two years to make. It's about Orpheus and Eurydice.

Of course I see a lot of things that I don't like in Ireland, but I'm very realistic. For example, at home in Germany I used to listen to the news on the radio and I knew who was in power in every country in Europe and even who was in opposition. Here, the news is an hour long but you'd have to work hard to gather any information about other countries from it. Poland might as well be on the other side of the moon. Of course, there's plenty about hogget prices. But there's no global view of things.

I'm an Irish citizen. I have an Irish passport. I had to swear allegiance to the State. It was so funny. For seven years I had to go to the Aliens Office in Baggot Street and they gave me an alien's book. Then I was called into the Garda Station, twice on Sundays: it must have been overtime or something. Some fatherly figure of a garda inspector asked me all kinds of questions about my political views and so on, but he seemed satisfied that I'd make a nice member of the Irish state. Then I had to go to Harcourt Street and be sworn in, while all my pals were sitting in the back row. At the time I was sharing a house with a bunch of female bikers and they were there in their black leather gear. And this little kid was there waving an Irish flag. They'd bought me this green, white and orange woolly hat with a bell on it but I didn't wear it for the ceremony. Anyway, I was surrounded by traffic offenders and defaulters of TV licences, you know, petty criminals. The judge called me up first and I was standing in a beam of sunlight coming through a window and felt like I was in an American film. And after I'd taken the oath, the judge came down and shook my hand, and all the bikers, the traffic offenders and the TV licence defaulters cheered and applauded. Then I put my woolly hat on and went off to the pub. The little kid was very disappointed with the whole thing and kept asking, 'And when is Edith going to be Irish?' I think she thought I was going to change before her eyes.

I'm still regarded as an outsider and always will be. I've been in relationships where the guys would be apprehensive about introducing me to their parents. It's amazing; guys in their thirties still afraid to own up to their parents what they do in their spare time. These are professionals, teachers, afraid to tell their parents that their girlfriend isn't Irish. That comes as a bit of a shock. Irish men have a lot to learn. They have to cut the apron strings: otherwise they remain charming little boys forever. Part of it is the education system which has males and females divided. They don't get to know each other at puberty, which is so important. It's breaking down, but very slowly. Most schools are still separated.

Schools are scary here. I stood in for a friend, an art teacher, for about two weeks, five years ago in Dublin. First, there are the uniforms — all these maroon kids. And you really had authority if you said something. I couldn't believe it. If you were nice, they ran riot: you had to be authoritarian. And then there would be this strange crackle and the kids would tell me to be quiet because they would have prayer through the intercom. I thought I was in downtown Teheran or something. I come from a country where schools are state-run and can't understand what religion has to do with education. The school system here holds back personal development. The argument that girls do better in single-sex schools is so sad: they'll have to come out of that school some day.

Ireland, like most countries, is in danger of losing its cultural identity to an ever-growing global trivialisation. From McDonalds to *Big Brother* and bland boy-pop. But I am more optimistic than my Irish friends about the strength and resilience of Irish culture.

Noor Poppers

Dutch

Noor sits at her desk in her modern house in a suburb of Galway city. Books on alternative medicine and new age studies fill the shelves. Attractive and slightly bizarre paintings hang on the wall. Noor is dark-haired with a thin face, in her late forties. She has a deep voice and speaks rapidly. One of her two daughters, a glamorous teenager, looks in briefly before heading out.

I come from a small town about twenty kilometres south-east of Amsterdam. Originally, I arrived with a man friend who knew Ireland well and loved it. We were going to live here together but split up. Later I came back by myself to visit an Irish woman who lived in Clifden. At the time I was working in Amsterdam: I had a temporary job restoring archaelogical pottery. The person I was filling in for was due to return after my holiday, so there was actually nothing for me back in Holland. Then I met John, who would become my husband, and got sucked into his world, so I decided to stay. Twenty-five years later I'm still here.

I was in Dublin restoring china until I realised that it was an extremely unhealthy life, working in an unventilated place with spray paints. Actually, I'd got good at the job. The thing I liked best was making things, adding things: arms on to angels, handles on to broken cups. So then I got into pottery, had a baby, had problems with the relationship, had another baby. It's not that interesting but it took up a lot of time and energy.

My life — I don't know how suitable these details are for a book — it's very personal. John was a drinker. I became very co-dependant and went down myself. But it was through getting involved in that side of the addictive life that I started looking at myself and got on to the road to recovery. Now I actually know what I'm doing; I'm working as a therapist, but that's only happened here in Ireland. When I came here, I had no idea where I was going. In fact when I left Holland I had no desire to have children. I had a really strong rational view that it was wrong to bring more children into the world. Coming here and meeting Irish people changed my view of that.

What I liked was that it all seemed uncomplicated. Nobody asked what are you, what do you do? I was just accepted as an odd foreigner, not for what I had achieved. That was appealing. I got to know people from their stories rather than from their deep psychological searching, or their status. Through my partner I was mixing with artistic people, poets, actors, musicians. It was all very exciting, even though I was only on the fringes of that world.

I lived in Dublin for five years, although what really attracted me was the countryside. After I separated from John, I moved to Cork, to Ross Carbery, where my parents had a house, and even got to know some Dutch people down there. Up to then I had stayed away from foreigners. The interesting fact was that in Cork it was more foreigners that I mixed with. It was quite hard to become close to the local people, even though on the surface they would be very friendly. I had one good Irish friend there, an oddball. Then she died and that was the end of that.

I'll always be a foreigner here. There are certain things conditioned by my upbringing which will never change. Even the way I do things in the house, the way I bring up the kids. They feel Irish but at the same time know they have a kind of edge, a different angle. Still, they had an Irish dad, which helps, and they were both born here.

I've a lot of gripes about Ireland: the education system in particular. I didn't want my daughters to do the Catholic thing because I'm not a Catholic, and as a foreigner I could get away with that. There was no big deal made of it down in Cork. I just said I didn't want them to do their communion and that was that. One of the girls was in fact easy about it and was even interested in sitting in on the class. The other one, for whatever reason, wanted nothing to do with it. But still it wasn't easy for them to be singled out like that. If I had to do it again, I'd do it differently. With regard to secondary education, Galway's funny. It's such a progressive place but there's really no nice secondary school. I tried to get my eldest daughter into the Jesuits which is at least co-educational, but couldn't. There was a big waiting list. I think my youngest daughter in particular suffered from the fact that the system is still based on punishment rather than encouragement. The way it's all geared to exams. This all-important Leaving Cert. The system really has to be changed. She hated every day she had to go to school and has now left, after her Junior Certificate. Somehow I feel it let her down.

How did I get into the healing? First of all I was a mess and was doing it for myself: homeopathy as well as a five-day course in re-birthing in, of all unlikely spots, Killary Harbour deep in Connemara, after which I was actually told I could start working with clients. My God! It's all much more carefully regulated now, of course. Eventually, because I came to feel it was something I was capable of doing, after a lot more training, I did get into it. Over the years I've got more proficient and more convinced that this is the direction I want to take. Now in my forties, at last I know what I want to do when I grow up. It's good position to be in. In Cork and here too I worked in a pottery and I still enjoy that, the practical, hands-on, creating thing. I never saw myself as an artist, more as a craftsperson.

It was a man brought me to Galway, what else! When I went to Cork, I was alone for about a year. Then, soon after my friend died, I met this man who was from Sligo and hated Cork. He persuaded me that Galway would be the answer to all our problems and in a very roundabout way, that has been the case, even though it was an equally disastrous relationship — why do I always pick lunatics? He was also a drinker and for the first year and a half I got the feeling that Galway consisted of nothing but drunks. It was a nightmare. The flip side was that I started going to Al-Anon and met all these people who were non-drinkers that I wouldn't have met if I hadn't touched rock bottom.

In the end it was very helpful for me. It gave me the boost to look at myself. Now I'm doing a women's studies course.

I practise rebirthing and voice dialogue. Rebirthing is a way of working with the breath. By using conscious breathing techniques, you bring up stuff that's blocked in your body, and learn to resolve painful emotional situations that could be recent or could stem from birth or even before birth. Every time I do it with people I think it's magic, what comes out of it. My function as a therapist is to make them feel comfortable with it.

Voice dialogue is more of a verbal thing and I've only got into it in the last few years. It combines very well with the rebirthing. In voice dialogue you learn to distinguish between the different voices you hear in your head. For instance, you dialogue with your inner critic and get to know him or her. With a woman, this is often a strong male voice or maybe a mother, characteristically repeating how useless you are — that sort of thing. Voice dialogue enables you to separate yourself from these inner voices, thereby creating an aware ego, which in turn makes it possible to transform these voices into positive energy. The voices I am talking about include the pleaser, the perfectionist, the pusher, the controller. You learn to honour the voices, not to argue with them. It's easier then to make considered decisions regarding your life. That's all very oversimplified, of course.

As far as my own life is concerned, I went from living in Cork doing the nature thing — I had goats and dogs and cats, did spinning, made cheese — to living on a housing estate, where I've been for the last ten or so years. It was a big change in direction. Actually, I do eventually see myself moving back into the countryside. There's a lot about Galway now that I dislike: the greed, the short-sightedness, the lack of planning, all this building of housing estates without providing a transport service or any adequate facilities, all these cars. The general attitude is that rules are made to be broken, which is charming at first. It's like in any relationship: what attracts you initially, ends up driving you nuts.

Matxalen R *

Basque

Matxalen is lean and tanned, in her mid-forties. Her apartment over-looks the wholesale fruit market in Dublin and the window of her liv-ing-room has to be kept closed because of constant bustle and noise outside. Across the road is a very Spanish-looking bar, 'La Hacienda', white-washed with black ironwork round the windows, its position completely fortuitous as it is owned by an Irishman who loves Spain and wants to bring a touch of it to Dublin. Matxalen speaks flu-ent English in a husky voice with a very pronounced accent and a mannerism of repeating the same word many times for emphasis. She smokes throughout the interview.

I've been in Ireland permanently about two years. For the two years before that I was coming and going. I've no idea if I'll stay on. At the moment I'm doing a Masters in Social Policy in UCD but that's not why I am in Ireland. The reason I am here is, as always, because of love. I came here first because my girlfriend was studying here. Over the course of my visits, I didn't come to like the country: I came to love it. It's something special.

From the environmental point of view I think it's the cleanest country in Europe. That's logical because there was never much industry here. That's important to me, the preservation of natural things. When I talk about Ireland in Bilbao, which is where I'm from, I always say that Ireland means music, joy — humour and jokes — and drink. In particular, music. It's good for everybody and any kind of music is a healing thing. Even when people have a lot of problems, they are always joking, not taking things too seriously. And in this country the individual still counts. For instance you go to pay your phone or electricity bill and they ask you, 'Are you paying the whole or just part of it?' For me, coming from the Basque country, this is incredible. If I don't pay the very last peseta, my water, my telephone, my electricity is going to be cut off. And the lack of ID, the fact that you aren't constantly being checked! It's wonderful.

I've lived in London, I've lived in Costa Rica for a year and in the States, in California, for another year. I can tell you, this country is something else. The social welfare isn't what I would call generous but it enables people to live with a degree of dignity. This system — the Third Level Allowance — has allowed me to study for two years: first for the Higher Diploma in Social Policy and then for the Master's degree this year.

So I came for one reason and stayed for others.

Originally I trained to be a doctor and was working in a small town as a kind of locum. But in Spain there's a huge rate of unemployment in the medical profession. When I was young there was a series on television a bit like *ER* and everybody wanted to be a doctor. I'm not joking. It was put on as a deliberate strategy to get more people to train in medicine. When I started studying in Bilbao there were one thousand of us in first year alone. Ten classes of a hundred people. Imagine!

So I was working as a doctor but without a permanent position. And I took the job too much to heart. I even gave money to patients of mine who were hard up. I took files home — which was completely forbidden — to do case studies. It was insane. Now I'm happy working in any job that doesn't involve responsibility for people's lives.

Do I miss anything here? Not the weather because I come from a region with a similar climate. Miss people, my family? Yes, sometimes. But I'm a survivor. If I'm here, I'm here. I can't be longing for my favourite fish dish, because otherwise I'm going to suffer. I don't miss my country from a political point of view, from an economic point of view, nothing. When you are working in Bilbao, everyone has a long face, as if they are in pain or anger. Here everyone is smiling.

And Bilbao is in a hole surrounded by mountains. It's claustropho-
bic. One of the first things I noticed here, where I was living at first was
that I could see the horizon, round 360 degrees.

There's nothing I don't like about Ireland although some things are
different. This Irish custom of not facing up to things, for instance,
people not saying what they think. Sometimes I have problems because
I am so open and say things the way they are. That's the only thing I
find a little strange.

I have a lot of Irish friends — even more than in Bilbao —people I
can confide in. But, you know, I think we are like a chest of drawers:
we reveal different things to different people.

The position of women is universal. It's always based on depend-
ency on men. I know about this from my studies. Even where the law
of a country establishes equality, that's not how it works out in
practice. I don't think there are differences between women here and
those in Spain, for example.

Regarding foreigners, even in the time I've been here I've seen
great changes. This was a monochrome country. Now there are more
and more colours. It's very good. The only difficulty is that the people
who are coming are bringing their problems with them. We are all rac-
ists. Some time ago, there was something in the papers which said that
refugees are welcome but they are going to be sent to an army barracks
to be accommodated: some welcome! Personally as a foreigner, I've
had no problems. On the contrary, as someone from the Basque country, I've always been made especially welcome. They see the similarities between the Basque/Spanish situation and the Irish/English. Sometimes, though, it's funny because the Irish aren't used to dealing with
foreigners. They don't expect to understand, so they close their ears
and you have to repeat yourself several times and even draw a diagram
if necessary. Like if you want to buy a £2 call card, you end up giving
them clues.

I was struck when I first started travelling on the bus into town how
people blessed themselves when passing churches. This would happen
only in very rural areas in my country. Here it's funny: many of the
customs are still from the sixties and seventies.

With regard to the gay scene, there are a lot of places to go and in general Dublin seems a gay-friendly city. But my friends tell me it wasn't always like this. It was very closed for a long time and the majority of gays had to emigrate to more open countries. They say that it's still quite homophobic but I've never experienced that. The grounds of discrimination are always the same everywhere: sex, gender, sexual orientation, religious beliefs. It seems to me that in this country there are big contrasts. Super-open people and bigots.

The lifestyle is simpler and I don't have a difficulty living here on very little money. Basically I get the dole. I live in the centre now and can walk everywhere or go by bike: one thing that is very expensive here is public transport. And something that surprised me was the patience everyone has waiting in a queue. Only once have I ever seen anyone complaining about a bus not coming. That's enough to make me realise I'm from a different country, that I have a different type of blood.

Martina S *

German

Martina is tall and thin and in her late twenties. She wears glasses and has light brown hair. The rented bungalow she lives in on the outskirts of Castlebar, County Mayo, is modern and functional. She laughs a lot and speaks good English with a pronounced Irish accent.

I'm from Recklinghausen, about fifty minutes drive from Düsseldorf in the Ruhr valley. It's a town of 130,000 people, so compared to Castlebar it's huge. My first time in Ireland was in 1988, on holidays down in County Cork. In 1990 I came for the summer, to work in a hotel in Mulrany. That's when I met my husband. I had two years of college to finish but during that time came over at every opportunity. I came to live here permanently in 1993 and we got married in 1994.

My husband's a chef, on the night shift. When I first moved here he was working in Knock but one thing I insisted on: no way would I live there. They have loudspeakers all over the village, so even when you're sitting outside the hotel reading a book, you can hear Mass being broadcast.

I've no regrets about the move but I miss the shops. You'd have to go at least to Galway to find anything similar. Sometimes I get these weird food cravings for something from home. My mother's over at the moment and I told her to bring bread and some of the different meats we have in Germany.

I've been working with FÁS on an archaeological scheme for two years. At first I was in Mayo Abbey which is a tiny little hamlet — if you closed your eyes passing through, you'd miss it. St Colman established a monastery there in the seventh century but there's not much to see now. Recently an exhibition in the church showed the work of the scheme. Now I'm based in Westport, to set up a similar scheme there. The plan is to visit all the local sites and record them with a view to producing a book. The archaeologist in charge at Mayo Abbey was sufficiently impressed with my work to promote me from trainee to assistant supervisor. I'm to be laid off again, because after eleven months' work you get certain entitlements. You're not supposed to be taken back on the scheme but usually are because they can't get enough new participants.

Nobody guesses I'm German, which I'm glad of. As long as you're a tourist, people will do anything and everything for you, but once you live here, it's a different story. I'm not saying that anything really bad has ever happened to me but at times there's a noticeable shift in attitude. For example, at work you have to call at different houses to ask the owners for permission to go on their land. They kind of close up when they find I'm from Germany. And people say things. One guy back in work in Mayo Abbey used to ask me, 'How's Hitler today?' He went on and on about it. I just couldn't believe it. He wasn't even a kid; this was a man in his thirties. At first I ignored him but one day I got really mad over it. 'My name is Martina,' I told him, 'not Hitler. Please remember that in future.' He never said it again but he wasn't as friendly to me any more. Probably he thought he was being funny and didn't realise what he was saying.

Now there's another guy in work — a lad of eighteen or nineteen — who's always slagging me, and he brings it up now and then as well. He'll say something like, 'I'll put you in the chamber and gas you.' That is actually worse than the Hitler thing. Usually I'd give him a smart answer but when he says that, I stay silent. It's horrible. Please don't think I'm being negative about the country. In general I like Irish people very much. They're warmer and much less formal than Germans.

Around here my husband is also regarded as an outsider, because he is from Belfast, but once he tells people that his grandmother is from Liscarney, which is just down the road, they immediately get more open and interested. He would actually quite like to move to Germany. He'd be earning much more money there. But I wouldn't want to go back at the moment. I visit once or twice a year, which is fine. I'm settled here now.

Agustina Santín Sánchez

Spanish

In her mid-twenties, Tina is whiplash thin with a cascade of dark curly hair. She is very animated and friendly but has some difficulty understanding the questions put to her. Her English is heavily accented and, though she speaks quite quickly, full of mistakes. She lives with her boyfriend in a small top floor apartment in inner-city Dublin.

My name is Agustina Santín Sánchez but to my friends it's Tina, just Tina. This year I am working in Bewleys Oriental Café but it's only to get a little experience of Irish people and improve my English. Next year I would like to teach, to be assistant teacher or voluntary part-time teacher. I don't need to be paid money, just for the experience.

What do I like? Well, here life is more peaceful and it's not too crowded. I was living with my Irish family in the suburbs for five months and it's nice that you can see green around the city. I also like, for example, that the pubs close early. People usually make parties at home. In Spain you start late and go to bed maybe at 4 a.m., which is a problem when you have to work next day.

I love the Irish people. They are very very truthful. But you have to spend time to get their friendship. Spanish people may not be truthful, they may be false, but you get to know them quickly. In two days you are best friends. I have been working in Bewleys for six months and only now I feel I am a workmate — with the girls especially. It's quicker with the boys. I don't know why.

Getting a job is easy, I think. Good jobs maybe not, but getting work in fast food restaurants or shops is much easier than in Spain. When I went to apply to Bewleys, they gave me an interview and the next day I was working. My friends here tell me that Irish people don't want to work. It seems most people prefer to stay at home. And when Irish people work, it's very slowly. I think they are not accustomed to it. Maybe one reason is that it's easy to get the dole.

I expected to improve my English much more quickly. The accent, oh my God! I thought English only had one accent or two until I started meeting different people from different parts of the country. I went to Wexford, to Galway and couldn't understand anything. Even in Dublin there are different accents.

Most of my friends here are Irish and Spanish. My boyfriend is Spanish, though I met him here. I had a small problem with the family I was staying with. I don't think they liked that I went to sleep at my boyfriend's house, so the woman came to me and said that their relations were coming from America and they needed the room. Irish people are more Catholic than the Spanish: they go to mass every Sunday; some don't even eat meat during Lent. They are more religious. Now things are changing: there is more information for the young people about sex. I had one experience with my Irish family. They have two children — the girl is twelve and the boy is nine — and one day we were watching a movie on the TV where there was a couple making love. The boy started asking me how do babies come and because I am a teacher I tried to explain to him like in a cartoon or in a children's book about babies. And quickly the girl came and said, 'Don't tell him that; he's small, he hasn't to know that. It's bad . . .' She was so upset. Here I think the people are not used to talking about such things. There is a lot of ignorance. I have seen many very young girls with babies. In Spain, in primary school at the age of nine, children are taught about protection, about AIDS and about venereal diseases.

The other day I was talking to an Irish girl who told me the government pay when you have a baby, they pay you money. I don't know why. Maybe the birth rate is low?

Monica Santos

Brazilian

Monica and her husband live in the Donegal fishing village of Rathmullan, on Lough Swilly, where they run a small restaurant. She also does most of the cooking. Recently she has had their first baby, a girl. She is a slim, tanned woman in her early thirties with rapid, fluent English but a pronounced Brazilian accent. She is emphatic and despite girlish prettiness, gives an impression of considerable toughness.

I come from a big city in Brazil called Belo Horizonte. Why I'm here: I married an Irish person. I met Martin in London and have been here five years now. Before we got married I came for Christmas, just for ten days. My idea was actually to go back to Brazil; I never really thought of staying. But then we were offered the job running the restaurant, and we decided to take it. It was short term at first; just to try really.

I didn't know much about Ireland, but the idea of leaving London was very attractive to me. We were doing a course there that was related to the environment, so it was romantic to think that we would stay in a small place and have our café and our herb garden and life would be sweet. In fact, it was a big shock to me, in terms of privacy. As a whole I find the Irish are extremely nosy people. You go to the supermarket in Letterkenny and meet your neighbour and then everybody knows what you are buying. Sometimes I wanted to be in a place where no one would know me.

The romantic idea soon disappeared. Here the season's short, so we couldn't survive on daytime opening and decided to go for evening meals: a restaurant and wine bar. It's very hard. For three months, all you do is just work, work, work and after that you think, *Oh my God, let me go back to my life again.*

Last year we stayed open during the winter at the weekends until after New Year, so we had a long season. It was the first time I'd been here in the winter. Because I was seven, eight months' pregnant, I couldn't do much anyway. It was quiet and I missed a lot of things but it wasn't too bad. When you're married to a person from a different country, one of you is going to have to make a decision to leave family and place. Last year, we tried to go and live in Brazil but for different reasons we had to come back. I'm happy. If I wasn't, I'd have to divorce Martin and I don't want to do that. But it was a tough decision.

Coming from a big family, I miss the warmth, the affection, of home. Here you might be acquainted with a person but you don't really *know* them. To me it seems relationships are rather superficial. There are certain things that you just don't talk about — like, for example, how you feel. I think I've learned to live with it but it's a hard process. The social life is the pub and I don't really drink. So because I don't go to the pub as often as our friends do, I feel not rejected, no, but not really part of it. I've never accepted why I have to go to the pub. For me, I'm happy enough with tea or coffee. Here I think alcohol breaks down the wall and then people start talking more freely.

It took me ages actually to say, right, I have a friend here. A few years ago I would have said I had no friends. Things have changed maybe because of the pregnancy and because of the baby. And maybe there was some sort of resistance as well, which I had. Now it's a lot easier and that makes life better.

Some of my neighbours were just great when they saw Martin and me with our first child, not always knowing what to do. They all came to see Kate, and the number of presents we got . . . they were very kind. Small things happened: one day the tap water was dirty and someone brought me a huge container with clean water so I could bath Kate, no problem. That sort of thing they don't really talk about but I don't know if it would happen in Dublin.

When Martin and I were in England, my visa was running out. I didn't want to be illegal in the country, so we had a talk about it. Because he has a British passport — he was born in Liverpool — we decided to get married in England because there was divorce there. Just in case. So we got married and then we told everybody else what we had done. The paper thing was just for legal reasons. We were already married in that we were living together. Then when we came here, the guards visited me. They asked for my passport and said I needed a visa. I told them that I was married to an Irish person but they weren't happy with that. So they took my passport away and gave me a visa which said that I couldn't work in this country. At that stage I was running a business and employing people, so it was just ridiculous. My British visa said that I could stay there for the rest of my days and have a British passport as well. It took two years to sort it all out here. In the end, we had to go and see a TD. Without a politician's support, we couldn't get anywhere. He wrote to the Minister for Justice and then I got an Irish passport, because I'm entitled to it after three years of marriage, and the guards left me alone. So now I have both passports, Irish and Brazilian, and everybody is happy. Basically they didn't have a visa to cover my situation, and didn't know what to do. But I said to Martin, 'If I can't work in this country, if I'm not welcome here, what's the point in staying?' I don't really need that.

London is such a mixed society that you don't feel so different. But it seems to me it doesn't matter how long I stay here, I'll never be part of it. First it's the language: as soon as you say hello, they know you're not Irish. Because of my accent, people think I'm French. I say, 'No, I'm Brazilian.' Then they start to think about this exotic place. I always get very strange remarks — about carnivals, samba, football, street children, stupid things. You have to have a sense of humour to answer back. For instance, in a bank in Belfast one day, I met this lady who had been to South America: she was working in one of those Christian missions for two or three months and she had stopped off in Brazil. She thought the bikinis in Rio were shocking and then the violence, and I said, 'Oh, funnily enough I thought the same thing when I came to

Belfast because I never saw an army in the streets before. It's terrible isn't it,' I said, 'how we get those ideas. I thought Northern Ireland would be like a civil war.' At first I was defensive but now I make jokes and say things like we don't have houses; we just live in the trees. Let them think whatever they want; I couldn't give a damn. At the beginning I was a bit sore because they're so ignorant about the world.

It's seems with the English language that you reach a point where you don't really improve any more and I start to make mistakes when I speak Portuguese. And I think, *Oh my God, such frustration.* But again it's just part of the process of being away.

It's very tranquil here. I wouldn't get that back home if I went to live in my city. It's huge, the third city in the country, and rich as well. We have a lot of pressure to make money, work work work. Here it's a lot more relaxed. You can leave your things outside and they'll be there when you go back. That I find positive. And yet there are some things in this country that are a joke. There's a lack, especially when you're dealing with business people: they're not professional, not well-trained. You want to do business with them and expect to receive your fax that day but you may not receive it for two weeks. They say, 'Oh yes, we're dealing with that.' And you think, *My God, I'm not doing you a favour.* That's a pain. We deal with some Germans, and it's completely different. It's there for you in the next half hour. Even the suppliers we have in Northern Ireland are a lot more professional than the ones we have here.

Last year we travelled to Cork and Dublin. It seems the grants all stay down south, even though we're dealing with tourism up here too, and we wanted to see what they have there that we don't have here. We were impressed: they work very hard for what they get. We visited a small village in Cork the size of this one but with a lot more to offer. Everyone was involved. There's a sort of laziness here but perhaps that will change.

Margriet Schouwenburg

Dutch

Margriet lives in a fine wooden house remotely situated among high pines on the shores of Lough Derg near Terryglass in north Tipperary. It's a beautiful place, although on a foggy winter evening, this has to be surmised rather than observed. She and her husband, Hank, own in addition two holiday homes, which they rent to fishermen and other seekers of tranquillity. Margriet has a warm and welcoming manner and speaks excellent English.

I was born near Rotterdam and have been in Ireland nineteen years, a long time. The first plan was to go to New Zealand. But I thought that was too far. Although I was actually enthusiastic myself until my mother said of New Zealand that we couldn't get any farther away if we tried, which set me thinking. So we compromised — we'd visited Ireland in the late seventies and said we would use it as a stepping stone. And we're still here.

I'm glad we made the decision but it was tough at first. When we tried to sell our house in Holland, the recession had just started, and between one day and the next, you couldn't sell property any more. We finally moved over for good in 1981, the house still unsold. But we had to leave at that point, because our daughter was twelve and we thought it wouldn't be fair on her if we left it any longer. Children shouldn't have to suffer as a result of their parents' choices.

In Holland we were living in the countryside but it was still a community of 8,000 people. When our children went to the local school here, there were just two classes, which was a huge difference for them. They saw it as a big adventure, particularly as this house wasn't yet built and we were living in a caravan. We had bought the land when we were over on holiday and Hank designed this house himself — he's a carpenter and had also worked in an architect's office. In the end it took him five years to build it because he was trying make a living at the same time. Wages here were very low, as well as which we were still paying the mortgage on the house in Holland. At times we even started to think that if things didn't improve, we'd have to go back.

Hank's quite versatile and can virtually turn his hand to any job that comes up. So things gradually turned around for us. Meanwhile, I joined together with some of the neighbours and we set up a village market, baking cakes and so on. In Holland I'd worked as a playschool teacher but there wasn't any call for that here in those days. Then in 1983 I had a bad accident with my fingers and had to take a year out. For six months I couldn't do anything and Hank was looking after me. So that really set us back quite a bit again; but you survive.

Before we came here a friend of mine in Holland, who knows that I can be quite outspoken, said to me, 'You'll have to bite your tongue sometimes.' And I must admit that I was shocked at first to find how different it was here in the countryside. Women still went to the pubs with their men and stood beside them. They wouldn't think of doing anything by themselves. And they would say things like, 'With the help of God I won't have any more babies.' It was very strange for me. Much later I helped to set up a self-help group for women and three of those who went along later got jobs and said they wouldn't have done it if it hadn't been for the meetings.

Initially I was advised by some Dutch women living round here to join the Irish Countrywomen's Association. I thought it was a crazy idea but they said it would be a good way to meet people. The members were lovely old ladies, who really welcomed you in. But they had very old-fashioned ideas as well. During the divorce referendum, head office asked that every guild should take a vote, so a meeting was set up locally at which nobody said a word. It was dead quiet. Then they asked us to vote. Two of us were for the introduction of divorce and the rest against. So then I asked if we could have a discussion about it. I rambled on, saying, 'Divorce isn't always bad.' They still didn't say anything and afterwards I asked a friend why no one had spoken out. And she said, 'Look, now they're all thinking there's something wrong in your house, that you and your husband aren't getting on.' Apparently they couldn't see that it was possible to have an opinion on something that might not relate directly to your own experience.

I respect everybody's beliefs and expect them to respect mine. Hank and I don't go to any church and in Holland the children attended the Protestant school because that's where most of the children went. In my view, it's important for kids to have their friends around them, so that was why I sent them to the Catholic school here. I explained to the teacher that we weren't Catholic and he said they could read a book during the religion class. He was very good. Only at secondary school it was something of a problem. Our son is a bit rebellious and the headmaster tried to push him in a certain way, to take him to church and so on. I think you stay a bit of an outsider no matter what you do. A lot of the time you wouldn't know what's going on in the village unless you went to church, because they announce everything from the pulpit. Our Dutch neighbour, who's a Catholic, is perhaps more accepted as part of the community than we are.

Managing the holiday homes is my job, and as well as that I give craft classes to children. I also run week-long summer schools for national school teachers. They learn all sorts of crafts and make a big folder that they can refer back to when they start teaching again. For a year I did voluntary work in an institution for mentally handicapped children. I couldn't believe my eyes at first. It was so basic, with so little stimulation. Kids just banging their heads on the walls. When I took them out to the craft room, it was great to see the smiles on their faces. But there seemed to be a thirty-year difference between practices here and in the rest of Northern Europe. Now Ireland has come on so much. Hank sometimes says to me, 'I think we'll have to move on. It's becoming too sophisticated here.'

For many years I've been involved in community development. For example, there's an old church in Borrisokane, which we leased from Shannon Development for £10 a year. We formed a limited company to preserve the windows. Then we formed another group — too many things were going on at that time! — an Area Development Management group, funded by the Department of the Taoiseach, to help the disadvantaged in the community. We had five target groups and it's still going, blooming in fact. Then there's something I did in Holland that I'd really like to develop here: school gardens. It's great to do that with the kids. To plant a few bulbs in the ground and see them come up.

Nature here is just gorgeous. We're right at the lake's edge and have our own quay. In summertime I never want to go anywhere else. When we came first and went swimming in the lake, you could see your own feet through the water. It's more polluted now, mostly with algae, although recently it seemed to be getting cleaner again. I was a member of An Taisce for several years and urged them to go out into the schools promoting ecology. They wanted me to do it but I wouldn't have been comfortable as a foreigner, telling the Irish what to do. Not that anyone's ever made me feel that way. It's perhaps more in myself.

People ask me, "Don't you miss things?" But you can always go out. The only thing you must have here is a car. Limerick, with all its facilities, is only an hour's drive away. We've been to the ballet a few times. I love that. It transports you to another world for the evening. And we were members of the Belltable Arts Centre for a couple of years. But then Hank remarked that all the plays they put on were harking back to old history and full of doom and gloom.

Last year there was an Arts Festival in Terryglass. I made masks with the kids. We had wonderful fireworks and a Limerick-based artist made a construction that floated on the lake, burning. There was also a barge on which musicians played classical music over the water to the audience on the quayside, and later from the same barge there was a jazz band. It was truly marvellous.

Family and friends come to visit sometimes and I go back to Holland quite a lot because my son is now living in Rotterdam. My parents are both dead. In fact, my father died when we were over there attending the wedding of a cousin. My sister said, 'He was waiting for you.' Then my mother was sick for a couple of years and I was able to pop over to see her quite frequently. That would have been impossible if we'd moved to New Zealand.

Most of my friends are Irish but, funnily enough, they tend to be Protestant. It's not that they go to church. I think it's to do with the way they were brought up. Perhaps they are more open. You can have more of a discussion with them.

One thing we noticed, that a lot of Irish people, when you are talking to them, talk with you. They never want to say what they really think. Perhaps foreigners have a rather rosy view of Irish people. We had some problems with the land here, from the man we bought it from, and had to go to court. It was a really awful time. So whenever we meet people who want to come and live here, we tell them to take their time, to rent something first and see. We went too quickly and were too trusting. And at the time we came, there was a huge influx of Dutch people like us, with the idea of living green and living clean. At first we had animals, a horse, two pigs, two sheep, ducks, geese, a bit of everything. But even though we were living in a caravan and working hard, we got the idea that some local people thought we must be very rich and therefore ripe to be exploited. It was funny because at the time we were struggling to make ends meet, even selling home-made toys and jewellery in the Galway street market. Actually it was a great experience because we would never have done those things in Holland. Dutch friends had thought we were crazy to move. We had a good life over there. But as Hank said, 'I don't want to grow old, doing the same things.' There were more possibilities here and I think there still are.

Bonnie Shaljean

American

Bonnie, who is a harpist of part-Armenian, part-Irish ancestry, has a dramatic appearance: long dark hair, a pale face and black clothes. Her manner is intense and she speaks rapidly, with a slight American accent. She lives at the very top of a big Victorian house overlooking Cork harbour. Her flat was once the servants' quarters in the attic and the windows disappear dizzyingly into the floor. The living room where Bonnie sits contains many laden bookshelves, a computer and two of her numerous harps.

I'm originally from a town called Stockton, about sixty miles east of San Francisco. I went to the conservatory in Boston to study piano and composition. Then I moved to London for nearly twenty years and now I live in Ireland. I've been here since April 1991.

With me it has never been a going from, but always a coming to. Boston was certainly a place where I could happily have lived my life — I had a lovely job there working in an antiquarian bookshop — but I'd always wanted to travel around Europe as a musician. I had a lot of romantic notions: the troubadour on the road, the writer in the garret, that sort of thing. Even in those days I used to go round coffee houses with my guitar, singing folk songs, wanting to be Joni Mitchell.

At that time I didn't play the harp. In fact there's a story connected to all that which sounds like something Bord Fáilte would make up, but it's God's truth. When I went to live in London, another friend from the bookshop was going to Dublin to study. I came over to visit her and went to Trinity College to see the Book of Kells, having always been interested in Irish culture. I walked into the Long Room, started looking at the different exhibits and literally bumped into a display case containing a five-hundred-year-old harp. I was transfixed. I think in so far as I had ever thought of Irish harps, for me they were kind of like leprechauns, a dream image. I couldn't get this particular one out of my mind. Later on that day, my friends took me to Glendalough. Now, even though there's always an instant Irish legend provided for visiting Americans, I think this one's true: an old stone obelisk stands there and the story goes that if you can get your arms all around it so that your fingers touch, you can have whatever you wish for. I tried it and succeeded. What I wished was that I could have a harp. With all my musical training, I thought I could probably make some job of playing it. So I wound up spending the money I was supposed to use for my ticket back to England on a little Irish harp I bought in Walton's Music Shop in North Frederick Street. Then I had to borrow the fare back.

I was able to start making music on my harp but decided to look for a teacher to avoid getting into bad habits. I was living in Kilburn and had a lot of Irish friends, so I started going round the pubs and *fleadhs* and the *Comhaltas* sessions, learning the music the way you do, hearing it and playing it. At the same time I managed to borrow the money to buy a concert instrument and began lessons with Tamar Warren and then Marie Goossens, who has quite a name in the classical harp world. Even though the music styles are different, one training will reinforce the two. In addition to playing Irish music around the session scene and studying concert harp, I was also touring the folk clubs with Packie Byrne, a traditional whistle player from Donegal. And it all arose from seeing the harp in the Long Room and from making a wish at Glendalough. I had walked into that room at Trinity with no more thought of harps than I would have of flying to the moon, and it changed my life.

I lived another nineteen years in England, but I'd always had my eye on Ireland and loved the music and literature. We live in a world of motorways and computers but there's something about the life of the past that I wanted to try and make as real as I could. Or perhaps I got an overdose of the Leonard Cohen song 'Suzanne' at an impressionable age. I'm that generation.

The reason I came to Cork is that Mícheál Ó Súilleabháin at University College Cork had been very helpful with suggestions regarding an article on the Dalway Harp for the journal *Early Music*, which I co-authored with Michael Billinge. I'd also recorded a CD of harp music, so, as a sort of thank you, I sent a copy of both article and album to Mícheál. They happened to land on his desk — again, it's funny the little things that can completely change your life — just at the time when UCC was planning to host a traditional music festival. They choose one instrument to focus on each year and that year it was the Irish harp. So here was my Irish harp record that just landed there, plop, as they were trying to set everything up. I was invited over and came with Michael Billinge, my partner at the time. He was a harpmaker and had made a copy of the Trinity College harp for me. We were treated like royalty. I remember liking the city at once, the way it's shot through with water. And I'd had enough of London: I'd just got tired of the fight of trying to survive in the economic climate of that time. So I was looking to move somewhere smaller but which was still big enough to be intellectually interesting and have a cultural scene of some sort. Here I can walk everywhere. I can support myself by playing harp and teaching. Also Cork is well connected: it has an airport and a ferryport. That's important too.

The unemployment came as a shock. This was 1991: it's not like that now. When I first arrived over, I had this naïve self-confidence that I could always get a job typing or something, but there just wasn't anything to be had. No one would hire for more than about three months at a time. What saved me was music. I saw a card up advertising a FÁS scheme with the Irish Operatic Repertory Company. So I went and auditioned. And they said to me that one thing they did was teach people to read music. When I told them I had college training in the subject, they offered me a job. I stayed with them for nearly a year,

took part in a few shows, played in the orchestra, and taught in the
Academy. Then I got a post with the Cork School of Music, and later in
the University music department, teaching both Irish harp and
concert harp.

It was pretty lonely for the first couple of winters because I was not
only living alone, which I wasn't used to, but had emigrated by myself
to an entirely new country. I'd done that years before when I moved to
England, but this was at a stage of life when most women my age are
settled into long-term commitments and have established families. I
loved the endless time and endless space that I now had, though they
could also be empty. But I got over that — not just accustomed to it but
actually *past* it. I still live alone, in the same flat, and it would feel
strange any other way. If I ever do pair up with someone, I'm only
going to be able to manage if I have enough private space. My issue
now is not how to deal with solitude, but how I'd deal with losing it.

I wouldn't want to gig for a living again. It kind of hijacks your
life. You have to be prepared to go on the road all the time and I like to
be at home because I need a lot of time for writing, which I also love.
That has always been a major tug-of-war for me, the Performer *versus*
the Writer, and I suppose the performer tends to lose out.

Everyone here is so musical. I play sometimes at Ballymaloe House
with Rory Allen, one of the owners, who is a guitarist and singer. After
doing a bit of music together, we'll go around the room and ask if any
of the guests want to give us a song. No matter who's there that night,
you just about always find someone — and usually more than one —
who can sing well. And they don't get hung up about it, or make you
coax them for half an hour. It's great when visitors bring such good
music with them and are willing to share it.

The only complaints I have are about things I'd hate wherever I
was living: the encroaching urban sprawl. I think part of me has always
been allergic to the twentieth century. OK, I like computers and I like
photocopiers and I like anaesthetics. I didn't come looking for utopia
because I wouldn't expect to find that anywhere. I like it here and I
think I'll stay.

Of course, there are times I wonder if I made the right decision.
I've turned down good management-level jobs; there have been guys I

might have married but didn't because I decided to go for this independent artistic thing. I never wanted to be a housewife and I never wanted children. I know for some women the issue of children *versus* personal work is a conflict, and it means they have to face tough choices that will affect them the rest of their lives. But I was spared that dilemma. So I can't really say I would have wanted anything different. I wouldn't go back and take any other fork in the road.

Yvonne Gaughan Sidler

Swiss

Yvonne is a tall, athletic-looking woman with long dark hair caught up in a plait. When she smiles, which is often, she reveals strong white teeth. The small rented bungalow in a remote village in County Mayo, where she lives with her Irish husband, is fairly primitive: shelves made of planks on breeze blocks and a lavatory off the kitchen with a door that doesn't close properly. She speaks English fluently but with the melodious lilt of Swiss German.

I met my husband when I was over on holidays with my father, who's been coming here for the last ten years for the salmon fishing. It was love at first sight. I've been living here three years now.

I was born in Lucerne and grew up in the Canton of Zug, which is in the middle of Switzerland. It's a small place but there everything is so close — it takes only forty minutes to get to Zurich. So it was very different when I came here: the remoteness, the people, social life, shopping.

Unlike Swiss people, who are very serious, the Irish take it easy. If you ask for something to be done, they'll say yes but it doesn't necessarily mean anything. It just shows willing. Then you wait for them to come. Also the standards are lower here. Even small things, like going to the toilet and you can't close the door. But you get used to it.

I'm the kind of person who takes life step by step and at first it was like being on holidays. After a few months I woke up and started thinking about the future. I always assumed that if you wanted work you could find it, but it's not like that. You can find work, but what kind of quality is it, and what about the money you're getting? In Switzerland I was a qualified legal secretary. Then after several years I started childminding. When I came over here first, I wasn't allowed to work because Switzerland is not in the EU and at that time we weren't married. I had to go to the Garda station and get an aliens' order, bringing my passport and bank statement to prove that I had enough savings to live on. Since we got married, I'm allowed to work but still have to get a permit. That's no problem, but you have to pay for it every year. I don't agree with the system and when I get an Irish passport — after three or so years of marriage — I'll go and talk to politicians about it. When I first came over here, my husband was studying to become a greenkeeper on a golf course. He didn't get a lot of money for that, so I was supporting him on my savings. And at the same time I had absolutely no rights. It's crazy, especially as I come from a very rich country. I might understand it if I was looking to the state here to support me, but I was always working in Switzerland, since I was sixteen. It was my intention to take a break but not like this, not forced on me.

Now I'm minding four children, between one and five. The mother's a nurse. Sometimes I work forty hours a week — it depends on her schedule. I'm also doing a correspondence course in Montessori studies, which is quite challenging because of the language. There are a lot of gaps in my vocabulary.

It's very backward here. I wouldn't mind leaving and going to a city. I love Cork. Down there my husband would get at least double the money he gets here for the same work. That's one thing I don't agree with: there are certain people round here who make great money but pay their workers nothing. They got EU funds to set up a golf course, to create jobs. Then they treat people so badly: they even refuse to recognise the union. I've noticed that, in general, workers here don't have a lot of rights, compared to Switzerland.

My husband works on a weekly basis, for example. When he was sick, he had to go on the dole. Because I'm not Irish, it's hard for me to get the right information about these things. I don't know where to go, whom to ask.

At first people seemed to be very nice, curious, generous. But I read in the newspapers about refugees looking for asylum, that the Irish don't like it: they stop them at the border and want to send them back. On the other hand, for centuries the Irish went to other countries to work. You can't discuss this. They don't like to talk about serious things. Everything always has to be nice. If you don't agree with them, they don't want to know. I've learned to keep my mouth shut sometimes about certain issues.

I have two good Irish friends here and know a lot of people. Social life means that you go to a pub and then to a nightclub. Sometimes I invite friends home but here people don't do that. It's all pubs, and it's more a male thing: men go out, women stay home with the children. The position of women isn't great. They have to be strong: they bring up the children, look after the house and work and handle the money. They tell their husbands what to do. It seems to me that the average Irish woman is hard, not female, not soft. Perhaps they have to be, with the men the way they are.

My feelings on Irish men: they're big boys, not very responsible, easily satisfied. And they don't like change. The first time we went to a Chinese restaurant my typical Irishman ordered chips and burgers. Now he'll take a spring roll. He's the sort of bloke who says: 'No problem, I'll sort things out tomorrow.' But it's happened quite often that I've had to sort it out. Like when the turf for the fire was building up: every time I wanted to hang out washing, I had to climb the turf hill. So I shifted it and then he said, 'You should have left it to me.' If I have something to do, then I do it and move on to the next thing. And he actually told me that it's a scientific fact that men have different brains from women; they don't see when the carpet needs to be vacuumed, when the dishes need washing. He was joking — but still. All the same, I'm getting used to it and we have great times together, too. Spontaneous. I often say that if I was looking for security or a normal life, I definitely wouldn't be here.

The very first time I came over, I said to my mother that I could live in Ireland. I wouldn't want to go back to Switzerland. I can't breathe there any more. Everything is so closed; everything's too perfect. And there's a certain energy in this country, a vibration. Here people don't touch nature. They leave it the way it is — brilliant. You can walk for hours without meeting anyone. And of course, we have no sea in Switzerland. I love the sea.

Sometimes, however, I feel that the place and the people don't go together. For example, after I was here a few months, I went looking for a stone circle. Nobody knew anything about it here — they couldn't be bothered. When I asked a farmer, he said, 'Are you talking about the few stones up in the field?' People don't know what they have.

A lot has to do with the power of the Catholic Church. I was brought up a Catholic but left when I was about twenty-three because what they said and what they did didn't go together for me. Of course I attend weddings and funerals but am quite shocked at the way it's done here. For example, at the first wedding I attended, there was this ceremony: the bride and the groom each held a candle, which they used to light a third. Then they each blew out their own candle. I found it strange, the way the priest was talking, as if the woman was losing her identity.

I've been doing meditation for several years and tried to get a group going here but it didn't work. I'll try again this winter. People are still so focused on the way they've always done things. They aren't interested in anything new. Of course, Ireland is an island, not like Switzerland, with so many different countries bordering on it, so you can't expect the same openness. And what's happening in Northern Ireland: it's like people are on a wheel and can't step off it. They're so set on the past. But you can't always be looking back. As I see the Irish mentality, it's, 'That's the way it is. What can we do?'

Peggy Smith

English

Peggy is a tiny, frail, elderly lady, perched on the edge of a big chair in a room with a long view over grass manicured like a golf course. The walls of the room are hung with watercolours, painted by Peggy herself, of landscapes, often with horses. A toy dog constantly jumps up, looking to be petted. Peggy speaks with a pronounced upper-class English accent and lets slip that she has been to several garden parties at Buckingham Palace. As a schoolgirl in Scotland she once literally bumped into Edward VIII on a hotel staircase, when he was Prince of Wales. He was, she recalls, very kind to her.

I've been here for twenty-five years. Our daughter got married and came over to live in Derry at a time when we could live wherever we wanted because my husband was semi-retired. I visited Donegal with my daughter and as soon as I saw this place, I knew it was right for us, even though it was in a frightful state. There was a bath in the drawing room of the big house to catch the water coming through the roof. But we just love doing up old places.

We lived in a cottage down near the fish farm during the alterations. Then, after about eight or nine years, we decided the main house was far too big for just the two of us, so we sold it and went down to the cottage for another short bit and altered all this. The other part of where we are now was a huge barn, and this was the stable block. They were all joined together. It's made an ideal place for us.

I've had horses all my life. Never been without until about five or six years ago. They were in this field here. And we started the fish farm. It wasn't something we'd done previously, so my husband went to Stirling in Scotland on a course and bought a book on the subject. We were the first to put fish in the sea: we put one in a birdcage down on Lough Swilly, just to try. I'm afraid we didn't realise what we were starting. Seriously, it's a mess now, all over the country. There was one fish farm near Dublin, but we were the first otherwise. After seven or eight years, the work got too much and we sold it on.

Going back fifteen, twenty years, all the people we knew then were that bit older. They've nearly all gone away now or died. But in those days we had marvellous parties. Once we were out for eleven nights in a row and we thought: *Now this is a bit much!* But it was great. Most of the people we mixed with were Irish — our very best friends, the husband was Irish, the wife English. There weren't all these people that come in now, none of that. There used to be a lot of sailing in Rathmullan. We often used to go out on boats pigeon shooting and I remember one particular day coming back on shore, the men all carrying their guns. There'd been some tremendous upheaval in Belfast — bombs going off and so on — and someone came up to us and said, 'You'd better put your guns away!'

My husband, Ian, has done so much to help local people with advice on how to get businesses started, general advice, that sort of thing. And they repay you three or four times over. This marvellous housekeeper we have, she started with us as soon as we moved here. For two or three years she hardly said anything. Then she'd say, 'Good morning.' Now she never stops talking. We've had her twenty-five years. It's a small house, so now she comes just four or five mornings, unless we need her at weekends. But everybody helps; you find that with the Irish, don't you?

Up until ten years ago, we used to spend four months in the winter in the Canaries. We had a house in Lanzarote. Then I was very very ill and everything stopped for about a year. We still go to the Canaries, but not quite so frequently. We don't have a house there any more.

When we first came we had forty-something acres . . . no, we didn't, that was somewhere else. We had twenty-eight acres. And we're down to six now. That's all we need. But we always wanted a long view. Funny, we always look at the view before the house.

Nobody's asked me whether I'm a Catholic or a Protestant. Somebody asked Ian fairly soon after we arrived and he said, 'Church of Turkey'. That shut them up. But everybody's been so kind. I mean, workmen will say they're coming and they don't, but you get used to that. And everybody calls you by your Christian name, not me so much but my husband. We found that a bit hard, a bit too familiar. But that's the way here. We're living in another country and we take it as it is. It's not for us to say why don't they do this or that.

My husband misses the pubs, which may sound strange but he doesn't like the beer here. He's a great beer man. And in England, you see, you go into a pub for half an hour on the way home to have a quick drink. But he finds here that people go in late and then they drink and drink and drink.

And then, Ireland's not as pretty as England. We miss the trees, the villages. Of course, we go abroad a lot, so we don't have much chance to travel here. We go round the coast in Donegal, but it's the bog that spoils it, isn't it? You don't have the lovely green fields.

In the early days you had to phone through to the operator to ask for your number. And she'd always say, 'Oh, that's all right, Mrs Smith.' Because immediately, with my accent, they knew who it was. And I'd ask if Mrs So-and-so was home and she'd reply, 'No, she won't be back till Thursday.' It was lovely then. And very little traffic, of course, in Ramelton village. It was beautiful. And when you see it now, with all these cars, it's been spoilt.

Some changes are for the better. You can buy so much more in the shops. Cheese, for instance. My husband is a great cheese eater. Even now we get our cheese from a little shop in Limavaddy, proper cheddar. That's where my husband came from, the West Country, near the Cheddar Gorge.

I'm eighty now. I had my eightieth birthday about a month ago. To celebrate, we had a party at our club in London. That was a huge success. And then afterwards, it wasn't until Gatwick Airport that I realised we were going to Florence. I had spent a year there before the war, but I'd never been back. I was afraid of all the alterations. There was no need — it was marvellous. If you were able to block out all the millions of Japanese, the cars and that sort of thing, the city was exactly as it used to be.

I was brought up in that funny age when women didn't work. I wanted to be a vet and did a lot of hunting and riding. I was obviously spoiled, you see, and had a sheltered upbringing. When the war broke out, I was twenty-one. I went into the Red Cross as an ambulance driver with an X-ray unit, so I was thrown in at the deep end and it was very good for me. I was in Exeter for a few years and then in Kent and thoroughly enjoyed it all. I met Ian on a railway station in Bristol and we talked on the train coming up. He had a terrific war — got an MC and a bar. We knew each other for four years on and off — he was busy going over to France and doing various things with the Resistance. Then he was posted to Yugoslavia, so we got married and a week afterwards he left and I didn't see him for a year. Now everything is on the news, but in those days you didn't know what was happening to people. If you had, you'd have gone mad with worry.

We're perfectly happy here and I don't think there's anywhere else I'd want to live. I like the south-east, going down to Wexford. We fly now when we're going anywhere but we used to drive down to Rosslare to get the ferry. The countryside, the trees, reminded us of England.

Irina T *

Russian

Irina is in her mid-thirties, small and plump with short brown hair and glasses. Her face frequently breaks into a warm and dazzling smile. She is a research chemist in a Dublin college and we meet in the laboratory. Her twelve-year-old son, Alex, sits in on the conversation, having just come from school. He is quiet and well-behaved and thumbs through a geography book while he waits. Irina has a soft voice and speaks quite fluently in English, although with a strong Russian accent.

I come from the middle of Russia. After obtaining a master's degree in chemistry from Moscow University, I worked in a military plant in St Petersburg for four years. Then, when I got married, I moved to another capital, Minsk, at that time in the Soviet Republic of Belarus, which is now a separate state. My husband was from Belarus and got offered a job back there, so I thought, *OK, I'll go with him, we'll start a family*. We stayed for three years and then went to England, then Germany, after that to England again and now Ireland. My husband is a scientist, a great one I think, and everyone invites him to work for them.

We've been here for two years. I couldn't say I like everything but some of the customs and attitudes remind me of Russia. For example, to be late, not to be very punctual, that's like in Russia. It's not necessarily a good thing, but it suits me, compared to Germany, for instance, where everyone is always on time. It's more free here, more easy-going.

What don't I like? When we came here first, it was from England. Everyone there said, 'Oh, you are so lucky to be going to Ireland. It's such a nice country, particularly the people. They are so warm, so open, you'll be really happy there.' I have to say, from that point of view, for me it has been a disappointment; not what I was expecting. It hasn't been easy to find Irish friends, even after two years. People are nice to you but don't seem prepared to go that one step farther. That's very different from Russia. And in all the countries we've been in, it's difficult for me not to be a housewife. If you have a good education, good qualifications, it's impossible to find a suitable job. In Germany and England, I wasn't allowed to work at all. Here in Ireland it's the same. The one plus is that I can study. I was a lecturer for six years and now, at my age, I have to start again. I have Russian women friends in the same position. Their male partners were offered jobs here and so they came too. Some are doctors, lawyers, everything, but they aren't able to work. They consider me very lucky to be a student and at least get out of the house. The question is, when I graduate, will I be able to get a permanent job? My supervisor has been honest with me: in the first place, I am foreign, and in the second, I'll be forty when I finish. Who will need me? As for teaching in schools, my English would have to be absolutely perfect. My husband is happy. He has a good job, status. He gets promotion. It's just me who has problems. I have given up a lot to be with him. I don't know, sometimes I wonder if I did wrong, putting the family ahead of everything.

When I first arrived, people were interested in hearing where I came from: Russia, where is it, what's it like? I never felt that people didn't like me. Now, since so many foreigners have started to come in, the reaction has become much more negative. People can tell from my accent that I am foreign. Recently, in this very college for example, a man asked me where I was from and when I told him, he asked in a not very friendly manner why so many Russians are coming over here now. What could I say? Perhaps it has all happened so quickly that Irish people have been unable to adapt to the new circumstances. They don't seem to see that all are equal. At first, I tried to find a job in my area of expertise and applied for the post of lab technician in a school. Of course, I was overqualified but I accepted that, because after all it's a new country for me and because English is not my first language. Anyway, at the interview, one of the teachers commented, 'You know, this is a very good job. Wouldn't you be better off trying for something in McDonalds?' At that instant, I understood my future here.

Each day, I ask my son how he got on at school. I am delighted to say he doesn't have any problems. And in my opinion, Irish people in general are very generous. They just need time.

When I meet together with Russian friends, there are two main topics of conversation: what is Russia like now and what is happening here? One issue is the problem of improving our English. Our neighbours don't want to talk to us. On the other hand, how can I criticise when I know that if Irish people go to Russia now they will experience similar attitudes? In the past, foreigners were regarded as gods coming to our country, but not any more. Both Ireland and Russia have become so nationalistic. I must say, I never had this problem in Germany or in England. The very first week in Germany, I made a good friend whom I am still close to. It wasn't difficult there, only here. We'll see. The future will tell us.

We live in Rathfarnham, near the mountains. The Irish landscape is absolutely wonderful: the most beautiful country that I've ever seen. And if you travel just a little outside Dublin, the people are very different. Much warmer.

I still have family in Russia. I tried to invite them to visit us but there are a lot of difficulties with visas and so on. We go back each summer for a few weeks to visit our parents. With regard to what's happening there, I don't think the near future promises well. There's about to be an election and the same things are starting again, all the corruption.

I have recently been thinking about the types of Russians who come here: there are those who come to work, like my family, ordinary people who pay taxes. Then there are the asylum-seekers — I know the situation in Russia and I don't understand how people need to seek political asylum from there. A third group are the New Russians — you understand what I mean by that? Capitalists, entrepreneurs, who have made money out of the collapse of the old system. In this country it's very easy to get identity papers, so such a person will bring his wife over to give birth here. They are still Russian citizens, living in Russia, but through their child they have rights of residency in Ireland too, so if anything bad should happen there, they have a fallback. These are three very different groups of people who in Russia would never mix, but because there are only officially about four hundred immigrants here, we all know one another. The interesting situation is that, among these three groups, no one talks about Russia because our backgrounds are so different. It's all about Ireland and how we are managing to live much better here. With my friends I can of course speak about everything, but even if one person from another group joins us, then certain topics are taboo.

Alex is starting to forget the Russian language. I am not happy about this. Some of us have organised a Russian school that meets once a month at the Embassy, to coach our children in their own language and give them a chance to chat to their friends. The Embassy also holds a small party whenever any writer or composer visits Ireland. It's nice to stay connected to the country in that way. Yesterday, for example, we visited the Stanislavsky ballet, which was performing here at the Point Depot. It was absolutely wonderful. All the Russians were there but I was even more delighted to see that the theatre was full. It's just great that so many Irish people are interested in Russian ballet. And it makes me think that perhaps after all it's possible to be optimistic about the future.

The food here isn't a problem for me because I have lived for so long abroad. One day recently I had a nice conversation with an Irish acquaintance about some dish which I considered to be typically Russian and she said, 'No, it's typically Irish.' It's a simple dish of grated potato mixed with flour and milk and then fried. Irish potato cakes. And in Russia we call them *draniki*.

Maria Tecce

American

Maria is in her early thirties, tall with a striking appearance, an animated and very friendly manner. She sits in a bar in the centre of Galway city, full of loud music but few people, sipping white wine. Maria is a singer and actor — she is currently working on the RTE soap, Fair City — *and her voice is strong and melodious. After the interview and despite a backache, she is keen to go out and paint the town.*

I was born and raised in Boston of Italian and Polish stock. Originally what brought me to Ireland was music, I suppose. I had spent a year in England in the late eighties and couldn't settle back down to life in America, so in 1991 I left and came back to England and Scotland. There was no music or theatre in my life at that time. I was making native American jewellery, going round festivals to sell it. I made enough money to visit Ireland on holiday and loved the music. When I was finishing grade school in 1985/6, I was doing kind of coffee-house stuff. Boston used to be hot on the folk-scene — it still is — but I never felt I fitted in, probably because I was singing on my own. In Ireland it's kind of group-oriented, jamming together, and that suits me. The longer I live here I see how much Irish music has in common with the blues, and maybe even jazz.

I was very lost at the time I was in England. I didn't know what I wanted to do with my life and went back to Boston for another year. There I worked with a theatre group called 'Shakespeare and

Company' and later with an Irish company, as actor and composer. That was the real beginning of my work as a performer and gave me a great training base. By then, I was already twenty-five, twenty-six. I feel like I've come to it late but, at the same time, it's exactly perfect. In hindsight, I realise that it was the right time for all those things to happen.

In 1995 I came to Ireland to work with bands. Ninety-nine per cent of everything I came over for fell through, as it does. So I was here for months just travelling round the country, going to traditional singing festivals, listening to the unaccompanied style. It was wild; I met some amazing people. At that point I decided that what I wanted to do was to become a traditional Irish singer. It's a tight community. Traditional singers are really hardcore, passionate about songs and storytelling, which for me is what singing really is.

I feel like my personal style is only just starting to develop. For the last year or two, I've really been getting into blues. Now I'm singing a lot of jazz, because my accompanist is a real jazz-head. The stuff I write is more folky. But I don't consider myself a singer-songwriter. There are so many fantastic songs that have been given me to sing that I'm more of an interpreter and I'm very happy with that. It's the highest compliment you can pay to a writer.

Ireland has been a proving ground for me. It's like it's a plateau and I've just crawled on to the edge of it. Every gig I learn something new. A few years ago, I was touring Sligo and Dublin with a show called *Eclipsed*, a theatre production about the unmarried mothers who ended up in the Magdalen laundries, washing dirty linen for the priests. I'm also doing two films at the moment. It's funny, my acting actually allows me to do my music, financially speaking.

How I got into film is interesting. There's a director here, Roger Corman, who does these B-movies, low budget stuff. The first film I ever did was with these guys. I fell into it by accident. If I'd been in America, I'd never have been considered in a million years for the role. It's just very different over here. I've had opportunities I'd never have had in America, especially as an actor. They're terrible films but I get good speaking roles and I've probably had to work about ten times as

hard. To quote the singer Sheryl Crow: 'No one said it would be easy /
but no one thought we'd come this far.'

Because I often don't work regular hours — if I'm not doing a gig
until eleven o'clock at night, if I'm not touring or doing a film — it's
sometimes difficult to find some kind of structure to the day. You
need a balance. The first stability I've had over the last ten years has
been just recently. I'm living in a house and not out of a suitcase. As
an artist, to have a base to work from leaves you a huge amount of
freedom. It's very difficult to be productive in any way when you
have no structure.

There's a funny thing here: people don't really think of me as
American. That's one reason I like it. Whatever it means to be
American, I've always felt more in tune with Europe, even though the
first year and a half here was probably the loneliest period of my life. I
love talking to people but I think I'm really quite shy. One thing that
helps me keep chilled out is listening to other people's stories. At the
beginning, I didn't have one single person I could call up.

Galway isn't the be-all and end-all. It's not the centre of the
universe — contrary to what people here might think. I suppose it
might be the crossroads. It wants to be a city but it has still got a small-
town mentality.

There's this begrudgery. When I first came here, people were
saying to me, 'Work hard, but be careful. Do well but don't do too
well.' That's not something I found out on my own. That was
actually said to me by Irish people. As time's gone on, I have
definitely experienced the truth of this and I've asked Irish people,
where does it come from?

Last year was a real roots thing. I'd performed with a Polish
company in London and made a trip to Poland, where my grandmother
was born. It has got to be one of the most welcoming and fascinating
places I have ever visited. I could happily live there for the rest of my
life. I even learned to speak a bit of the language when I was there. It's
a language to be sung. I also went to Sicily last September when my
parents were there. I was worried about missing work just when I was
starting out, but I'm so glad now that I went. There's a small village
near Naples, where the family comes from. I'm very proud of my heri-

tage on both sides. That's one thing that Irish people find so interesting about Americans, that we're all such mutts, such mongrels.

What surprised me here? Irish men! Actually it's been less of a surprise than a gradual disappointment. I have never been asked out by an Irish guy since I've lived here. I think that, with just about every guy I've gone out with, it was me who did the asking. Any other men I've been involved with are people who have been here on holidays. I've talked to Irish women about this and we all agree it's this mother thing. Like, men would be attracted to you because you're full of life, passionate about things. You go out with them and then gradually they get anxious about the very qualities that attracted them in the first place. They start to hate that about you, that you're so independent, whatever. And then all these head-games begin, a power thing, and they turn into little kids. I end up feeling like their mother: not the most sexually inspiring experience. I see it in so many of the Irish men that I'm good friends with.

One thing I've learned in my travels, wherever I've gone: you meet the most wonderful people and also the biggest assholes everywhere. No matter what country you're in. And that's cool.

Turning thirty was one of the best things that happened to me. I was so excited. Life begins! You finish a chapter and turn the page and there's a lovely kind of blankness. Something new.

I had a shoot recently in Rossaveal harbour and it was pissing rain. It was a 6 p.m. to 6 a.m. schedule and I said, 'Look, can you get me out of here for 10.30 p.m. for a gig I really want to do.' At 10.15 we were still shooting this one shot; 10.30 on the nose, they said 'OK, Maria, you're wrapped. Let's go.' I rushed off. It was a bit messy but we were all laughing on stage: it was a great gig. Afterwards, looking at my day, I said to myself 'Jesus Christ, what an incredible life.' I'm so lucky to be doing something that makes me feel electric.

Joanne Toolan

American

Joanne is in her fifties, with short dark hair and a wide smile. She wears strong glasses that make her eyes look bigger and has a soft voice and gentle manner. She lives in Coolock, a suburb on the north-side of Dublin, in a street named after an American astronaut.

I was born in Illinois, in a very small town one hour from Chicago. When I was thirteen, we moved to South Bend, Indiana, but I've been in Ireland thirty years now. The reason I came was that I was a qualified nurse and I wanted to get experience working somewhere else. I told my parents that I would be gone six months, and that if I liked it I'd stay for another six months. But it was in that period that I met the man who was to become my husband.

Why I chose Ireland rather than anywhere else is a nice story. Before I did my nursing training, I was raising money by working in the cafeteria at Notre Dame University. I had to get up at six in the morning for the three-and-a-half-mile journey and my bicycle tracks were always the first in the snow. There were some wonderful women there, all much older than me: among them, Beulah, who was sixty-four and about to retire, and Cissie, who was in her fifties. I loved them dearly. The manager of the cafeteria was called Jimmy McGerrity and he said to me one day, 'Before you do anything permanent in life, go see Ireland. You'll love it and it'll love you. I see how you cycle up every morning and how you get on with people.' He was American but I think his roots were in Connemara because later in life he'd come over for two or three months at a time. It was he who planted the seed in my brain and it stayed there through the years of my training and work.

I knew nothing about the place. I've no connection with Ireland at all, being pure Yugoslav on both sides. I'm second generation American. My parents' first languages were Croatian and Slovenian, which are very similar. The reason I don't understand them myself is because we grew up in a one-room caravan and the only privacy my parents had was in speaking their first language to each other. It's a sad thing, because I love foreign languages.

After coming here I joined a cycling club and it was through that I met my husband-to-be. I'd never been interested in boyfriends, even at Notre Dame, where, in those days, there were seven thousand men and no women. In Dublin in 1970, the ratio of females to males was ten to one, because the men still stayed on the farm and it was the girls who came to the city. That didn't bother me and it came as much of a surprise to me as to anybody else that I fell in love. And now we have four boys and one girl, most of them scattered to the four winds. But what can I say when I did the same myself?

When I first arrived here, I had to go to the Aliens Office every six months to get my work permit renewed and always saw the same man. He collected stamps and I used to give him any foreign ones that I had. When I told him I was getting married to an Irishman, he said, 'Well, that's you and me quits.'

I worked for about six months after my marriage but then I got pregnant, and that was it. I hung up the uniform. For me, mother-hood was a full-time job. Even now, the only work I do outside the home is my volunteer work, as a Jehovah's Witness. We go door-to-door. Most people have their own lives and are very busy and/or have their own religion but, on the whole, the response is good and people are friendly. As for myself, I was reared a Catholic. How I came to the Jehovah's Witnesses: twenty-five years ago, my own door was knocked on. And I didn't say I wasn't interested; I opened the door.

When I first came, I found the pace of life very slow compared to America and I had to adjust to that. In those days, there was one car in ten families. Imagine that! I liked it because I never drove a car in America. Everybody in South Bend knew me because I rode my bike everywhere. They'd call out, 'Hi, Joanne' as I went by. I carried on with the bike here and now it's easier to navigate through Dublin by bike than by car.

Over the years, standards have got higher: food safety in restaurants, for example. Education has broadened out. More people speak better. Then again, the principles people live by are falling apart, but I'd say that's just on a par with the rest of world.

I loved rearing my children here because there was still a sense of family. By the time I was leaving America, that was already splintering. People my age then, twenty-six, were already married and broken up. And the draft system was still in operation there, so it was wonderful to come to a place where you wouldn't be afraid to rear boys. A neutral country seemed like heaven on earth to me.

Shortly after I arrived, two important things happened here. Dana had just won the Eurovision Song Contest and a Garda Fallon had been shot dead. It had moved the heart of the whole country: first the ecstasy, then the grief. I thought, 'Wow! These things really mean something to these people. This is a good place.'

I was struck even by something as seemingly insignificant as the size of a packet of crisps. Here you can get a small packet. These don't exist in the States. And that's the root of the problem there. Everything is on a massive scale. Everyone here looked so skinny to me, so healthy. In the States, I'd never seen a person walking along eating an apple.

I earned much less money, of course. In fact I worked out that I was earning exactly one quarter of the wages here that I'd get in the States as a staff nurse.

All our married life, we've lived in the same house, but in those days, Coolock was outside Dublin proper. I used to cycle along Skelly's Lane, which now leads past Beaumont Hospital. In those days, it was just a teeny path and in some places not much more than a ditch. When it rained, it filled with water and you'd have to put your bicycle on your shoulders and carry it across. Travelling people were camped there. It's now a very busy road.

We used to go on youth-hostelling holidays with the children and, now that they've grown up, my husband and I visit independent hostels. We've been attending a bird-watching course several times a year in Corofin, County Clare. The winter is a great time, of course, because of all the migrants. But it's such a wonderful place that we've taken to visiting it at other times. It's like going to another world.

The telephone system, now that is one huge difference from the time I first came here. I was so frightened of it because either it never worked or the people on the other end of it never worked. In the States, I was a telephone operator before I went into nursing and we were required to give one hundred per cent commitment to the job, a perfect service to the public. Here, if you were trying to do official business, they'd say, 'Hold on a minute,' and then never come back. It's a good service now but I can't get used to all these recorded messages. I'm a dyslexic and I'm pretty sure it affects how I hear things. I have to read very slowly to get the meaning of anything. And if someone is giving me instructions over the phone, a timetable or something, I find they speak too fast for me to grasp it. I generally get one of my friends to do it for me. She'll ring up and get the information and then ring me back and give it to me at my pace. It doesn't mean you're stupid. It's just a disability.

The year my mother died, my father got on a plane for the first time in his life and came over to visit us. He stayed for a fortnight and the next year he came for a month. The children would have been aged between five and fifteen at that time and he just absolutely loved them. My brother stayed in Indiana and was married there. He has two girls, now aged about thirty. I met them for the first time last year when I went back. They're lovely people. This family that I'd left, all of a sudden I had flesh and blood belonging to me. It was amazing.

I had adopted Ireland so thoroughly, you see. Some foreigners stay a bit aloof, but I wanted to find out everything about the people. I remember when I was first nursing here, I was in a children's hospital and those babies couldn't understand my accent. I had to have a crash course on how to speak. The other nurses were mostly from the country and I started copying their accents so that these little children would understand what I said and respond. For example, if myself and another nurse had to put them on their potties in the middle of the night, I noticed that the one she had would do the business while I'd get nothing until I copied what she said. It was like pressing a button.

I appreciated Ireland even more when we went to visit our son in Germany two years ago. Germany has cities, towns and villages and nothing in between. It's not permitted to build anywhere else. You know, when you're in the Irish countryside at night, you see little lights in the darkness — welcoming lights. There's nothing like that in Germany. It's eerie. I was so happy to come back here.

Eriko Uehara

Japanese

Eriko is in her mid-thirties, small with very long black hair hanging loose. She lives in the centre of Galway city, in a modern house tucked into a small mews. Her two-year-old daughter, Caoimhe Mariko, vies for attention throughout the interview and is only briefly distracted by a model Santa Claus which plays 'Jingle Bells' when wound up. Eriko speaks softly, in fluent English, an occasional Galway intonation overlaying her Japanese accent. She explains that she was married in Japan but is now divorced.

I am from Okinawa, which is in southern Japan, near Taiwan. I suppose it was music that brought me to Ireland to live, the old style of singing. Ten years ago I came here by accident: myself and my sister were travelling together round the world. She had some Irish friends, so we stayed in Dublin for a week and went to a pub where they played traditional music. People were singing *sean nós* in Irish and everyone was holding hands, the way they do. I had studied classical music, opera singing. As in Ireland, music in Okinawa is a living tradition. At the end of the Second World War, there was a terrible battle and everything was destroyed except for the culture, which is really strong: craftwork and music and dancing. My grandparents used to sing every night; my father as well. So I grew up with music.

The songs I had heard here were very similar to mine, so I started to read books about Ireland and got more and more interested. I came here maybe eight times afterwards, on private trips or as a travel co-ordinator. I was working really hard in Tokyo, so five years ago I thought it was time to quit and maybe try to live here, to study *sean nós* singing. It was kind of fieldwork, mostly in Connemara where the *sean nós* is different from that of other Gaeltacht areas. I felt it was very Asian, quite different from European music. It's been said that there's some Arabic influence. Okinawan music is influenced through Indonesia by Arabic music as well. It's very dramatic and emotional.

I'm trying to learn Irish. I have to if I want to sing the songs. My teacher is a native speaker. I suppose some people are surprised when I start to sing, especially as many young people aren't interested. Caoimhe has begun to play music already. She likes the fiddle and draws the bow across the strings herself while I play the notes. Her father is also a musician.

On the whole, I like living here. It's a very relaxed place, a nice place for kids to grow up. I don't like the Japanese education system; it's too strict. But I go home maybe twice a year and perform Okinawan traditional music in concert: I play the snakeskin banjo and sing. I also play Irish music for them. They love it. Of course, there are loads of Irish pubs now as well — there's even a 'Murphy's' in Okinawa. I also write articles for Japanese news-papers about Irish life, traditions, music.

I think I'll stay here. I don't miss Japan. I miss Okinawa but wouldn't want to live with my family now. My husband was a nice person; for a Japanese man he was independent and not conservative at all. But his parents were country people, very old-fashioned, and their ideas were completely different from mine. They considered that women have to be behind their men. He was the only son and I was expected to fall in line. In many ways, it's very similar to here: the sons bending to their mothers. When I was visiting as a tourist, I wasn't aware of these things. I don't want to be a Catholic, at least not automatically: I want to be able to choose. So anyway, I had an argument with my Irish partner, because he wanted our daughter to be christened. And then there was his mother and his granny and so on: they felt that if Caoimhe wasn't christened, she couldn't go to heaven. In the end, I gave in, because I didn't want to hurt them: and now I suppose she'll want to wear a white dress for her first communion. I'll have to think of some trick when that comes up, something to distract her. I'd rather she made her own choices when she's old enough.

Although the position of women seems to me similar in Ireland to Japan, it's changing more quickly here. I know many young Japanese girls studying here and they're quite different from Irish girls. They are very innocent and immature, shy. Still, most of them want to change their lives; that's why they come here. One girl I know was going to college but started playing the fiddle last May. She's very good at it and mad for music, so she quit the language school. In general, these Japanese girls don't want to go back home and work in an office. But the pressure is still there to get married before they reach twenty-five.

I'm interested in Irish history and politics. Japan took over Okinawa a hundred years ago. Before that, we had a strong connection with China. After the Second World War, we belonged to America, so I had a US passport until I was twelve years old, and was using US dollars. Then we became Japanese again in 1972. So our attitudes are very different from Japanese ones. Shinto is the main religion of Japan but in Okinawa we follow Buddhism. We have our own language, which is ancient, perhaps an older form of Japanese. Okinawa is comprised of a million people spread over thirty-six tropical islands, every one with its own dialect. My mother and father speak different variations, so at home we use Japanese for convenience. Before 1972, we were fighting about whether to be independent, whether to go back with Japan or stay with America. There were lots of different movements, some of them similar to the IRA, although it wasn't ever really violent. So I am very interested in the Irish situation, especially since Caoimhe's father is from Donegal, from Buncrana, and grew up just beside the border. We went to the funeral of the Buncrana children who died in the Omagh bombing; my partner's family knew them. It was very sad.

I have a daughter now and this is her country and her future. Before that, I was an outsider. Even now, I'm not eligible for social welfare benefits. But things are getting easier. Next year, Caoimhe will go to school and I'll have more free time.

It's really funny: a friend came over here on her honeymoon and asked me, 'Eriko, where are the vending machines?' In Japan, they are all over the place, every ten metres. You don't need to talk to people to buy things. Even the convenience stores are open for twenty-four hours. I love the fact that, even now, it's so much less materialistic here. And I was working recently as an interpreter for the sailors on a Japanese tuna fishing boat. They were nice people, country people. They asked me where they could go to have fun at night. They wanted to know about *karaoke* bars, bars with girls. When I said that there's nothing like that, only pubs, they were amazed and asked, 'How can you live here?' But of course, that's why I came.

It's changing, though. When I visited a friend of mine in Clare for Christmas, all people wanted to do was watch TV. My friend's father owns an old-style pub, which used to be really popular, with lots of musicians singing and playing. Now when young people come back from Dublin or London, they go to a fancy pub with TV screens, and this man's place is deserted. I was sitting there by myself feeling nostalgic. But maybe that's just the sentimentality of the tourist.

Bridget Uhuegbu

Nigerian

Bridget is a plump woman in her thirties, of slightly formidable appearance until her face breaks into a charming smile. Her hair is composed of many thin plaits, tied back. She speaks accurate but heavily accented English. She has been living and studying in Dublin for eighteen years and, as well as her many academic qualifications, is writing a novel entitled Commandments and Chronicles.

I'm originally an Ibo but after school I moved to Enuguland. That's where the family home is now. In Nigeria, there are many tribes and about five hundred dialects. You learn English in school and most of the books are in English. Some in Ibo, some in Yoruba, some in Hausa. These are the major tribes. The Hausa and Yorubas are dominated by Muslims and the Ibo are Christian. The missionaries came everywhere in my country but the Ibos were more receptive than other tribes. I was born a Catholic but have become Anglican.

In Nigeria, the comprehensive school I attended followed the English system of education, instead of the WAEC, the West African Examination Council, which is less broad. When I finished my GCE, I was teaching but I didn't like it, so I decided to further my career. I chose to come to Ireland because I had friends in Maynooth. They provided me with a letter confirming that I was coming over to study. So I flew in, thinking I'd be here for a year, and I'm still here. I plan to go back eventually, but not yet.

Initially, I did a secretarial course at Rathmines Senior College and after that studied Personnel Management at the College of Commerce. I'm now a member of the IPM[*]. Next I took up law and got my diploma. Then I did a postgraduate course in Criminology, which I obtained in 1997. I've done other courses too: as the result of a correspondence course, I'm a member of the British Psychological Institute, and I also have a Certificate of Supervisory Management from the Irish Management Institute in Sandyford. At present, I'm doing business studies and am now in my final year. I suppose I'm something of an eternal student, but eventually I want to be a barrister. I've applied to King's Inn and am trying to sort myself out. My problem is that I don't have Irish, which is a formal requirement. So I have to sit down and study it. Not that they use it much.

I've been mostly self-sponsored. My family helped me at first but when I decided to stay on, it wasn't their problem financially any more. Now I get nothing from the state and nothing from home. At present, I've a part-time job as an editorial assistant. I've been working for this firm since September. Before that I had a clothes shop in Capel Street but it didn't do well and I had to close up.

I'd never been to Europe before I came to Ireland. It was hard for me to get used to cold. I only had light clothes. Now I dress the Irish way and have got used to the weather.

I quite like it here but one thing I've learnt about the Irish is that they are internalised. English people tell you if they don't like you. The Irish wouldn't say anything, but it would be in their hearts. I find them a very jealous race. That's not part of my culture and I find it difficult to understand. You can go from house to house in Africa in a relaxed and social way. Here, Irish women in particular are very jealous. If you are friendly with a man — I'm not talking about a boyfriend here — an Irish woman will do all she can to upset things. In my country, people can be friends for years, no problem. Here, that's not possible. I've never actually considered having a white boyfriend. I've nothing against any whites because I'm a Christian. At the same time, I've noticed how Irish women try to prevent even an ordinary friendship.

---

[*] Institute of Personnel Management.

There's something I don't like about Irish men. When you meet one, they aren't straightforward about asking you out. Instead, they start twinkling their eyes [*she demonstrates and then giggles*]. It's one of the silliest things I have seen in my life. It would be hard for a mature woman to go with a man who does that. It indicates that he thinks the woman is easy. It's not that my culture is very strict but certain standards are maintained. In the Book of Proverbs it says that a good woman is hard to find; her price is above rubies. This means that you have to work at it. It makes a woman cheap if she follows a man too fast and I think Irish women tend to be a bit like that. That's why they are easily dumped. Lots of relationships here break down.

I'm talking of course about city women. In the countryside, they are more like African women, with a sense of their own dignity. They are more honest because they are closer to nature. City women find it hard to say no to a man and that's why, for example, the refugees use them to change their status. Many form relationships with Nigerian men and have their children. The general view is that Irish women are easy, which is insulting. I think women should be strong for their own good.

There's a lot of begrudgery here, too. Even if you have nice clothes, people are resentful. If they see something good, they will call it bad. Why is this? I don't know.

African people are much more generous. They look after each other. Here, if someone is poor, it's only the state that looks after them. In Africa, everyone supports everyone else, even if it's only with spiritual uplift. For example, whereas here you'd have to pay for a babysitter to come in, in my culture it would be part of family duties. I looked after two children for my aunt for nothing. Here you have to pay for everything. I find that very strange.

Or friends might ask you to the pub but you haven't got any money. In my country, that wouldn't be a problem. Your friends would pay for you to have a drink. Here, if you don't have money, you don't go out.

Most African cultures are rooted in religion, in kindness. And when I say that, I mean something from the heart, a spirituality. Here, people wouldn't care if you were lying dead in the street. A pagan in Africa would have more true religion. He would have the fear of God in him even though he doesn't go to church. These pagans actually observe a strict moral code. And maybe it's even stronger with them. If you go to church regularly, you tend to relax and say, 'God will forgive', whereas those pagans are afraid of sin.

When I came here first it was very hard to get a job. Now you can pop in wherever you want and find something. And, of course, there were very few blacks over here in those days — mostly people who came to study law and medicine. They didn't intend staying. Now they come and don't want to go back. The economic balance has changed. When I first arrived, the value of the nira and of the pound sterling were about the same. Now, to buy £500 sterling in Nigeria I'd have to pay 100,000 nira. I'll be rich when I go back, if I have it.

I don't mix with the Nigerians who have come here recently. They say they are refugees but they are not. The word 'refugee' is very specific. There is no war in Nigeria, so why would they have to escape? They just want to get out. Ninety per cent of them come from another EU country anyway. They come to Ireland for papers, status, which they think the Irish government will give them. Only a few come straight from Nigeria. But if I was one of those, I'd do everything not to use the word 'refugee', because it brings shame to us.

Now Irish people think we are all refugees. It has created problems for those of us who came over years ago. But what can you do? You can't keep on explaining yourself. And then you see the way some of these so-called refugees behave. They seem to think everything is due to them for nothing. Most of them don't use their real names, either. I don't know if you're aware of that. The only contact I have with them is to go to their shops and buy stuff. Of course, I don't ignore them and when I meet them, I say hello. But as for a more tangible relationship, I'd be worried that it might affect me adversely. The Department of Justice knows me personally by now; I have established my credentials, so I'd be stupid to go there and say that my boyfriend or partner is a refugee.

When you're black, people here don't think you're a human being. Or they think 'this is a black woman' rather than treat you as a person. But your colour has nothing to do with it. When you take a knife and open us up, we're all the same underneath. If I need blood, I can take yours if we're the same group. Racism here hasn't got worse, only more obvious. Years ago, there was a young girl, a neighbour's daughter of about seventeen, who used to call in to visit me and one day I was talking about flying back on the plane, and she asked me if it was really possible for a black man to be a pilot. In college too I had this experience that they expect black people to lag behind. But once I am ahead of them, they get confused and can't understand what's happening. I just wonder why white people think they are superior. It doesn't hurt me because I have never accepted it. But I see that when you are black they give you an inferior job, even if you have the same qualifications as white people. I remember when I was working in a place as an administrative assistant, there was a woman boss who, when she had finished eating, would dump her cup on my table. Or she'd throw her rubbish on the floor, dirty wrappers and so on, and then she would expect me to clean it up. Although there were white people with the same qualifications as me, she never asked them to do it. It was just because I was black. So I took her to court. I even brought a cup into the court to show the judge. In the end, I won the case. It wasn't for money; it was for the principle of it.

Hilary Wakeman
English

Hilary is quite tall but frail in appearance, a very young-looking sixty-two with short hair and clear blue eyes. She is a rector of the Church of Ireland and sits in her office with an up-to-date computer, a wall of books of a theological nature and her cassock and snow-white surplice hanging on the door. She wears a thick sweater and trousers against the winter weather, with not a dog-collar in sight. She speaks in a serious and considered way, but frequently bursts into merry laughter. Her church is remotely situated near Mizen Head in West Cork, at the edge of a rocky bay.

I'm from everywhere, but mostly from Norfolk. I've been in Ireland for four and a half years now, because, having worked in the Church of England for about ten years, I felt that the whole ecumenical scene was opening up here and wanted to be part of it. Once I got here, I found that this was actually a totally false impression. I still have the press clippings that had influenced me and I take them out and look at them from time to time and think, 'Journalists have a big responsibility.' They seemed to be saying that the Catholic Church in Ireland was on the verge of becoming more independent, lessening the ties with Rome. And at the same time, the peace process in the North seemed to indicate that a healing of relationships between the Catholic and Protestant communities was possible, and if it was happening there, then surely it would be happening all over. All that made me think a united Christian Church in Ireland was possible and I wanted to be on the spot, to help it forward.

I should say that I was brought up as a Catholic. I left the Church because of the usual teenage doubts and then underwent what was for me a very important conversion process when I was about thirty. I went into the Church of England for no other reason than that it was the local church: there seemed to me no good reason for getting into a car and driving ten miles to another building. I became a practising Christian again and gradually got more and more involved. I was ordained in 1994, the year that the first women priests were ordained. I'd been a deacon for seven years and then a deaconess before that. Coming from this background, it really is very important, for me, that the churches move together.

When I arrived here I was told that ecumenical relations were great, but I soon found out that was all relative because they weren't nearly as far forward as I'd been used to in England. That was a bit of a blow, even though everyone was well-intentioned. The two communities live side by side with few problems. The way I've been treated by local Catholic clergy can't be faulted, but it's all played very much by the book. We have the week of prayer for Christian unity, the Women's World Day of Prayer and we have a united carol service. Those are the three events of the year where we mix with each other's churches in this parish. But if I try for further activities, they tell me they're too busy and I think that's genuine enough. My Catholic counterparts are very hard pushed without any extras. It's difficult to say how much the general attitude is influenced by the conservatism of the present pope. Colleagues of mine have said that they have had no problem receiving communion in a Catholic church, even though it was only recently that the pope re-emphasised that this was not to happen. Personally, I've never wanted to put a Catholic priest in the position of having to say no.

My congregation here is roughly between one and two hundred people. The parish covers the peninsula and is about fifteen miles long and six miles wide at the widest point. That's another thing I find so fascinating about the Church of Ireland, in contrast to the Church of England. It took me a long time to realise that a large factor in church-going here — and I don't want to belittle people's spirituality or their religiousness or whatever — is the preservation of a sense of cultural identity. In an odd sort of way, the Church of Ireland feels besieged, although they've also tended to be the people who've had the big businesses, the shops and the land. In my view, this siege mentality holds the church back and needs to be brought up to the surface and dealt with. Of course, I'm only talking from the experience of one parish, but I feel there's a tendency to live in the past, to continue to do things the way they've always been done, almost out of a sense of loyalty to their grandparents. Many of my congregation would have been here for generations, though not all. This is a mixed parish in that, westerly, it's very much a farming community, but going towards Schull it's comprised much more of blow-ins, retired people from Cork, Dublin and England, as well as Europeans. They tend not to go to church on a regular basis but will put their noses round the door the odd Sunday.

When I decided I wanted to come here, first I had to get John, my husband, to agree, which he did after I explained my reasons to him. Next I had to square it with my bishop in Norwich diocese and after that I applied for any jobs that came up. I sent my CV to three of them. One didn't answer at all. The other two called me for an interview and this place was the first. John and I had decided to accept the first offer, no matter what. It was a gamble.

I'd been on holiday in Ireland before, though not to West Cork. My mother's family come from Galway and we'd been to Dublin a few times. But coming here to live, we both suddenly realised that we were in a foreign country. The things that struck us straight away were this landscape of rocks that I've been looking for all my life, that I thought existed only in the north of Scotland, and the people, who are wonderful. Most of all we were struck by the way of life, the way people relate to each other. I don't think I'm looking through rose-tinted spectacles. Of course, people don't always say what they think but there's no particular harm in that. It's a tremendous privilege having an official role here. It's a privilege to be clergy anyway, because you're let into people's lives and into their emotions at key moments. I've never felt a barrier either among the Protestant or Catholic communities, and John by extension feels the same, even though as an agnostic he doesn't go to church. I think people actually find that quite interesting.

I'm retiring now for health reasons. I had ME about ten years ago and recently the symptoms have been returning. I could continue here doing half a job but that doesn't seem right, even though the parishioners urged me to stay. Neither John nor I want to go back to England, so we're moving down the road to a retirement cottage we bought just after coming here. My daughter and son-in-law have been living in it, but I've warned them they'll have to start looking for somewhere else.

Rosie is the only one of our five children who came with us, and that was only because she'd broken up with her then boyfriend. Two weeks after we arrived here, we were in a pub and this tall handsome fisherman came in and that was it. Rosie married him a year later. The only problem was that Richie's a Catholic. Although it took me a while to see what was happening, both communities had trouble coming to terms with it. The Church of Ireland community in particular thought it was appalling that a rector's daughter should marry a Catholic. They cope with their own sons and daughters marrying out because it's happening more and more, but for a while, they really felt let down.

I myself conducted the ceremony and married them. It was wonderful. What I didn't realise was that if there were any Catholic clergy present, they would expect to take part too, so we ended up with four priests in the sanctuary. There was Richie's parish priest from Schull and Richie's uncle, who is a missionary priest in Nigeria, and his friend, also a priest. The other side of it was that one or two young Catholic men said very nasty things to Richie after they'd had too much to drink, things he wouldn't even repeat to Rosie. At least one of them apologised after the wedding. It was the prejudice coming out under the influence of drink, and just shows it's still there.

The only other unpleasantness I've experienced was when we had the one-hundred-and-fiftieth anniversary of this church here. It was built during the Famine by the Rev. William Fisher, who was a Souper. He dispensed soup to famine victims, as a result of which some Catholics became Protestant. In fact, Eoghan Harris wrote a play on the subject about this very parish, and it was performed at the Abbey Theatre. A Catholic colleague asked to be excused from our celebrations, because there are still hard words expressed locally. He said to me, 'I have told them that sort of talk is of the devil.' But I've heard there's even someone who spits every time he passes the church.

I suggested a service of reconciliation, maybe during the anniversary year. But the parish priest said that would be too soon. What he was willing to do was set up a study group — not on the history of the place, which was what I wanted — but a Bible study group. That's been going for two years now and has been very useful in clearing up misconceptions. Part of my work has been to teach RE at the local community college to twelve- to fifteen-year-olds and I usually do a session on what they think each community believes. All sorts of strange things come up. For example, Catholic children say to Protestants, 'You don't believe in Mary' or 'You don't believe in Jesus'.

I miss being so far from a city. The social life here is totally different from England and it took us a while to realise that there's none of the having two or three couples round for dinner that we've been doing all our lives. We couldn't understand how people got to know each other without that. People are so friendly to each other and yet it always seems to be in public places. We missed the dinners at first but now I find it a great freedom, maybe because I'm getting older and I don't really want to be cooking for eight to twelve people. Because of my health problems, I'm going to really enjoy being lazy for a while after I retire but at the same time don't want to become an instant geriatric. There are a couple of books I want to write — my background, as much as I have one, is in journalism — but I'm thinking in terms of one non-fiction, one fiction piece, both to do with religion. A 'Murder at the Vicarage' perhaps — I read one of those recently. It was appalling. I hope I can write something better.

Tracy and June Wasserfall
South African

Tracy is in her late thirties, a stout woman with blonde hair and a pale complexion. She has been living in a suburb of Limerick city for seven years after her husband moved there with his job. She has three children, the youngest, Siobhan, having been born in Ireland. Tracy's mother, June, an active-looking woman in her early sixties, has recently retired and come to live near her daughter.

June: I think the quality of life in Ireland is great. It's a happy country. You get such a relaxed feeling here. I've been over on holiday many times, twice for a six-month duration, so I'm used to it. Of course, it's different when you come here to live, but the country and the people don't change. You change, you have to adapt, to make a new life.

Tracy: When my husband was moved here, I knew nothing about Ireland and didn't want to come. I wouldn't let him sell our house in South Africa in case I wanted to go back. But I just fell in love with it here. Now I'm glad we moved and plan to stay. I actually surprised myself at how quickly I adjusted. And the children have a much better life. On the other hand, I don't interest myself in the politics here. When we first came, I found it all rather silly compared to South Africa.

June: Africa's very vibrant, while Ireland's gentler. I miss the cultural life, concerts and the theatre. With the children being so small, it's difficult for us to get to Dublin and there isn't much happening in Limerick, although there's one theatre, the Belltable. In Johannesburg, there were lots of small orchestras playing concerts everywhere. But quite a lot goes on at the University. I'll have to get on the mailing list.

Tracy: One thing that struck me immediately was the choice in the shops here. Even the range of breakfast cereals! The quality of clothing is much better. And everywhere is so clean! We're living in the same sort of suburb here as in Johannesburg. Obviously, there we had a much bigger house, a much bigger garden. I didn't have to clean and my husband didn't have to do the gardening. It was quite a culture shock having to do my own housework.

June: But you've got very used to that now.

Tracy: I have. But my maid and I were great friends and I miss her. I went back to work when each of the boys were three months' old and she brought them up. When I had Siobhan, I was at home with her from the beginning, which was a new experience for me. The changes in South Africa make me sad because it's such a beautiful country. I had a wonderful childhood, which children there haven't got now. I'm glad my mother has moved here because I worried about her on her own. It's got very violent in South Africa.

June: It'll be all right in about fifteen years' time, when these little black ones who are now going to school grow up. There'll be a middle-class black population by then.

Tracy: I'm impressed with the quality of education here. One thing, though, it's very relaxed regarding rules. In South Africa, the children would never be allowed wear runners to school, and girls would have to tie their hair back. I remember we even had to lift up our dresses to show that we were wearing the regulation green knickers. It was very regimental. Here, I don't know that it's always a good thing to be so laid back. There's a lack of discipline. My son Stephen keeps telling me he wishes I was Irish because Irish mothers don't care what time you come home. I'm much more aware of where my children are and who they're with. It's not that the Irish mothers don't care, but they just don't imagine that anything bad might happen. I used to worry, when my children were out playing, that they might get kidnapped or molested and my neighbour used to laugh at me. 'They'll be fine,' she'd say.

June: I think the reason the majority of Irish people are so happy and self-confident is that as children they're always being told, 'Aren't you the best! The best in Ireland!' So the child develops good self-esteem. It's not like that in South Africa. I don't ever remember hearing that. Here, even strangers will stop and say, 'Aren't you a beautiful child! Aren't you a little dote!'

Judith Wilkinson

Australian

Judith is in her early forties, with a healthy outdoor complexion. She sits in a pleasant café in Clontarf, on the northside of Dublin, amid busy lunchtime clatter on a sunny St Valentine's Day. A neighbour is minding her year-old baby girl, to give her a break. Her manner is warm and she is very articulate, giving considered replies to the questions asked.

I'm from Perth in Western Australia, although it's a long time since I lived there. I left in 1982 to do my obligatory year abroad but stayed away a bit longer than intended. I went back in the mid-1980s and left again, thinking I would return, but didn't. I settled in Oxford in England for several years. Then I went on holiday and met my husband.

It's a great St Valentine's Day story. We were both trekking in the north-eastern fjords of Iceland, part of a group of people on an adventure holiday. I'd had a bad fear of flying and thought I should try to overcome it. So I decided to treat myself to this rather expensive trip and filled in the form. Then I chickened out, but in the meantime, my secretary had sent it off for me, something she had never done before. I doped myself up with valium, got on the plane and set off. And then, at midnight at Keflavik airport, there was Ultan. He was looking out for someone who'd be in the same little group. 'You must be Judith Wilkinson,' he said. 'I claim my prize.' Those were his first ever words to me. I'd seen his name on the list but I'd never heard of 'Ultan' before. So my reply to him was slightly less romantic. 'Oh,' I said, 'I thought you were a woman!' Anyway, after two weeks trekking, we were well and truly in love. There were a couple of years spent commuting between Ireland and Oxford, and then six years ago I moved over here for good.

I left my career behind in England. I was in management in Social Services and there was nothing equivalent here. It was a big change. In addition, I got married. Up to then, although I had lived out of Australia for years, I never felt like a migrant. I always had the possibility of going back. Suddenly, here I was settled in another country. On the other hand, I knew I wasn't condemned to a life sentence, that if I couldn't live here, then Ultan would come to Australia, even though he's never lived anywhere else. He was born in the Coombe in the oldest part of Dublin.

He's Catholic but we were married in our local Church of Ireland by a woman. A Catholic priest friend of Ultan's family assisted. We said our vows in Irish, the only Irish I can speak. My mother and my sister came over for the ceremony, although my father wasn't well enough to travel.

What struck me very forcibly at first was how ignorant the English are about the Irish. I was gobsmacked when I started learning about the complexities of Irish history, where terrorism came from. The English have no idea, even after the hundreds of years they've been messing with Ireland. Now, when I hear even the BBC news, I realise how uninformed it still is. And when people in Oxford found out I was coming over here to live, it was amazing how many asked me whether Dublin was in the North or in the South. These were educated people, people in official capacities. Quite a few of them actually thought I was taking a risk coming here. My family in Australia knew much better at least.

I expected Ireland to be different, and culturally it is. But in many ways I felt that I had come home. And I could see how much Australia's character is derived from the Irish, how *Irish* Australia is. For instance, if I was standing at a bus stop in Oxford and started talking to people next to me, they'd be likely to move away, thinking, *Weirdo in the queue*! Whereas people here talk to each other like in Australia, like in most other countries in the world, actually. I was also struck by the way Irish people are intensely interested in each other. I enjoy that. When Americans meet, they ask each other, 'What do you do for a living?' but when Irish meet they say, 'Where are you from?' They want to place you. When I came first, my experience was of not belonging in that sense, especially when I went for jobs. Then I knew what they were dying to ask was, 'Who's your husband?' I could read those signals because Perth is like that.

Another similarity: when I was working in England, a colleague told me I should meet this woman from Perth. 'You might know her,' she said. I laughed because Perth is a city of a million people. It turned out that we grew up within a hundred metres of each other but never met because she was Catholic and I wasn't. She went through a totally different education system from me. There was a real segregation in Australia in the 1960s. I don't know what it's like now.

But the thing is, the longer I stay here, the more I come to realise how these similarities are purely superficial and how fundamentally different the Irish are from the Australians. There's a streak of anarchy in the Irish that the Australians don't have. In fact, Australia is a highly regulated society, with rules about everything. And furthermore, people obey those rules. I remember when I was here first seeing how people parked their cars near corners. And I asked Ultan, 'Isn't that against the law?' He explained that although there are rules, it's all a matter of interpretation. On one level, that's good. On another level, it makes for a frustrating place to live, especially if you've been used to something quite different. I'm finding it increasingly difficult to deal with. Particularly the way they treat their environment. No one in Australia drops litter because it's been drummed into them that they shouldn't. The litter in Dublin is disgusting and it's getting worse. I'm ashamed to show my visitors around. When my mother was here, we were walking in the street and someone ahead of us dropped something. Thinking it was accidental, she called their attention to it. The look she got! The countryside's not much better. It's very depressing to climb a mountain and find litter on the top. I don't understand the mentality of people who take the trouble to climb 3,000 feet and then leave litter.

There should be a national waste management policy. It should, for example, be compulsory to recycle glass. But there are no votes in a tax on plastic bags.

Another thing: the way politicians are elected makes for a very clientele-style system. You look after your voters because you may be competing even with someone from the same party for the one seat. Even more amazing is the fact that everyone's so open about it. If your local member happens to be a minister, you get a four-lane highway. People don't seem to see this as corruption. On the other hand, there's a good side to it in that people do feel they have a say. I like the fact that the Taoiseach lives in his own house, goes to local pubs — the lack of ceremony, the lack of hierarchy. My problem in England was that people couldn't place me, because they go by the way you speak. Here you're categorised not by your class but by education and how much money you have. Anyone can make it to the top here, and that's like Australia.

I was pleasantly surprised here at first to go out to lunch with people who'd talk about books and theatre and other people. Visually, the Irish are a complete disaster. Look at the way they treat their architecture. But the oral tradition is alive and well: the way they tell stories, the way they express themselves. There was a notice that some Sligo farmer put up banning hill walkers on his land. Instead of saying 'Trespassers will be prosecuted' or some such, he'd written: 'As Yeats said, *Arise and Go Now*.'

And I love the way the Irish use language. They don't tend to use shorthand. I went on a tour of the House of Lords in the Bank of Ireland, and someone asked the guide if the place was haunted. An Englishman would have said, 'Oh yes, I think so.' But this man described a night he had been there by himself. 'And sure,' he said, 'weren't the spirits lepping out of the panelling.' Some of these expressions are wonderful. And the Irish are much more careful about the way they speak. They articulate all the sounds.

With regard to the position of women, the years before I came here saw the biggest changes. The condom train, all that, happened long before my time. When my husband's mother got married, she had to give up work and didn't think anything of it. I have an Irish friend my age with several children. She lived down the country and, after her first child, her mother insisted that she be "churched". She didn't realise the significance of that until afterwards: that new mothers are somehow unclean. To me it was shocking. Now things are still a little bit behind — the phenomenon of the Irish mammy is alive and well — but among young women here, I think their opportunities are much the same as anywhere else.

But even since I've been here there have been enormous changes. Six years ago, if you saw a black person you knew they were either a diplomat or a medical student. I couldn't believe how homogeneous the place was — the only visible ethnic group that was here was extremely badly treated. I mean the Travellers. Coming from a cosmopolitan society, I found it very sterile. Things are getting better in that respect. The new nationalities coming in are bringing with them their traditions — their foods, for example. There's a much wider range than there used to be and restaurants are much better now. On the other hand, we're seeing how racist the Irish are, which is very disappointing. I actually can't understand it: it seems out of keeping, because in many ways the Irish are kind and considerate.

Of course, racism isn't only a matter of black/white. The Irish themselves have long been subjected to discrimination. As for me, I've heard all the drunken Aussie jokes. And I had this Irish friend in Oxford who went to Melbourne and came back saying, 'I couldn't believe it. Australia's such a cultured place.' I replied, 'What did you expect? You've known me for thirteen years.' 'I thought you were an aberration,' she said.

Having the baby here was a disappointment. My first question to the gynaecologist was, 'When do I meet the midwife?' I was told that I'd meet her in the delivery room. One thing I hadn't been aware of was that, while the hospital services here are very good, the community services are lousy. They hardly exist. Everything is very centralised, very medically dominated and once you're out of the hospital, you're on your own. I had problems breast-feeding, as many women do. It's not surprising so few babies are breast-fed in Ireland when you see how little community support there is for it. In Australia, there's a twenty-four-hour-a-day helpline. They pay lip service to it here but don't have the back-up either in hospitals or in the community.

There's another side of things, however. We lost our first child at the age of ten weeks and it was brought home to me very strongly then that the Irish know how to handle death. The community doesn't stay away as people would in England or Australia — I'm talking about Anglo-Saxons here. They'd tiptoe around you. When Daniel died, neighbours came with flowers, bringing their children, wanting to see the body, to say good-bye to him. Food appeared on the doorstep, we were taken care of. The whole street came to the funeral, even people we didn't really know. They talked to you about it and shook your hand. It was wonderful.

I was very anxious about the second baby, even after she was born, expecting something to be wrong with her. But she's perfect. Except sometimes it seems to me that's the only thing the Irish ever write about: there seems to be one novel after another about dead babies and drowned babies.

It's awful when you're a foreigner because you don't want to be critical of the country that you live in, as you're so glad that they've accepted you. You feel a bit like a traitor saying bad things about them. The Australians have this thing about the old whinging Pom. I don't want to be like that. It's only that my deepest despair is that some of the best things about Ireland are being spoilt.

Shamsiah Yasin

Malaysian

Sham, who is in her thirties, is a small and delightful person with plenty of warm smiles. Because she is a Muslim, she wears a silk scarf that entirely covers her hair. She sits in the Parents' Room at her children's school in central Dublin. She and some of the other mothers have been making buns and biscuits and there is an appetising smell of baking, spices and vanilla in the room. Her English, for which she apologies, is somewhat broken but she makes up for this with laughter and gestures.

I'm from Malaysia, Kuala Lumpur. I came here a year ago because my husband was continuing with his studies in the Royal College of Surgeons. He's an anaesthetist. Once he's fully qualified, we will go back to Malaysia because everything is there, my house, my job, my family. I'm a nurse. I met my husband when I was still at college, a long long time ago, seventeen years.

Kuala Lumpur's a big city, the size of London. The highest building in the world is there. It's very modern and busy, with bad traffic jams. It would take me an hour and a half to travel three or four kilometres from my home to the hospital where I was working. That's by bus. I would be scared to drive. Here, my husband walks to work in ten minutes.

I'd never been to Europe before but I knew what to expect because my husband had already been here several times and told me about it. On the whole, I've been happy in Dublin. Irish people are very nice.

And my husband has had no problems with his work. All the same, sometimes I've been a bit homesick. I miss my house. And we have two cars. I left my car with friends so that they could keep an eye on things. My husband went back for two weeks just to check everything was all right and he found that somebody had broken in and taken the computer, the hot water filter — something that's very necessary to us because in Malaysia we have a lot of dust. I think the thieves must have had a master key because nothing was broken.

We have four children, one son and three daughters. They speak English fluently now and don't want to go back to Malaysia. They are all in this school and are happy. In Malaysia, there might be forty students in one class, so it's difficult to get the teacher's attention. And my children actually prefer the cold weather. In my country it's very hot. As for me, I like the spring and summer here but not the winter. Luckily, our house is close to the school. Only three minutes' walk away.

We have a lot of friends from Malaysia who come here, especially medical students. At any one time, there might be up to a hundred people. They come with the support of our government because there's a special relationship between the two countries. The Royal College has connections with a university near Penang.

We're Muslims. We can practise our religion here because there are two mosques, one on the South Circular Road and the other in Clonskeagh. It's a good place to meet our friends. And here too we have Malaysia Hall, where we hold parties and other activities. It's somewhere new students can go when they arrive. Mostly they are very young, undergraduates. My husband and another person are the only postgraduates here at the moment. Graduates mostly go to England. I was in Birmingham last year and met fifty families of people who are studying there.

I know some very nice Irish people, in the refugee centre, for example. Of course, I'm not a refugee but I asked if I could go, just to meet people, and they said I could. Last summer they arranged a party and then a picnic, a barbecue. There was also a Christmas party where we all mixed together, no problem.

I had very little English when I came here but I have been going to classes, even though I don't have much time. They are organised in a small church near where I live but are in the afternoons when my children finish school, so that's a bit difficult. It was unusual for me to find that I could get English classes free. In Malaysia you'd have to pay a lot of money for that. My husband went to an English school but when I was growing up, my parents lived in a village, so there was no opportunity for me. Now there are no English schools in Malaysia any more. I suppose it's because they want to promote the national language. On the other hand, at university all the textbooks are in English, so that's a problem. Now when I go back my children can teach me English.

I like to go out — it's better than staying at home. That's why I come to the cookery class. Then tomorrow they will have a computer class. Sometimes I go to the library for a few hours to read a storybook to improve my English.

If I stay at home, I watch television. I like the cookery programmes because I enjoy cooking so much. It's easy for me to get the ingredients for Malaysian food here. There's the Asia Market. And there's also a shop attached to the mosque.

My husband thinks he might like to stay here. There's a shortage of anaesthetists in Ireland. Here he's studying and working at the same time, so gets more money. On the other hand, the taxes are very high. In Malaysia, tax is only ten per cent. If we stayed on, I could get work as a nurse, but my English would have to be much better. At the moment, I could get a job not as a staff nurse but maybe in a nursing home. But just now I don't want to work. I want to rest.

We recently travelled around Europe a little, London, Paris, Brussels, Amsterdam. It was a wonderful trip. I can't wait to tell my friends about it. And we're planning to go to Switzerland to see the snow. Although I already saw it here this winter, for the first time in my life. So perhaps after all we can save our money. Who needs to go to Switzerland when there's snow here! The children loved it.

We've also travelled around Ireland: Wexford, Cork, Galway, Glendalough. It's really beautiful.

Everything is OK here and if I didn't have any ties in Malaysia, it would be nice to stay on. I've no problem with the fact that I go to a Catholic church for the classes and that my children are learning about Christianity. Catholics read the Bible and I read the Koran: they are very similar. And there's only one God.

Christina Z *

South African

Christina is a largish, middle-aged woman with a broad, attractive face and light brown hair. Her accent is soft but when she laughs, which is often, it's a big belly laugh. She is white but the remote County Wicklow cottage where she lives with her family is full of native African artefacts — carved figures, weaves, bright prints.

I am fifty-one years old and I am from Cape Town. We first came to Ireland in January 1980. We lived here until August 1983 and then went back to Africa, to Zimbabwe, for three years. Coming back, we stayed in London for six months or so. We're here in County Wicklow since August 1987.

Why did we come to live in Ireland? Yeah, that's the question everybody always asks. Basically because we had to leave South Africa. This goes back to the apartheid era and the mixed marriage problem and what they called the Immorality Act. My husband, Anthony, is Cape-coloured and at that time whites and non-whites weren't allowed to marry, so we got married in Lesotho. Then, when I got pregnant, we decided to go to Australia, where we knew people. But after trying to get visas from March to November, finally we got turned down. We'd given up our jobs when we thought we were going to leave in March, so all that time we were living on our savings. And Paul was born in the meantime. Anthony was at the birth but his name was never put on the certificate, because Paul would then have had to be classified as coloured and that would have created enormous problems: it was legally impossible and might have resulted in the baby being taken from me or even me being jailed. So Paul was registered as the child of a single mother, father unknown.

Anyway, we had to decide what to do. Now, OK, we were looking for an English-speaking country just to make things easier. Neither of us knew much about Ireland, but what we knew we liked. I wanted to have a rural setting near a city and that's not always easy to achieve.

We arrived in England in December. Anthony came over to Ireland straight away after Christmas, while Paul and I stayed with friends in London. Then Anthony kept saying he couldn't find a job, he couldn't find accommodation; he was living in youth hostels. Finally, he got a job with this guy who was a tax-dodger and charlatan and Anthony was the perfect victim — the immigrant with no rights, illegal — and after a few months he didn't even get paid and couldn't complain about it. But one thing this man did: he got Anthony a work permit, and also introduced him to a computer company in Dublin. Anthony later got a job with them. That kind of set us on the road to redemption. At first, though, we were miserable: so poor we could hardly afford to put the tenpences in the heater. This was January and it was freezing. I was trying to get nappies dry. Disposable nappies were the new thing then but I couldn't afford them.

There was a woman living on the ground floor. She was very young, about eighteen. She'd had to get married, you know. We had nothing in common except babies but she was really so kind. I'd go down to her in the afternoons and watch telly, just so Paul could play with the little girl. I can remember there was one stage when this charlatan let us down and didn't pay us. And we thought, *God, how are we going to get by?* At the end of the week Jenny came up to me and said, 'I can spare a pound from the housekeeping.' That's as bad as it was. And they didn't have much. It was very touching.

After that first miserable year, we decided to go back to Africa and finally took a contract through APSO[*] to go to Zimbabwe. That's

---

[*] Agency for <u>Personal</u> Service Overseas.

another long story. But at the end of the three years, we weighed up the pros and cons and decided to come back here. For once, we had a few thousand in the bank and were able to buy a place. Now the one thing I said to Anthony when we were in Zimbabwe was that I'd go back to Ireland on condition that we live in north Wicklow. When we came first in 1980, we took a bus out to Enniskerry and walked all the way to the waterfall, carrying Paul in a back-pack. It was February but it was a sunny day, and I looked around and I said, 'Wow, yeah, maybe I could be happy here after all. This looks like how I imagined it to be.'

We were back in London when a friend sent us a little slip from the paper, advertising this cottage. He said to us, 'It's up in the hills. You probably wouldn't want it because maybe you'd have water problems there. It could snow in June.' So anyway, we came over and looked at it and said, 'Right, that's it.' At that stage it had only two big rooms and a kitchen and bathroom, so it was quite small for us with three kids — Aisling had been born in Ireland in 1982 and Conor in Zimbabwe in 1984.

When we moved here, Conor was really scared. There were woods all around and he kept on imagining there were bears. When we first got to London, he was mad about it. The kids were so used to Zimbabwe and wild animals that the first time we went across the Thames, they were asking were there crocodiles in it. And when we went to the south of England on the train Conor saw cattle in the fields and said, 'Oh, look at the zebras.'

Up until recently, being about five or six miles from the nearest village, the kids had to be taken and fetched every day to primary school. Now Aisling is in sixth year at an Irish school. Conor is in third year. So we've got Irish-speaking children, which is strange because I don't know if I have half-a-dozen words in the language. But it's lovely for them.

Paul actually won a scholarship to a music school in Mullingar — they take people from all over the country and hand out something like four or five scholarships a year — but when they found out he wasn't a Catholic, they wouldn't admit him. Now he's at college in Dublin.

We haven't really experienced any racism. Anthony looks as though he could be Portuguese or Spanish, so people are always amazed when you tell them the stories. Everybody's heard about apartheid but they've never really thought about how it worked in practice.

People always ask, 'Will you go back to South Africa?' and I suppose when we first came I thought, well, maybe someday. I loved Cape Town. We lived on the slopes of Table Mountain and my heart dwells there in the mountain. So coming here at first was hard and we were desperately homesick. And I felt very angry. I felt like I'd been hounded out of my mother country, that I was a victim. Then you'd hear people saying: 'You're not suffering, you've run away.' I felt there was a lot of suffering involved.

So came Majority Rule in South Africa. I really felt more disoriented than ever. I watched Mandela on the television and talked to people on the phone and they were all on about the celebrations, the street parties, and I felt I wasn't part of it.

OK, you asked me, do I like Ireland? I absolutely love Ireland. I love Glendalough: it's just one of the most magical places on earth as far as I'm concerned. There's a priest who lives there — he calls himself a hermit but he's hardly that. He takes people on spiritual walks. The first year they ran it, South Africa was just going through these big changes. He took about thirty people on a walk and one of the things he said was that, after seven years, your life changes; you move on. At that time, we'd been seven years in this house. Now there's a certain stone at Glendalough where the roads meet, with the symbol of the cross on it, like the crossroads of your life, and you choose the one or the other fork. Everything seemed to say to me: this is the time of choice. I went around with a big heartache. And, funnily enough, on this walk there was a black woman and it turned out she was a nun from Cape Town, principal of a coloured primary school. I said who I was, that I'd also taught in a coloured school, and we looked at each other — well, we fell into each other's arms crying. It was so embarrassing, but I was just so emotional and she knew exactly how I felt.

Anyway, it was then the choice was finally up to me — I knew Anthony would go along with what I decided — and another friend said to me, 'I don't think you are really worried about choosing. I think you only now are grieving for South Africa.' It was true. The grief had been kind of postponed for years because it was a decision still to be made. But our home was now here; the children were Irish. I had to face for the first time that I had already made the decision. Last year I went back — first to Malawi where Anthony was working on contract and then on to South Africa. Everything was changed, of course. You go back after twelve years to your beloved birthplace and suddenly realise that the world isn't the same any more.

I'd been elated in Malawi. It's so wide and mountainous with spaces forever. It brought tears to my eyes. Then you come back and Ireland is a park landscape. Wherever you are here, you only need to walk for an hour or so and find people. In Africa, you can walk for hundreds of miles and not see a soul. Still, coming back to Ireland after nine weeks, I was so happy to see the family. It was the first and biggest break I've ever had away from the kids. My first feeling was relief to be home.

There's one thing I really miss: the mix of people, although of course it's changing here at last. But people don't realise what a mix South Africa is. There are fourteen official languages. Not only are there a great number of black tribes — there are even people called Rehoboth Bastards, that's a classification — there are coloureds, a great variety of white or almost white people, Chinese, many Portuguese, Germans, British, large numbers of Dutch. I myself am three-quarters French, of Huguenot stock. I've even a great-great-grandmother who was an Ellis; for a long time I thought she was Scottish or Irish, but in fact she turned out to be Norwegian. One day I might dig into that. But I wonder sometimes is there some subconscious recognition of the Europe of our origin. We went out three hundred years ago: now I feel that in some strange way I've closed the circle and returned to the place we originally left. But very very changed in the process.

Coming back from Zimbabwe the second time, I arrived in London once again in December. And again it struck me as so strange, so built up, grey, dreary. Cape Town is Mediterranean. The winter, however bad, is three months. Then it's over and you are assured of a good summer, but I actually enjoy the springs and the autumns more, which would be more like a good Irish summer. That's the kind of weather I like. I love the Irish summers, I love the long evenings. When my Mam was here, she couldn't get over it. At ten o'clock at night, she could thread a needle outside. That kind of thing. The long, long dusks that seem to go on forever.